Transmodal Communications

TRANSLANGUAGING IN THEORY AND PRACTICE

Series Editors: Li Wei, *University College London*, Angel Lin, *Simon Fraser University*, Yuen Yi Lo, *The University of Hong Kong* and Saskia Van Viegen, *York University*.

Translanguaging in Theory and Practice aims to publish work that highlights the dynamic use of an individual's linguistic repertoire and challenges the socially and politically defined boundaries of languages and their hierarchy. We invite research from across disciplines by both established and emergent researchers in multifarious settings, including everyday use, educational, digital and workplace contexts. We will also actively welcome and solicit studies on translanguaging in contexts where English is not the mainstream language and where other modalities and semiotic resources take prominence over speech and writing. The series is transdisciplinary and encourages scholars to publish empirical research on translanguaging, especially that which aims to disrupt power relations, to create new identities and communities, to engage in the discussion of translanguaging theories and pedagogies, and/or to help the field of translanguaging consolidate its scholarship.

Topics to be covered by the series include:

- Theoretical underpinnings of translanguaging
- Translanguaging pedagogies
- Translanguaging in assessment
- Translanguaging and language policy
- Translanguaging in everyday social practices in different contexts and communities, including digital/ social/ media

All books in this series are externally peer-reviewed.

Full details of all the books in this series and of all our other publications can be found on http://www.multilingual-matters.com, or by writing to Multilingual Matters, St Nicholas House, 31-34 High Street, Bristol BS1 2AW, UK.

TRANSLANGUAGING IN THEORY AND PRACTICE: 1

Transmodal Communications

Transpositioning Semiotics and Relations

Edited by
Margaret R. Hawkins

MULTILINGUAL MATTERS
Bristol • Blue Ridge Summit

DOI https://doi.org/10.21832/HAWKIN6362
Library of Congress Cataloging in Publication Data
A catalog record for this book is available from the Library of Congress.
Names: Hawkins, Margaret R., editor.
Title: Transmodal Communications: Transpositioning Semiotics and Relations / Edited by Margaret R. Hawkins.
Description: Bristol, UK; Blue Ridge Summit: Multilingual Matters, 2021. | Series: Translanguaging in Theory and Practice: 1 | Includes bibliographical references and index. | Summary: "This book explores transmodal communications, particularly those that are technologically-mediated and transglobal. Using examples and data analyses from a project that digitally connects youth to share their lives across global communities, authors offer new theorizations, approaches and understandings for semiotics, meaning-making and relations"— Provided by publisher.
Identifiers: LCCN 2021014876 (print) | LCCN 2021014877 (ebook) | ISBN 9781788926355 (paperback) | ISBN 9781788926362 (hardback) | ISBN 9781788926379 (pdf) | ISBN 9781788926386 (epub)
Subjects: LCSH: Modality (Linguistics) | Youth—Language—Social aspects. | Multilingualism—Social aspects. | English language—Study and teaching—Foreign speakers. | Semiotics—Social aspects. | Language and culture. | Intercultural communication. | Education—Effect of technological innovations on.
Classification: LCC P99.4.M6 T73 2021 (print) | LCC P99.4.M6 (ebook) | DDC 302.2083—dc23 LC record available at https://lccn.loc.gov/2021014876
LC ebook record available at https://lccn.loc.gov/2021014877

British Library Cataloguing in Publication Data
A catalogue entry for this book is available from the British Library.

ISBN-13: 978-1-78892-636-2 (hbk)
ISBN-13: 978-1-78892-635-5 (pbk)

Multilingual Matters
UK: St Nicholas House, 31-34 High Street, Bristol BS1 2AW, UK.
USA: NBN, Blue Ridge Summit, PA, USA.

Website: www.multilingual-matters.com
Twitter: Multi_Ling_Mat
Facebook: https://www.facebook.com/multilingualmatters
Blog: www.channelviewpublications.wordpress.com

Copyright © 2021 Margaret R. Hawkins and the authors of individual chapters.

All rights reserved. No part of this work may be reproduced in any form or by any means without permission in writing from the publisher.

The policy of Multilingual Matters/Channel View Publications is to use papers that are natural, renewable and recyclable products, made from wood grown in sustainable forests. In the manufacturing process of our books, and to further support our policy, preference is given to printers that have FSC and PEFC Chain of Custody certification. The FSC and/or PEFC logos will appear on those books where full certification has been granted to the printer concerned.

Typeset by Nova Techset Private Limited, Bengaluru and Chennai, India.
Printed and bound in the UK by the CPI Books Group Ltd.
Printed and bound in the US by NBN.

This book is dedicated to all of you who have believed in and supported Global Storybridges over the past years, and given so generously of your time, effort and spirit. It could not be what it is, and we could not have done this work, without all of you around the globe: community folks; educators; researchers; graduate students; professional and technical support; and most of all the youth participants and site facilitators. What an amazing journey we are sharing!

Contents

	Acknowledgements	ix
	Contributors	xi
1	Global StoryBridges: Being and Becoming *Margaret R. Hawkins*	1
2	Building Scalar Frames of Understandability in 'Trans' Practices within a Catalan Global StoryBridges Site *Emilee Moore, Claudia Vallejo Rubinstein, Júlia Llompart-Esbert and Miaomiao Zhang*	22
3	Cosmopolitan Aims/Cosmopolitan Realities: How Immigrant Youth Negotiate Languaging and Identity in One After-School Program *Anneliese Cannon and Sarah J. Turner*	43
4	A Place-Based Critical Transmodal Analysis of Chinese Youth's Digital Storytelling *Rui Li and Jiayu Feng*	64
5	Navigating Transnational Transmodal Terrain: Perspectives from Ugandan Lugbara Youth *Willy Ngaka*	80
6	Youth Transmodally Indexing Social Discourses: A Vietnam Video Narrative Analysis *Gordon B. West, Bingjie Zheng and Trang D. Tran*	109
7	Critical Cosmopolitanism and Sustainable Education: Primary Educator Perspectives from Uganda and the United States *Sara J. Goldberg and Sarah Nazziwa*	134
8	Developing Decolonizing Pedagogies with Mexican Pre-Service 'English' Teachers *Mario E. López-Gopar, Vilma Huerta Cordova, William M. Sughrua and Edwin Nazaret León Jiménez*	152

9 Positionality Revisited: A Critical Examination of Meaning-
   Making and Collaboration in a Transnational Research Team   176
   *Patricia Ratanapraphart, Lisa Velarde, Nikhil M. Tiwari and
      Suman Barua*

10 Coda   196
   Li Wei

   Index   200

Acknowledgements

This book exemplifies collaboration at its best, among partners and stakeholders across the globe. Without the intensive collaboration there would be no Global StoryBridges (GSB), and no research or theorizing around it. Many, many thanks to all involved, with particular shout-outs to the following:

For the hands-on workings of GSB, the role of the site facilitator is especially critical, and we deeply appreciate the commitment and hard work of those who serve in this position. These are folks who are community members and/or educators, and each contributes great heart and significant time to working with project youth with no recompense. Several have contributed to chapters in this book – Sara Goldberg, Sarah Nazziwa, Trang Tran and Miaomiao Zhang. Others have not, and at the risk of leaving out some who have worked with us over the years, I'd like to acknowledge the contributions of: Rhobert Kennedy Afhema, Christine Alitura, Izaro Aruti, Esteban Benites, King James Bwambale, Eliseo Hernández, Zixuan Hou, Wenxia Huang, Dũng Huỳnh, Fabio Murillo, Wendy Nagilla, Darcy Poquette, Noel Sánchez, Ravikumar Shahu, Heather Thone, Yun Wang, Pat Wongkit and Juan Zhang.

Thanks also go to those who, although not site facilitators, have helped to connect us with sites and facilitate their initiation. These are community members, university faculty and/or those affiliated with NGOs, and include some of our authors: Suman Barua, Jiayu Feng, Mario López-Gopar and Willy Ngaka. Those who are responsible for the existence of some of our sites but who are not members of the research team are: Amos Kambere, Li Yanping, Cristián Meléndez and Maurice Simanyu. We also want to give a special mention to Herkimer Media – Nathan and his crew have worked generously, closely and patiently with us on website design and maintenance, and to Jason Erdmann, who has supported our technology needs in every way imaginable, including responding to trouble-shooting calls at all hours of the day and night in response to pleas for help from across the world.

We each have professional networks with colleagues who have expanded our thinking and understandings of this work that we do. Although they are too numerous to mention individually, their names will likely appear in references; we are so grateful for our communities of practice! We would, though, like to give a special thanks to Li Wei (who has contributed the coda to this volume) for his unwavering enthusiasm and support over the past several years.

A huge dept of gratitude, of course, goes to the team at Multilingual Matters – Tommi Grover, Laura Longworth, Flo McClelland, Anna Roderick, Elinor Robertson and Sarah Williams – who have deftly shepherded this book through the entire publishing process. Tommi – thanks especially for the initial encouragement, and to all for your professionalism in seamlessly coordinating all of the bits involved in the production process. We hope that you are as proud of this volume as we are!

Contributors

Suman Barua has a Masters of Education from Harvard University. He has worked in NGOs in the field of education for eight years. Currently he works at Street Child, supporting programs in 20 emergency/crisis countries in Africa and Asia. Previously, he was the Director of Education at Reality Gives, a community-based non-profit in Mumbai, India. As a Teach for India fellow in 2013–15, Suman taught for two years in a low-income school in Mumbai. He has worked as a teacher-trainer, and done projects with UNICEF India and the Swedish government.

Anneliese Cannon is an Associate Professor of Education at Westminster College in Salt Lake City, Utah, and currently teaches classes in teaching methods, TESOL, literacy and research methods. She received her PhD from the University of Wisconsin-Madison. Before teaching at the university level, Dr Cannon taught in diverse settings, including public K-12 schools in the US and internationally. In her research, she explores how innovative pedagogies from digital storytelling, the arts, and computer science can enhance teaching and learning for linguistically diverse students. She is also interested in issues of representation and ethics in qualitative research.

Jiayu Feng, PhD, graduated from East China Normal University. He is an Associate Professor at the School of Education of Shaanxi Normal University in Xi'an, China. He serves on the Membership Committee of the International Association for the Advancement of Curriculum Studies (IAACS). He has conducted a number of national, provincial and ministerial research projects. Publications include a monograph entitled *Research on Children's Autobiography from the Perspective of Autobiographical Curriculum Theory,* and more than 20 articles in journals such as *Journal of East China Normal University, The Chinese Journal of Education,* as well as several provincial education policy documents.

Sara J. Goldberg is an English language/bilingual teacher for the Wausau School District in Wisconsin, USA. She has been a public school educator for 13 years and has taught in both rural and urban communities. In 2019 she was awarded the Herb Kohl Fellowship for teachers. She is currently earning a Doctorate in Education through the Educational Sustainability

Program at the University of Wisconsin-Stevens Point. Her research interests involve utilizing technology to facilitate transnational projects that support educational equity while supporting the development of global citizenship. She explores language, culture and context in formal and informal learning environments.

Margaret R. Hawkins is a Professor in the Department of Curriculum and Instruction and in the PhD Program in Second Language Acquisition at the University of Wisconsin-Madison. Her work, centered on engaged scholarship around issues of equity and social justice, focuses on languages, literacies and learning in classroom, home, and community-based settings in domestic and global contexts. Published work examines: classroom ecologies; families and schools; language teacher education; and new destination communities' responses to mobile populations. She currently explores semiotics and relations in transmodal communications. She received the Erwin Zolt Digital Literacy Gamechanger Award from the International Literacy Association (2019).

Vilma Huerta Cordova is a Professor in the Faculty of Languages of Universidad Autónoma Benito Juárez de Oaxaca (UABJO), Mexico. She has a PhD in Critical Language Studies, UABJO. Her research focuses on collaborative learning, peer tutoring, and interpersonal relationships in the classroom to promote equity in education. She has published in national and international journals on collaborative learning and peer tutoring.

Edwin Nazaret León Jiménez is a Professor in the Faculty of Languages of Universidad Autónoma Benito Juárez de Oaxaca (UABJO), Mexico. He is a member of the Critical Applied Linguistics Academic Group, and he has a PhD in Critical Language Studies, UABJO. His research interests are: language; communication; hegemony; racism; critical thinking and cultural resistance in educational spaces.

Rui Li received her PhD from the Department of Curriculum and Instruction at the University of Wisconsin-Madison. Her research explores relationships between language, literacy, communication, technology, and educational equity in formal and informal learning contexts. She foregrounds how voice, status, inequities and power are allocated in digitally-mediated multimodal communications that reshape learning and social relations for linguistically and culturally diverse youth. Recent publications include: 'Figured Worlds in Transnational Transmodal Communications' (2020, *TESOL Quarterly*) and 'Creating Multimodal Design Spaces for English Learners' (2020, in *Chinese-Speaking Learners of English*, Routledge).

Li Wei is Director and Dean of University College London (UCL) Institute of Education, where he also holds a professorship in applied linguistics. His research covers different aspects of language contact, bilingualism and multilingualism. His publications have won the British Association of Applied Linguistics Book Prize twice: *The Blackwell Guide to Research Methods in Bilingualism and Multilingualism* (2009, with Melissa Moyer), and *Translanguaging: Language, Bilingualism and Education* (2015, with Ofelia García). He is Editor of the *International Journal of Bilingual Education and Bilingualism* and Principal Editor of *Applied Linguistics Review*. He is a Fellow of the Academy of Social Sciences (AcSS), UK.

Júlia Llompart-Esbert is a postdoctoral researcher at the Universitat Autònoma de Barcelona for the LISTiac project (*Linguistically Sensitive Teaching in All Classrooms*) and a member of the Research Centre for Plurilingual Teaching & Interaction (GREIP). Her research focuses on plurilingual practices in education, language mediation, and teaching and learning in non-formal settings, and her work combines ethnography, collaborative and participatory action-research and conversation analysis. She is also a part-time professor at the Unit of Language and Literature Teaching of the Faculty of Education. She has participated in national and international projects and has published several articles related to her research interests.

Mario E. López-Gopar (PhD, OISE/University of Toronto) is Professor in the Faculty of Languages of Universidad Autónoma Benito Juárez de Oaxaca (UABJO), Mexico. Mario's main research interest is intercultural and multilingual education of Indigenous peoples in Mexico. He has received over 15 academic awards. His latest books are *Decolonizing Primary English Language Teaching* (Multilingual Matters, 2016) and *International Perspectives on Critical Pedagogies in ELT* (Palgrave Macmillan, 2019).

Emilee Moore is Serra Húnter Fellow (Associate Professor) at the Universitat Autònoma de Barcelona. She researches interactional practices in multilingual and multicultural educational contexts. She is coordinator of the BA in Primary Education, preparing early childhood, primary and secondary school teachers to educate children and youth in contexts of linguistic diversity. She is a member of the Research Centre for Plurilingual Teaching & Interaction (GREIP) at the UAB and co-convenor of the AILA Research Network on Creative Inquiry in Applied Linguistics. Recent publications include the co-edited: *Translanguaging as Transformation: The Collaborative Construction of New Linguistic Realities* (2020, Multilingual Matters).

Sarah Nazziwa has a Grade III teaching certificate from Kyambogo University in Uganda, and is a sixth grade social studies teacher in the Mukono District. She has been a public school teacher (in Uganda) for 19 years, and is earning her Diploma in Primary Education credential at Uganda Martyrs University-Nkozi. Her current interest is in exploring and learning about new technologies, and how to effectively utilize them for teaching and learning.

Willy Ngaka received his PhD from the University of KwaZulu-Natal. He is a Senior Lecturer with Makerere University and Coordinator of a UNESCO/UNITWIN Cooperation Programme on 'Literacies, Green Skilling and Capacity Development for Sustainable Communities in Africa'. He was the National Coordinator, Makerere University Centre for Lifelong Learning, from 2011 to 2017. Some of his publications in the field of literacy and language education include: 'The Role of Communities in Uganda's Mother Tongue-Based Education' (2020, *Applied Linguistics Review*) and 'Generational, Cultural, and Linguistic Integration for Literacy Learning and Teaching in Uganda' (2016, *Journal of Language and Literacy Education*).

Patricia Ratanapraphart is a PhD student in the Department of Curriculum and Instruction at the University of Wisconsin-Madison. Prior to her graduate work, Patricia worked as an early childhood educator and adult ESL instructor in central Florida. Her research is focused on studying the affordances of classroom-based play for bridging home and school experiences and supporting young English language learners' linguistic, academic, and social development.

William M. Sughrua holds a PhD in Applied Linguistics from the University of Kent. He is professor in the Faculty of Languages of Universidad Autónoma Benito Juárez de Oaxaca (UABJO), Mexico. His research interests involve critical pedagogy, qualitative research, epistemology, and autoethnography. His numerous publications include the book *Heightened Performative Autoethnography: Resisting Oppressive Spaces within Paradigms* (2016, Peter Lang).

Nikhil M. Tiwari is a PhD candidate in the Department of Curriculum and Instruction at the University of Wisconsin-Madison. A former high school English teacher and consultant for nongovernmental organizations and education technology enterprises in South Asia, his current research interests are in the languaging, literacies, and racialization of South Asian youth in the United States.

Trang D. Tran has a Master's degree in in English Language Teaching from Can Tho University in Vietnam and is currently enrolled in the

Master of Science Program in Education at the University of Wisconsin-Madison. She has extensive experience teaching EFL at primary, secondary, and postsecondary levels in Vietnam. She was awarded a Fulbright Fellowship in 2016 and has four years of experience teaching Vietnamese at the tertiary level in the US.

Sarah J. Turner researched Global StoryBridges as an undergraduate student of Education at Westminster College. She is fascinated by the complex interconnections of language, cultural identity, and education, and hopes to further study the topic in the future. She currently teaches first grade at a linguistically diverse school in Salt Lake City, Utah.

Claudia Vallejo Rubinstein is a PhD candidate, adjunct lecturer and member of GREIP (Research Centre for Plurilingual Teaching and Interaction) at the Universitat Autònoma de Barcelona, where she teaches subjects on plurilingualism for pre-service teachers. She has participated in local and international projects on plurilingualism and social inequalities in education. Her PhD research analyzes an after-school program for children categorized as being 'at-risk' of not meeting established curricular objectives on language and literacy, and the transformative potential of their plurilingual practices and pluriliteracies for creating more inclusive educational environments.

Lisa Velarde is a PhD candidate in the Department of Curriculum and Instruction at the University of Wisconsin- Madison with a focus on languages and literacies. She has taught middle school Language Arts in Salt Lake City, Utah, and English to adolescent and adult language learners in Mexico. Currently she is working with the Secondary Education dual certification program at UW-Madison as an instructor and supervisor of pre-service teachers and as a research assistant on an educational project with local youth. Her research focuses on digital literacy practices and cross-cultural communications of youth in transnational contexts.

Gordon B. West is a PhD candidate in the Second Language Acquisition Program at the University of Wisconsin-Madison. He has an MA in Second Language Studies from the University of Hawai'i at Mānoa and worked previously as an English language teacher and teacher educator in the US and South Korea. His research interests are in transmodal communications, narrative analysis, and critical pedagogy. He has published in journals such as *Applied Linguistics Review*, *Critical Inquiry in Language Studies* and *Linguistics and Education*.

Miaomiao Zhang is completing her PhD in Education at the Universitat Autònoma de Barcelona. She has a postgraduate major in International Chinese Education and a dual Master's degree in Teaching Chinese as a

Second Language to Spanish Children from Zhengzhou University and the Comillas Pontifical University. She has worked as a foreign language teacher for almost six years, and currently teaches Chinese and English to children from Chinese migrant families at the Confucius Institute in Barcelona.

Bingjie Zheng is a PhD candidate in the Second Language Acquisition Program at the University of Wisconsin-Madison. Her research interests include linguistic anthropology, sociolinguistics, bi/multilingual education, and language policy. She recently completed a comparative ethnography of two disparate Chinese-English dual language schools in the US, exploring intersections between policy, teaching and learning, and scales of socialization. Recent publications include: 'Neoliberal Multilingualism and "Humanitarian Connections": Discourses around Parents' Experiences with a Mandarin Chinese Immersion School' (2020, *Language & Education*) and 'Translanguaging in a Chinese Immersion Classroom: An Ecological Examination of Instructional Discourses' (2019, *International Journal of Bilingual Education and Bilingualism*).

1 Global StoryBridges: Being and Becoming

Margaret R. Hawkins

Introduction

Once upon a time there was a primary school in a rural Ugandan village, a community-based learning center in a subsidized housing development in the Midwestern US, and a woman – an educationist, in Ugandan parlance – who worked with both. The synergy from their connections catalyzed a project – Global StoryBridges – which, in turn, launched a transglobal education and research initiative. This book is one production emerging from that journey.

However, this is not a fairy tale. This is in part because it's a very true story, but it is also because it doesn't have a happy ending. In fact, it doesn't have an ending at all; it is a story of continual becoming.

So what is Global Storybridges (GSB), why does it matter, and what can we say about its process of becoming? It began approximately 10 years ago as an educational project, digitally linking youth from the two places introduced above, with the intent of having them learn about, with and from each other. The youth, in site-based groups, virtually shared and discussed digital stories they created to represent their lives and communities. As they communicated across time and space, issues and questions became salient; in fact, pressing. For example: How (through what semiotic means and modes) do youth communicate digitally, and to what effect? What meanings do they intend to encapsulate, and convey, and what meanings get interpreted and negotiated? What happens to messages as they travel through time and digital space, across languages, cultures and contexts? What understandings do youth construct as they make sense of one another, and why and how does it matter? What sorts of relationships can/do they forge, and what are impacting factors? How can we define and analyze languaging and learning in transglobal digital communications, and what is the impact on project participants? And so on.

As the research endeavor got underway, rather than encountering straightforward research analysis and outcomes, the questions increased in number and complexity. We realized that, although transglobal digital communications are now a hallmark of our world (Douglas Fir Group,

2016; Hawkins, 2018; Lam & Warriner, 2012; Stornaiuolo et al., 2016), we know little about how they work and what they accomplish from semiotic and relational perspectives. The project and the research on the project are completely entangled, and mutually dependent and informative. The conceptual framings that we use shape our understandings and recursive (re)design of the project, and new insights and theories are ever-emerging from the workings of the project-in-action.

Along the way, GSB grew, such that at present there are 16 active sites in 10 countries, all in under-resourced communities, and a robust transglobal research undertaking involving a research team comprised of university researchers, graduate students, place-based educators and community members that not only enables continual improvement of the project, but also serves to transform understandings of meaning-making in transpositional transmodal communications.

This book has chapters from various members of our research team, some working in tandem, some alone. Given our various positionings as researchers, community members and/or educators working with and across specific global sites, our foci, roles, interests and framings differ, but these collaborations transcend our individual, unique vantage points to demonstrate the power of transglobal interactions and communications both for learning and for researching, as we bring diverse social and cultural perspectives and identifications, and diverse conceptual lenses, to our explorations of how people communicate, encounter each other, make sense of one another, and navigate difference within and across distance and diversity.

This chapter takes up the what, why and how of GSB; I detail its journey of becoming up to and through the point in time of this particular writing. As may be apparent, I am the afore-mentioned 'educationist' – I created and coordinate the project, giving me one particular view of what we are, what we are accomplishing, and what we are becoming. Below, from my vantage point, I first address the titular term 'transpositioning', setting a framework for all that follows. I then describe the *what*: the foundational goals, terrain, sites and participation processes of GSB, information that readers will find helpful to make sense of the project and the discussions in the ensuing chapters. I next discuss the *why*: the critical importance of the project, especially at this particular moment in time, through introducing *critical cosmopolitanism* – one theory that, although building on existing literature, has emerged from the project. Finally, I take up the *how*: the ways in which the project is enhancing understandings of meaning-making across space, time and modalities. For this I invoke *transmodalities*, another conceptual lens emerging from this work, which takes up the 'trans' turn in communications (Hawkins & Mori, 2018), building on work in translanguaging, multiliteracies and multimodalities, extending them to account for the semiotic particularities of transglobal, digital, transcultural (and perhaps all) communication. These lenses serve as guideposts, though not sole guideposts, for the chapters that follow. The following eight chapters, Chapters 2 to 9, are each written by various members of our transglobal research team from their own (single and multiple) vantage points, and, while leveraging transmodalities and critical cosmopolitanism, they invoke a variety of unique and disparate theoretical and conceptual lenses, and focus on analyses of diverse and varied sites and exchanges. The final chapter is a reflection and commentary on our journey-in-motion.

Transpositioning: A Cohesive Framing

As readers may have noted, the concept of positioning has already – both explicitly and implicitly – been central to this discussion. The project, and the research, are premised on a perspective that holds being, becoming and meaning-making as sociocultural processes. That is, who we are, how we make meaning in communications, and how we see the world and understand ourselves and others in it, are always-emergent processes co-constructed with others through social interactions that are situated – or positioned – in particular times and places, between particular people (and things), and located in (and shaped by) particular histories, trajectories and movements of ideas, ideologies, resources, information, goods and people. Everyone and everything are emplaced in particular ways – positioned – in any interaction, and meanings being made are contingent on that positioning. Further, all flows, environments, contexts, encounters and interactions are laden with power dynamics – a theme that permeates this work.

The concept of 'trans' can, at its most basic, be taken to mean 'crossing'. Hawkins and Mori explain:

> Trans can be understood to mean crossing borders or boundaries, and this move toward a 'trans-' disposition signals the need to transcend the named and bounded categories that have historically shaped our thinking about the world and its inhabitants, the nature of knowledge, and communicative resources. (2018: 1)

When combined with 'positioning', 'trans' signifies the multiple and interwoven layers of positioning that are entailed in this and all communicative endeavors. It points to the erasure, and even the transcendence and transformation, of discrete, bounded labels and categories for identifications, subjectivities and positionalities. Here I will identify two dimensions of particular relevance to this project and research.

(1) Spatial transpositioning. In this project, communications and interactions occur both locally and at a distance (translocally and transglobally), both within and across diverse geographic locations. However, the flows of communication and the meanings under construction are not *either* translocal or transglobal nor *either* within or across locations.

The situated intra-site (translocal) interactions are mediated through in-site activities and engagements, available resources, pedagogical and interactional norms, imaginaries of audience, and so on, all of which are located within transglobal flows. Simultaneously, the inter-site (global) interactions are contingent on and mediated by (and therefore inseparable from) those that are translocal. It is worthy of note that the project website itself is transpositional, as representations, ideas and exchanges flow through it on their journeys across space and time, and its design, layout, affordances and constraints transpose what is and can be conveyed, negotiated and understood. What is created and interpreted cannot be considered in isolation from transglobal flows, as meaning-making within each site, within its own socially and culturally mediated ecology, is transformed through artifacts, dialog and exchange with other sites, and other aspects of the transglobal communication and flows within which it is emplaced. Thus the two – translocal and transglobal – rather than being binaries, are so mutually constitutive and informative that the boundaries blend and are transcended, leading to the transpositioning of flows of communications.

(2) Relational transpositioning. All participating members of the project can be seen as transpositioned through their participation. Here I make three particular claims about aspects of relational transpositioning.

As the chapters in this volume will show, youth are emplaced in various ways in their lives, shaped by families, communities, histories, affiliations, experiences and so on. Some have always resided in a community that is comprised of others with similar backgrounds, affiliations, practices and beliefs, and have little or no direct exposure to ethnic/racial/cultural diversity. Others live in multicultural or pluralistic environments, may have resided in multiple locations, and so on, with significant exposure to diversity. Each is emplaced in specific (if complex) ways within networks that shape their identifications and affiliations, and how they perceive of and value those of others. Through in-depth interactions and dialog afforded by GSB – both with local peers and those at a distance – they encounter, experience and reflect on diverse lives, communities, beliefs and practices in ways that lead to transcendence of simple categorizations and stereotyping, leading to a transpositioning of social perceptions, relations and subjectivities as they construct new understandings and interpretations of their own and others' civic and global identifications.

As noted above, there is no simple way to account for researchers' identities and roles. We can apply some labels to research team members' professional roles: teachers, university-based researchers, community educators, graduate students, and so on. Sedimented across these are a variety of national, ethnic and cultural labels that could be applied: Indian, Mexican, Thai-American, African, White/Anglo, Western, indigenous, and so on. And yet the various emplacements when combined with researchers' lives, experiences and personal and professional trajectories complicate and render inadequate any of these labels for understanding what an individual researcher brings to the research. The collaborative nature of the research project further blends and blurs available descriptive categories for researcher positioning, leading to the transpositioning of researcher roles and identities.

Adult participants' roles are complex in this project. Some are site facilitators, responsible for supporting the youth in their engagements (these may be local educators, local community members, university faculty, or undergraduate or graduate students). Some are focused solely on research, are 'attached' to a particular local site, and attend (often somewhat irregularly) for data collection. Some are not attached to a particular site, but rather look across all sites and forms of data as an academic exercise. But most serve multiple roles. That is, they may be a local community member, facilitate a site, *and* be a member of the research team. Each role impacts, and transposes, the others. Many are researching their own sites, their own communities, and their own actions, beliefs and communications, assuming the roles of 'researcher' and 'researched' simultaneously. Further, because the research is collaborative, a particular adult may be conducting a particular inquiry while at the same time serving as an informant (in anthropological terms) to contribute emic perspectives to their global research teammates. Thus the binary of researcher/researched is erased, leading to the transpositioning of researcher/researched positionings.

I could point to other facets of transpositionality – including the transpositioning of messaging, of resources, of locations across space and time, of project/research, and so on, but it is my hope that those aspects will come through both this introductory chapter and all of those that follow. One last observation: it is the hope of all of us involved with GSB that this work will serve to transposition discussions of education and languaging, breaking down and transcending boundaries between disciplinary areas (e.g. language studies, literacies and education) to show how they are mutually dependent and informative, as well as between disciplinary divides within applied linguistics. At heart, teaching, learning, knowing and understanding are human endeavors, and occur through situated/emplaced communications and interactions. Meanings made are shaped by and constitute our social worlds, and transpositioning – crossing, erasing and transcending arbitrarily-constructed boundaries – is transformative, and serves to foster open, robust and caring human connections and relations.

The What: Global StoryBridges

While our two original sites, introduced briefly above, had many differences, they had some similarities as well. Although worlds apart, both were set in low-income, or under-resourced, communities, and both were comprised of youth from families who by local standards were living in poverty. One site – the US site – served predominantly immigrant (English-learning) youth, while the other – in Uganda – served youth who shared a heritage, culture and language (they were Baganda, and spoke Luganda as their home language). Yet the youth in Uganda were schooled in English as a legacy of colonialism, having never spoken it outside of school. So both sets of young project participants were learning English, although their histories, contexts, forms of language and processes differed. GSB put them in communication with one another, providing access to digital resources and opportunities for authentic language and literacy engagements in multimodal transglobal communications.

Over the past 10+ years, as noted above, the project has grown. There are currently 16 sites in 10 countries (China, Honduras, India, Kenya, Mexico, South Africa, Spain, Uganda, the US and Vietnam). Each is located in a low-income community. It is important, though, to realize that what counts as 'poor' is variable and contingent on context and perception; this will be discussed below (and throughout chapters in the book) as it affects understandings and relationships under construction among global youth participants. Some sites meet in schools, some meet in NGOs, some in community-based sites of learning, but the project is never part of the formal school curriculum.

Our original youth participants were approximately 11–13 years of age, as were participating youth at all of the early sites. After several years, however, there were requests for older youth – high-school aged youth – to participate. Thus there are currently two 'clusters' of sites. Some are still populated by youth in the younger age group, the rest by youth aged approximately 14–18 years of age. The younger group only communicates with sites at their age level, and the older group with their same-aged peers.

All youth are in the process of learning English. As demonstrated by the examples above, this means differently in different contexts. In some locations, youth are living in predominantly English-speaking environments but their home languages are not English; these groups are sometimes heterogeneous in terms of ethnicity/home languages, sometimes homogeneous (e.g. in the US). In others, youth live in communities where everyone speaks the same local language, and it is the only language spoken in youths' homes and communities, but schooling is in English (e.g. Uganda). Some sites are located in communities where the local language and the language of school may be the same, and English is a school subject (often taught in under-resourced schools with teachers who are not proficient) (e.g. Vietnam). And in yet other sites there are one or more local languages (the language of home and community), schooling is in a different language, and English is an additional language taught as a school subject (e.g. India). In each of these scenarios, project youth have different proficiencies in English, different forms of English, different access to English, and differing values and outlooks attached to English. Yet, for all, it is seen as a 'status' language, and one that is important for their futures.

We are cognizant, however, of issues attending to linguistic imperialism and the imposition of English (and values around English) (Canagarajah, 1999; Pennycook, 2017; Phillipson, 2012). While website interactions are predominantly in English, because it is the lingua franca of the project and the only relatively mutually intelligible named language among participants, interactions and communications within each site occur in multiple languages. Multiple languages, too, are represented in transmodal communications in a variety of ways, and have at times become a specific focus for the youth in cross-site communications. And from a transmodalities perspective (discussed below), in communication with audiences who are culturally and linguistically diverse and at a distance, youth hone translingual/transmodal communication and literacy skills as they move between and integrate aspects of languages and other semiotic resources.

The project has three 'official' goals. They are to foster:

(1) language and literacy development of participating youth (including but not limited to English);
(2) development of technological abilities and expertise;
(3) awareness and understanding of global others and of oneself as a global citizen, through fostering (equitable and open) global relations.

Similar to the diversity in languages, youth participants arrive with varying levels of familiarity and proficiency with technology. For some, it is an everyday part of their lives, and even their school lives. For others, they have never seen or touched a computer, or had access to internet, prior to participating in GSB. Many do have access to cell phones, but some do not. For all, the integration of digital and other semiotic resources, and learning to create multimodal stories that embrace and transcend place and diversity, enhance their technological/digital literacy skills.

Each site is comprised of approximately 8–12 youth. In site meetings, youth collaboratively (within their site) create digital stories of their lives and communities, using all of the semiotic resources, including digital modes, available to them. They then post these to GSB's dedicated website, where youth in other sites watch then discuss them together with their site-based peers, ultimately collaboratively composing comments and questions in response, which they post via a dedicated chat space/comment section the website provides below each video. The video makers, in turn, read the comments, discuss them, and respond. In this way they collaboratively (within and across sites) engage in video-sharing and dialog.

An important aspect is the collaboration, as, in alignment with socio-cultural and critical approaches to learning, GSB is premised on dialogic, collaborative, task-based learning (Freire, 1985; Gibbons, 2014; Hawkins,

2019). This is not social networking; youth do not access or post individually. The collaborations offer opportunities to learn with and from one another within sites through negotiating meanings and practicing emerging language, literacy and technology skills while navigating civic identities and constructing understandings of one another and of global peers; and these opportunities are mirrored in the transglobal collaborations by design.

Each site has an adult facilitator. Again instantiating a sociocultural approach, meetings and tasks are not teacher-fronted nor teacher-led, although this sometimes is challenging in contexts where learning and teaching historically and traditionally have only that structure. The facilitator, who is a local teacher, educator and/or community member (depending on location), is there to support the work of the youth but not direct it. Initially the facilitator is instrumental in selecting participants and helps with familiarizing youth with the project and technology, including the digital story platform (IMovie, as we provide Mac laptops and video cameras for each site). Their role in interactions is to guide and scaffold thinking and dialog as necessary (often not so necessary once the youth get the hang of it), and to ensure that everyone has the opportunity to participate, smoothing/guiding social relations if needed. There are times when transglobal (or sometimes local) interactions are controversial, or represent/reify inequitable positionings, and at those times the facilitator's role is to manage and mediate controversial issues and discussions (Ho et al., 2017; Noddings & Brooks, 2017), and also to draw attention to ways in which the messages composed by youth may or may not be appropriate to and respectful of their audience.

The Why: Critical Cosmopolitanism

In early years, I was the sole researcher; the research enhanced my understanding of what the project was and could do, and the research questions emerged from what I observed and data I collected. I soon discovered that, while there were conceptualizations around languaging, literacies (including digital literacies), globalization, mobility and more that had a bearing on the project, there was virtually no research on transglobal communications and/or education-oriented initiatives such as this. It became clear to me that, while language, literacy and technology development might be important goals in the project, what was most interesting, and arguably most important, were the encounters between global youth themselves: the ways in which they were and weren't encountering and understanding one another and making meaning together; the resulting impact on their perspectives towards and emerging relations with one another; and their understandings of themselves and others within a global terrain. In our increasingly hostile, biased, and distrustful world, understanding not just how these youth encounter each other across diversity and distance, and how they make sense of and understand each other, but how to cultivate attitudes and stances of valuing, caring, respect and equity among them was and remains the ultimate goal and foundation of the project. These social justice-oriented goals of the project – both the youth-centered interactions and the research – are its center and pivot-point.

In trying to make sense of the youth's transglobal encounters and exchanges, I consulted literature on globalization (e.g. Appadurai, 1996; Hall, 2006; Held, 2001), coming to see that a hallmark of an increasingly globalized world was the mobility of people, things, languages, ideas, ideologies, and so forth, and the resulting new configurations of geographies, people, knowledge and resources (Hawkins & Cannon, 2017), all of which are encompassed and reflected in GSB. However, multidisciplinary literature on globalization did not address the nature and becoming of human relations within forces of globalization. For this I turned to the literature on cosmopolitanism.

There is a large and diffuse body of work, from a variety of disciplines (e.g. philosophy, sociology, geography, education, and so on), addressing the nature and import of cosmopolitanism. Many scholars attribute its origins to Diogenes in the 4th century BC, who described himself as a '*kosmou polites*' (citizen of the world), and Socrates who, in the 3rd century BC, declared himself '... not an Athenian or a Greek, but a citizen of the world' (as cited in Ong, 2009: 452). Yet most scholars of cosmopolitanism, across disciplines, perceive the world as divided into nation-states, with discrete boundaries, and cosmopolitans as those who move across them. This, clearly, is not generative for understanding GSB, where youth themselves do not move across national boundaries but rather are fully implicated in the global physical, material, knowledge and ideological flows and trajectories that shape who they are and can be, their identities and worldviews.

More relevant, especially in a project for under-resourced youth and communities, were conceptualizations of 'cosmopolitanism of the above' and 'cosmopolitanism of the below' (Hall, 2006), echoed in the work of other scholars as 'cosmopolitanism on the ground' (Hansen, 2010), 'rooted cosmopolitanism' (Appiah, 2005), 'elementary cosmopolitanism' (Kromidas, 2011) and 'everyday cosmopolitanism' (Hull *et al.*, 2010). These theories began to shed light on the transglobal nature of the GSB encounters among youth who, in the words of Hall (2006), were 'living in translation every day of their lives' (n.p.), albeit often without crossing physical and spatial boundary lines.

I found particularly compelling work that spoke to intersections between cosmopolitanism, global encounters, and civic identities and engagements, such as that of Rizvi, who reflected:

> (while) interconnectivity (is) becoming a norm ... it is not always clear as to how particular communities and people experience and are affected by global interconnectivity, how they interpret its various expressions and how they work with this understanding to forge their sense of belonging, and their social imagination. (2008: 19)

Ultimately, I have been most influenced by work that attends to social and relational aspects of cosmopolitanism from an ethical perspective/stance, such as that of Appiah, who tells us that, 'we have obligations to others, obligations that stretch beyond those to whom we are related by the ties of kith and kind, or even the more formal ties of a shared citizenship' and that we must, 'take seriously the value not just of human life but of particular human lives, which means taking an interest in the practices and beliefs that lend them significance' (2006: xv).

This is, at least in part, the goal of GSB – to instill a sense of civic obligation in youth participants for the welfare of others and of our world, and to support them to value their global peers and seek for deep understanding. Yet cosmopolitanism in this guise does not account for the workings of power, positioning and status that are always and everywhere fully bound up with human relations (Apple, 2012; Freire, 1968). In GSB, it is clear, as mentioned earlier, that while all youth live in (relative) poverty, poverty is, indeed, relative. And youth, though perhaps they are not themselves mobile, are entangled in global flows of information, resources and ideologies that privilege some forms of knowing, being, doing and having over others. This plays out, over and over again, in the ways that project youth perceive one another, and themselves, as these provide the lenses through which they interpret the messages and communications from and with others. Thus I offer *critical cosmopolitanism* (e.g. Hawkins, 2014, 2018, 2020) as a heuristic for transglobal (and other) encounters across difference, to take into account the identity and positioning work that ensues from imaginaries of privilege, power and status, and to endeavor to foster attitudes and stances of equity, openness and caring (following Appiah, 2005, 2006) as we re-organize and re-distribute the knowledge, power and status that create inequitable conditions and relations.

Perhaps closest to this in terms of GSB is the work of Canagarajah, who calls for a dialogic cosmopolitanism, in which cosmopolitanism is 'interacted and negotiated ... treat[ing] power as open to negotiation and realignment' (2013: 196). This is the *why* of GSB: to foster journeys towards critical cosmopolitanism.

The How: *Transmodalities*

While critical cosmopolitanism embodies the core and the goal of the project, it matters little, especially in the design of an educational project, if we cannot understand how messages are crafted, travel, are received and negotiated, and (or put another way) the means and modes through which meanings are being made, carried and interpreted. This is perhaps especially obvious in research endeavors where we have limited tools for data analysis. How, when looking at (and across) artifacts such as youth-produced videos and chat texts, or when viewing video recordings of site meetings, can we subject them to analysis if we don't understand what, exactly, it is that carries a semiotic load? In conversation or discourse analysis there are now tools for unpacking and analyzing talk and text (e.g. Rogers, 2004; Van Leeuwen, 2008). Guided by a different understanding of semiotics – where language is not central, but is one of a vast array of resources and modes for communication, and human communicative tools are fully entangled with objects, space and time – what, then, are approaches and tools for analysis and understandings of meanings-under-construction?

The work of multiliteracies scholars perhaps first turned our gaze to the multiplicities of literacies: the need to shift our focus from 'reading' and 'writing' to understandings of literacy performances as integrations of multiplicities of languages/literacies/resources in 20th- and 21st-century worlds (New London Group, 1996). The current focus on the 'trans-' turn in applied linguistics also points to the importance of destabilizing discretely defined resources (such as language, or culture), instead focusing on the performativity of languaging and literacies, and the multiple, shifting resources that are fluidly intermingled and leveraged in communications (Canagarajah, 2013; Hawkins & Mori, 2018). For GSB, it was important to move beyond language given that youth were co-constructing meanings through assemblages of resources that included but went far beyond linguistic components as sole conveyors of meaning in these GSB blends of digital and face-to-face, transpositioned, interactions – and for this I first turned to work on multimodality. Similar to cosmopolitanism, the literature on modes is extensive and multidisciplinary, with a variety of views and approaches. What was most compelling to me, because it was most aligned with GSB and semiotic understandings and interpretations, was the work on modes by Gunther Kress and various colleagues (e.g. Jewitt, 2017; Kress, 2010), following a Hallidayan social semiotic approach (Halliday, 1978). Jewitt, for example, offers this definition of multimodality:

> Multimodality describes approaches that understand communication and representation to be more than about language, and which attend to the full range of communicational forms people use – image, gesture, gaze, posture and so on – and the relationships between these. (2017: 15)

Yet the concept of modes, while informative, still had limits in its heuristic power. First, the work on modes tends to focus on identifying modes (e.g. gaze or color), and analyzing in a given interaction, or set of interactions, what role the mode plays or what meaning it carries. Yet in GSB the modes, following the 'trans-' discussion above, were intermingled such that they mutually constituted a message, and were not separable. Moreover, messages and meanings were made between the modes used in videos, the text responses to them, and the discussions that occurred within sites, and were therefore cross- or trans-modal, and implicated space and time. Further, modes, as Kress claimed, are, 'a socially shaped and culturally given resource for meaning-making' (2017: 60), and were often not consistent, coherent or even interpretable across diverse social and cultural contexts. And, in line with the discussion above, they did not account for the workings of power, privilege and status that shaped and were embedded in messages and their interpretations. Thus I developed a theory of *transmodalities* (Hawkins, 2018, 2020).

There are five 'complexities' that I identify within a theory of transmodalities. They are meant to account for transpositional communications, although they are now being taken up and applied in promising ways in research on face-to-face and in-situ communications. They are:

Complexity #1: Modes intertwined. As discussed, it is important to be able to identify modes, and the meanings they carry, in communication, moving understandings of semiotics beyond talk and text to all of the available resources for meaning-making. However, a focus on an individual mode does not explain the ways in which modes are always inextricably entangled in communication, and interact together to form something different than what can be understood by considering each in isolation.

Complexity #2: Relations between modes, language and material objects. This, aligning with work by Latour (2005) and others, de-centralizes the role of language in human communications, turning instead to 'networks' or 'assemblages' of resources that constitute communication and production. New materialist scholars (Barad, 2007; Braidotti, 2013), in line with Latour, claim that humans and 'non-human actors' (Latour, 2005) have their own histories, networks and semiotic weight and potentials in communication and meaning-making.

Complexity #3: The arc of communication. Much of the work in multimodalities, and that in literacies, focuses on composition and design-work in assembling messages. This assumes human intent, and that meanings that creators, or producers, intend are actually those conveyed. Because this is not, in fact, what happens in GSB, we draw attention to the importance of considering the full 'arc of communication' (Hawkins, 2018, 2020), so that rather than analyzing only a production, or multimodal ensemble, we follow the chain of semiosis across the spaces through which the message travels, and its reception and negotiation, in order to more deeply understand the emerging co-construction of meanings.

Complexity #4: Culture and context. There are two aspects here worthy of note. One is that when considering context, one identifiable context is that of the multimodal artifact itself. Each mode is mutually dependent and formative, and also they are given meaning through the whole of the artifact. In this way the constituent parts, intertwined, shape the meaning of one other, and continually shape the meaning of the whole while only being understandable within the context of the whole. Another aspect, addressing both culture and context, are the places and spaces within which the arc of communication occurs. Space, itself, is a semiotic resource, and ontologies and epistemologies of place shape what can be done, communicated and understood within them (Hawkins, 2014). Culture, as discussed earlier, is tied to place, and modes and the meanings they carry are always interpreted and reinterpreted within specific cultural contexts. We must be cautious, though, not to essentialize 'culture' – interrogating what it is and means, and what role it plays in meaning-making, is a critical part of this work.

Complexity #5: Transglobalism and relations of power. In introducing the concept of multimodalities, Kress claimed, '… there are times – perhaps many times – when communication isn't really the issue, and power is' (2010: 3). Yet within literature on modes, multimodal ensembles and productions, little attention in subsequent analyses and research has been paid to political dimensions, power dynamics and status relations. However, as discussed earlier, they infuse all human interactions and communications. There has been some attention to access (e.g. Archer, 2017; Stein, 2008), whereby different people and communities have differential access to digital resources, as is the case in GSB. However, beyond economic capital, social, cultural and political capital and their associated resources also shape what modes are used, what messages are created, where and how they travel, how meanings are interpreted, and how various actors (or participants) are positioned vis-à-vis one another in communications. In the words of Sherris and Adami, 'If sign-making is at bottom relational, entangling and dynamic, it is no less political' (2019: 2). This takes us back to critical cosmopolitanism, and the need to attend to the differential and inequitable valuing of people, signs and resources in communications and interactions.

Transmodalities provides a conceptual framework for considering, and exploring, the transglobal communications that occur between youth participants in GSB. When applied, it enables us to see how the project becomes: the interworkings of communication, meaning-making and relations-under-construction between project youth.

Transglobal Research

By now, the historical trajectory, underpinnings, processes, and theoretical frameworks that have emerged along our journey have been explained. What remains is a word about the nature of transglobal research, especially transglobal research into meaning-making in (digital) communications across time, space and diversity. Critical cosmopolitanism delivers a clear mandate for understanding emergent meanings and relationships being forged as global youth encounter and exchange messages with one another. Transmodalities offers an explanation of the extraordinary complexity of analyzing such communications. So the question remains: how do we gain access to the meanings and understandings under construction? Full disclosure: we do not yet fully know; we're working on it. We do believe that qualitative, ethnographically-informed research offers us windows into dimensions of social understandings, positionings, relations and communications. Kress (2011) and Flewitt (2011), in fact, have called for ethnography to complement multimodal research.

Our data includes the videos that are posted on the project website, the texts of the chats they engender, observations (sometimes participant observation) of meetings in sites documented through video and field notes, group interviews with youth (per site), literacy artifacts collected from sites, and individual interviews with facilitators and youth.

Yet, while investigating participants' emergent understandings, perspectives, contexts and processes can offer insights into what meanings and relationships are being forged, or are in the process of becoming, there are significant challenges in transglobal research. A major one is access, another is perspective. Ethnography, quite appropriately, calls for gaining an emic perspective of the group or people under study. GSB itself stems from a Western imaginary and set of beliefs about what goals are important in a transglobal project for youth, and what appropriate means and processes might be to reach them. As will be apparent through the chapters of this book, the project is taken up quite differently in non-Western locations, and across the diversity of the places where sites are located. It is the height of arrogance to assume that a white, Western, university-based researcher can drop in on a site, gather data, and then adequately interpret that data. Further, with the expanding number of sites, it isn't possible to gather data from each on a regular basis. And lastly, there is, again, the not-inconsequential matter of (trans)positionality. Being an American university professor, and in fact an American project, means differently in different contexts and is relationally different depending on who the particular facilitator/set of students are, and that affects responses and interactions.

In response, several years ago we launched a transglobal research team. As mentioned earlier, it is comprised of university researchers, site facilitators (who are in some cases local teachers, in other cases community members who may or may not be educators), and graduate students. Some work directly with the sites, some have research as their primary activity. Initially we held a three-day workshop, learning about one another and our respective sites, setting goals, discussing research interests, and undertaking collaborative data dives to ascertain that, in fact, multiple perspectives (from multiple global locations and positionalities) would be fruitful and enable us to see more and more deeply than we could individually. Since then, we have engaged together in e-seminars (three times per year), come together in various configurations for conference panels and presentations, and co-authored publications (e.g. Li & Hawkins, 2021; Vallejo *et al.*, 2020, this volume). As we progress, we continue to become – to become co-designers, co-thinkers, co-researchers, collaborators and colleagues that inspire and enlighten one another, leading to continual expansion of ideas, approaches and productions as well as continual expansion and improvement in the design of GSB. This book is one example of our evolution.

The Book

In these chapters you will see the power of transglobal perspectives coming together to inform analyses of data. Each chapter, authored by a member or members of our research team, focuses on a different site or a set of exchanges between specific sites, thus representing different geographic areas and contexts. Each draws, foundationally, on the concepts of critical cosmopolitanism and transmodalities – to lesser and greater extents – in portraying deep, nuanced accounts of various aspects of transglobal communications. Yet each, also, uses its own approaches, framings and analytic tools in exploring different facets of the work. Some chapters are deep explorations of a particular site and its interactions; some have a sharper focus on transglobal exchanges and interactions. All are empirical; through these pages you will come to see the sorts of representations, communications, and co-constructions of meaning that the project engenders, and through the various analyses the power of research to shed light on what they mean and do. What emerges is a complex portrait of ecologies – the components of transpositioned transglobal engagements, the ways in which their entanglements and scales matter, the historical and current sociocultural and sociopolitical contexts, and their critical nature as they shape perceptions of identity, belonging and relations of project participants. We hope that this rendering of our present thinking in our journey of becoming will catalyze more (and more robust) engagements in transglobal educational exchanges, in conceptualizing and understanding languaging, literacies and learning in such exchanges, and in transglobal research. We invite you to join us in this work.

Chapter overviews

Chapter 1. Global StoryBridges: Being and Becoming. Margaret R. Hawkins.

This introductory chapter, authored by the US-based university educator who created and coordinates GSB, offers its foundational principles, design, and processes; describes its trajectory as both an educational and a research project; and shows its current and potential power and promise for (critical) theory, research and practice.

Chapter 2. Building Scalar Frames of Understandability in 'Trans' Practices within a Catalan Global StoryBridges Site. Emilee Moore, Claudia Vallejo Rubinstein, Júlia Llompart-Esbert and Miaomiao Zhang.

Drawing on the notions of sociolinguistic scale and transidiomatic practices, chapter authors – three researchers from a university in Barcelona, and a Chinese PhD student with the dual role of site facilitator and researcher – analyze scalar complexities in both translocal and transglobal communications in GSB, showing the importance of considering behind-the-scenes engagements and interactions in crafting understandings of meanings being constructed. Data from unfolding transmodal interactions between both human and non-human (digital) actors illuminate how people, place, languaging, resources (including technological resources), social roles, activities and imaginaries at various scales are intertwined and shape emerging understandings of and relations with local and global others.

Chapter 3. Cosmopolitan Aims/Cosmopolitan Realities: How Immigrant Youth Negotiate Languaging and Identity in One After-School Program. Anneliese Cannon and Sarah J. Turner.

Authors of this chapter are a faculty member and an undergraduate student from a small liberal arts university in the western US, who serve dual roles as facilitators and researchers at a community-based GSB site. Analyzing data from meetings, videos and chats involving five young female project participants from the Middle East, South and East Asia, and Africa, they explore how GSB supported both negotiations and representations of the cosmopolitan tenets of identities, citizenship and belonging for these immigrant youth as they made sense of themselves and others in light of their new community/homeland.

Chapter 4. A Place-Based Critical Transmodal Analysis of Chinese Youth's Digital Storytelling. Rui Li and Jiayu Feng.

A research collaboration between a US-based researcher and a faculty member from a Chinese university, this chapter demonstrates how and why place and context matter. Situating GSB goals and activities within a broader Chinese sociopolitical and sociocultural context, the authors identify the structures and hierarchies of power inside and outside of school within which their site is emplaced and show how Western-driven GSB criteria and processes conflict with local 'societal norms around inclusion and opportunity'. This critical inquiry blurs the lines between culturally-laden concepts of supports and constraints, showing why research into place, context and culture is necessary to comprehend what is and can be accomplished through both learning design and transglobal transmodal communications.

Chapter 5. Navigating Transnational Transmodal Terrain: Perspectives from Ugandan Lugbara Youth. Willy Ngaka.

Focusing on a rural village site in northwestern Uganda, this chapter analyzes youth-produced videos, chat texts, observations and interviews of GSB youth participants as they create a video about a local activity and then engage in dialog about it with youth from Barcelona and Vietnam. The author is a researcher from a Ugandan university who founded the site in a community library in his heritage community. Contextualizing the site within discourses of globalization and cosmopolitanism, he showcases its uniqueness in terms of lack of resources and the remoteness of the location and relative isolation of the population. Invoking multiliteracies and transmodalities, he demonstrates how differences across sites in semiotic representations and understandings, cultures, and ideologies led to miscommunications, cultural misperceptions, and complicated positionings and relationalities. Yet the arc of communication, as meanings were represented, received and negotiated, led to digital and transmodal learning, explorations of identities, and nascent understandings of and relationships with global peers.

Chapter 6. Youth Transmodally Indexing Social Discourses: A Vietnam Video Narrative Analysis. Gordon B. West, Bingjie Zheng and Trang D. Tran.

This transglobal research team, consisting of two US-based researchers (one from the US, the other from China) and a local teacher from Vietnam who served as site facilitator, conduct a transmodal narrative analysis of interactions between youth in the Vietnam site and their global peers, in order to better understand the relationships between the use of modes in video construction and the narratives they construct, and how these, in turn, serve to position youth both in terms of their own national identifications and in relation to their global peers. Drawing on Bamberg's (1997) three levels of narrative analysis, they examine transmodal elements in youth-produced videos and subsequent chat exchanges, in particular those between GSB youth in Vietnam and Kenya, to explore representations and stories-under-construction of national and cultural identities, the youth's locations within them, and how these were navigated and reified through their communications with global peers.

Chapter 7. Critical Cosmopolitanism and Sustainable Education: Primary Educator Perspectives from Uganda and the United States. Sara J. Goldberg and Sarah Nazziwa.

In this unique chapter two GSB facilitators who are primary school teachers, one from a small Ugandan village and one from a mid-sized town in the Midwestern US, analyze and discuss the global learning that occurs within their GSB sites through a lens of 21st-century learning and skills

(Williams *et al.*, 2013). They contextualize processes and interactions in their respective sites and offer both in-site and comparative cross-site analyses to elucidate learning affordances that GSB offers for youth. They suggest implications for schools and classrooms, and trace GSB's impact on their own development as educators.

Chapter 8. Developing Decolonizing Pedagogies with Mexican Pre-Service 'English' Teachers. Mario E. López-Gopar, Vilma Huerta Cordova, William M. Sughrua and Edwin Nazaret León Jiménez.

In this Mexican site, GSB served as both an educational project for youth and as a resource and location for pre-service teacher education. The four chapter authors, all researchers and educators at a Mexican university engaged in language teacher education, situate teaching, teacher education and GSB within the local educational and languaging context. They describe how the geopolitical context – including the effects of national ideologies and policies that reflect the legacy of colonialism – shape teaching, learning and schooling in Mexico, reproducing colonial difference. They provide a close analysis of one video produced by youth in their site in which youth represented their local activities, which were facilitated by pre-service teacher education students, and responses from peers in the US, Uganda and China. Through this, they illustrate the power of transmodal global engagements to empower indigenous youth through affirming identities, transgressing colonizing discourses, and promoting multiliteracies. Further, they recognize their potential to disrupt colonial discourses through alternative approaches to teacher education.

Chapter 9. Positionality Revisited: A Critical Examination of Meaning-Making and Collaboration in a Transnational Research Team. Patricia Ratanapraphart, Lisa Velarde, Nikhil M. Tiwari and Suman Barua.

Unlike previous chapters, this chapter directly analyses how meanings are constructed among diverse members of a transglobal research team. It is authored by three US-based researchers, one of whom identifies as American, one as Asian American, and one Indian, together with a community-based research team member from India. Together, they analyze the compositional choices of youth from a site in Mumbai for a video about a holiday celebration in honor of Ganesh, a Hindu god. Data consisting of the video and interviews with youth and the facilitator were collected, and the group analyzed it in various configurations over time. Rather than focus solely on that analysis, however, they use their collaboration as data to show how their 'differing and layered identities and positionalities' intersected with their collaborative explorations and understandings of the data, blurring boundaries between 'insider' and 'outsider', and leading to a theorization of 'spectrums of emicity' in ethnographically-oriented research. This chapter articulates the power and affordances (and also limitations) of conducting collaborative transglobal research.

Chapter 10. Coda. Li Wei.

In this concluding chapter, Li Wei – a linguist who is not affiliated with GSB – reflects on the power of GSB to promote critical reflection, support exploration of identities, educate, and forge transglobal linkages and relations. His musings on globalization, world order, human relations and social change offer an 'arm's-length' view of the value of the work presented in this volume, and the promise that it holds.

References

Appadurai, A. (1996) *Modernity at Large: Cultural Dimensions of Globalization.* Minneapolis, MN: University of Minnesota Press.
Appiah, K.A. (2005) *The Ethics of identity.* Princeton, NJ: Princeton University Press.
Appiah, K.A. (2006) *Cosmopolitanism: Ethics in a World of Strangers.* New York, NY: W.W. Norton & Co. Inc.
Apple, M.W. (2012) *Knowledge, Power and Education: The Selected Works of Michael W. Apple.* New York, NY: Routledge.
Archer, A. (2017) Power, social justice and multimodal pedagogies. In C. Jewitt (ed.) *The Routledge Handbook of Multimodal Analysis.* London: Routledge.
Bamberg, M. (1997) Positioning between structure and performance. *Journal of Narrative and Life History* 7, 335–342.
Barad, K. (2007) *Meeting the Universe Halfway: Quantum Physics and the Entanglement of Matter and Meaning.* Durham, NC: Duke University Press.
Braidotti, R. (2013) *The Posthuman.* Cambridge: Polity.
Canagarajah, A.S. (1999) *Resisting Linguistic Imperialism in English Teaching.* Oxford: Oxford University Press.
Canagarajah, A.S. (2013) *Translingual Practice: Global Englishes and Cosmopolitan Relations.* New York, NY: Routledge.
Douglas Fir Group (2016) A transdisciplinary framework for SLA in a multilingual world. *Modern Language Journal* 100, 19–47.
Flewitt, R. (2011) Bringing ethnography to a multimodal investigation of early literacy in a digital age. *Qualitative Research* 11 (3), 293–310.
Freire, P. (1968) *Pedagogy of the Oppressed.* New York, NY: Seabury Press.
Gibbons, P. (2014) *Scaffolding Language Scaffolding Learning.* Portsmouth, NH: Heinemann.
Hall, S. (2006) Interview of Stuart Hall. See http://www.youtube.com/watch?v=fBfPtRaGZPM (accessed April 2021).
Halliday, M.A.K. (1978) *Language as a Social Semiotic.* London: Edward Arnold.
Hansen, D.T. (2010) Cosmopolitanism and education: A view from the ground. *Teachers College Record* 112 (1), 1–30.
Hawkins, M.R. (2014) Ontologies of place, creative meaning making and critical cosmopolitan education. *Curriculum Inquiry* 44 (1), 90–113.
Hawkins, M.R. (2018) Transmodalities and transglobal encounters: Fostering critical cosmopolitan relations. *Applied Linguistics* 39 (1), 55–77.
Hawkins, M.R. (2019) Plurilingual learners and schooling: A sociocultural perspective. In L.C. de Oliveira (ed.) *Handbook of TESOL in K-12.* Hoboken, NJ: John Wiley & Sons.
Hawkins, M.R. (2020) Toward critical cosmopolitanism: Transmodal transnational engagements of youth. In E. Moore, J. Bradley and J. Simpson (eds) *Translanguaging as Transformation: The Collaborative Construction of New Linguistic Realities* (pp. 23–40). Bristol: Multilingual Matters.

Hawkins, M.R. and Cannon, A. (2017) Mobility, language & schooling. In A.S. Canagarajah (ed.) *The Routledge Handbook of Migration and Language*. New York, NY: Routledge.

Hawkins, M.R. and Mori, J. (2018) Considering 'trans-' perspectives in language theories and practice. *Applied Linguistics* 39 (1), 1–8. doi:10.1093/applin/amx056.

Held, D. (2001) Globalization, cosmopolitanism and democracy [interview]. *Constellations* 8 (4), 427–441.

Ho, L., McAvoy, P., Hess, D. and Gibbs, B. (2017) Teaching and learning about controversial issues and topics in the social studies. In M. Manfra and C. Bolick (eds) *The Wiley Handbook of Social Studies Research* (pp. 319–335). Hoboken, NJ: John Wiley and Sons.

Hull, G.A., Stornaiuolo, A. and Sahni, U. (2010) Cultural citizenship and cosmopolitan practice: Global youth communicate online. *English Education* 42, 331–367.

Jewitt, C. (ed.) (2017) *The Routledge Handbook of Multimodal Analysis*. London: Routledge.

Kress, G. (2010) *Multimodality: A Social Semiotic Approach to Contemporary Communication*. London: Routledge.

Kress, G. (2011) Partnerships in research: Multimodality and ethnography. *Qualitative Research* 11 (3), 239–260.

Kress, G. (2017) What is a mode? In C. Jewitt (ed.) *The Routledge Handbook of Multimodal Analysis*. London: Routledge.

Kromidas, M. (2011) Elementary forms of cosmopolitanism: Blood, birth and bodies in immigrant New York City. *Harvard Educational Review* 81, 581–605.

Lam, W.S.E. and Warriner, D.S. (2012) Transglobalism and literacy: Investigating the mobility of people, languages, texts, and practices in contexts of migration. *Reading Research Quarterly* 47 (2), 191–215.

Latour, B. (2005) *Reassembling the Social: An Introduction to Actor-Network Theory*. Oxford: Oxford University Press.

Li, R. and Hawkins, M.R. (2021) Figured worlds in transnational transmodal communications. *TESOL Quarterly* 55 (1), 5–28.

New London Group (1996) A pedagogy of multiliteracies: Designing social futures. *Harvard Education Review* 66 (1), 60–92.

Noddings, N. and Brooks, L. (2017) *Teaching Controversial Issues: The Case for Critical Thinking and Moral Commitment in the Classroom*. New York, NY: Teachers College Press.

Ong, J.C. (2009) The cosmopolitan continuum: Locating cosmopolitanism in media and cultural studies. *Media, Culture & Society* 31 (3), 449–466.

Pennycook, A. (2017) *The Cultural Politics of English as an International Language*. London: Routledge.

Phillipson, R. (2012) Linguistic imperialism. *The Encyclopedia of Applied Linguistics*. Oxford: John Wiley & Sons. See https://doi.org/10.1002/9781405198431.wbeal0718.pub2 (accessed April 2021).

Rizvi, F. (2008) Epistemic virtues and cosmopolitan learning. *The Australian Educational Researcher* 35, 17–35.

Rogers, R. (2004) *Critical Discourse Analysis in Education*. New York, NY: Routledge.

Sherris, A. and Adami, E. (2019) *Making Signs, Translanguaging Ethnographies: Exploring Urban, Rural and Educational Spaces*. Bristol: Multilingual Matters.

Stein, P. (2008) *Multimodal Pedagogies in Diverse Classrooms: Representation, Rights and Resources*. London: Routledge.

Stornaiuolo, A., Smith, A. and Phillips, C. (2016) Developing a transliteracies framework for a connected world. *Journal of Literacy Research* 49 (1), 68–91.

Vallejo, C., Moore, E., Llompart, J. and Hawkins, M. (2020) Semiosis y cosmopolitismo crítico: Un análisis transmodal de un dilema ético en comunicación transnacional entre jóvenes. *Profesorado. Revista de Currículum y Formación de Profesorado* 24 (1), 304–325. DOI: 10.30827/profesorado.v24i1.9130.

Van Leeuwen, T. (2008) *Discourse and Practice: New Tools for Critical Discourse Analysis*. Oxford: Oxford University Press.

Williams, C., Gannon, S. and Sawyer, W. (2013) A genealogy of the 'future': Antipodean trajectories and travels of the '21st century learner'. *Journal of Education Policy* 28 (6), 792–806.

2 Building Scalar Frames of Understandability in 'Trans' Practices within a Catalan Global StoryBridges Site

Emilee Moore, Claudia Vallejo Rubinstein, Júlia Llompart-Esbert and Miaomiao Zhang

Introduction

While the Global StoryBridges project's overarching aims are to promote critical cosmopolitan and transmodal communications between youth at different global sites, significant exchanges in relation to these goals also emerge within sites. In this chapter we zoom in on interaction occurring locally during a project session at the site in Catalonia (Spain). We examine how the participation of a graduate researcher from China in the facilitation and research at the site prompts meaningful possibilities for learning and communication by the youth and adult members. Analytically, we draw on the notion of sociolinguistic scale – or the 'spatiotemporal scope of understandability' – to enquire into how participants build scalar frames in their discourse (Blommaert *et al.*, 2015). We also employ the notion of transidiomatic practices to consider the 'comingling of localized, multilingual interactions and technologically mediated, digitalized communication' (Jacquemet, 2016: 8), as site participants deploy full linguistic repertoires and digital and embodied modes in constructing meaning. The ethnographic data we analyse include video-recordings of interactions and participant observations. The chapter contributes an understanding of how participants build understandings of themselves and others as they confront different worldviews, and of how interaction in the setting challenges monolingual, monocultural and monomodal approaches to education.

The chapter is structured as follows. We begin by outlining the main theoretical notions that guide the analysis in relation to the conceptual framework presented by Hawkins in the opening of this volume. We then frame our participation in the Global StoryBridges network as one of several collaborative educational initiatives in the municipality where our site is located. The research methodology is then presented, together with two extracts of video data, which are analysed and discussed in order to later draw conclusions in the final section of the chapter.

'Trans' Practices across Modes, Languages and Participants

In introducing the transmodalities framework, Hawkins (2018: 55) refers to the 'trans-' turn in studies of language and communication – partly thrust forward by scholarship on translanguaging (e.g. García & Li, 2014; Vallejo & Dooly, 2020) – to refer to 'the current era of globalization in which communication occurs with ever-increasing rapidity among ever-expanding audiences, through rapidly changing semiotic means and modes'. Hawkins claims that this 'trans-' turn also highlights 'the significant increase of attention to the ways in which language is enmeshed with other semiotic resources in constructing meanings in communication' (2018: 55) in fluid and unpredictable ways. In her work on transmodalities, similar to the scholarship on translanguaging, Hawkins builds on the notion of repertoire originally proposed by Gumperz (1964) and later developed by scholars such as Blommaert and Backus (2013) and Rymes (2014). Transmodalities also extends work on multimodality rooted in social semiotics (e.g. Kress & Van Leeuwen, 2001; Kress, 2011; Jewitt, 2017). While the emphasis in translanguaging work tends to be face-to-face encounters, in the case of transmodalities the emphasis is on the complexities of multimodal and transnational communication exchanges in which languages and other semiotic resources necessarily co-exist and are co-dependent, each having the potential to contribute equally to the construction of meaning.

Until now, transmodalities work has proved a powerful theoretical and analytical framework for analysing the processes of production and reception of the digital stories created and shared as part of Global StoryBridges. For example, in a recent article (Vallejo *et al.*, 2020) we draw on the transmodalities approach to untangle an ethical challenge that emerged in the production of one particular video at the site in Catalonia. In the analysis presented in this chapter, however, our focus will not be on a video production for transnational exchange, but rather on interactional data involving participants from our site only. Our in-depth account of what takes place 'behind the scenes' during a project session contributes to the multilayered ethnographic analyses which Hawkins (2018) refers to as a necessary development for transmodalities research.

A key characteristic of the data we present in the analytical section of this chapter is the participation of the Google Translate tool on the laptop computer that the youth have at their disposal and which they used, in this data, to mediate communication between themselves and a Chinese project facilitator/PhD student. The data also reveal how the young people are informed by the global circulation of and access to Asian popular culture (music, fashion, etc.), through digital technologies and global social networks of communication and information. Thus, in our work we also draw on the notion of transidiomatic practices as put forward by Jacquemet (2005) and defined by him as 'the multilingual communicative practices found at the intersection between deterritorialized people and digital interfaces' (Jacquemet, 2016: 8). This notion complements those of transmodalities and translanguaging and helps us to consider more closely the 'comingling of localized, multilingual interactions and technologically mediated, digitalized communication' (Jacquemet, 2016: 8). Jacquemet frames the notion of transidiomatic practices within work on sociolinguistic superdiversity and migration and has developed it in his work on asylum processes in particular. While the context of our work is quite different, Jacquemet's attention to the ways interactions involve both human and non-human (digital) actors, and to the role of communication technologies in transforming interactions (e.g. Skype or Facebook) and access to knowledge (e.g. Google) in these processes is informative. His work describes, for example, how digital translation tools such as Google Translate or internet search engines become significant participants in asylum processes, not without their challenges and imprecisions.

The Interactional Construction of Places and People

While the notions introduced above help describe how languages, modes, and human and non-human actors come into play in complex interactions, Hawkins (2014) also proposes the concept of critical cosmopolitanism, developing the work of Appiah (2005), Delanty (2006) and Hansen (2010, 2014), among others, to consider how diverse individuals encounter one another in contexts of mobility of people, materials and resources, messages, etc., guided by ethical principles of care, respect and openness to otherness (Hawkins, 2018). This critical disposition is particularly important when reflecting on how youth in different global locations and with different cultural and moral frames of reference face each other in the process of producing and receiving digital stories as part of the Global StoryBridges project. It is also relevant in our site to consider how young people and facilitators with dissimilar geographical, cultural and linguistic backgrounds engage in day-to-day interactions within sessions and come to know themselves and each other. In particular, we are interested in how they discursively construct indexical understandings of where they come from and who they are in relation to place.

The notion of scale was introduced into sociolinguistics by Blommaert (e.g. 2007) as a way of handling the complexities of 'context'. In a more recent development of the notion, Blommaert *et al.* (2015: 123) define scales as the 'spatiotemporal scope of understandability; we are thus looking at the degrees to which particular signs can be expected to be understandable'. Scales, according to these authors, are a particular form of 'indexical order', or normative frames of expectation with regard to meaning (Blommaert, 2005). In their discussion piece, Blommaert *et al.* (2015) refer to Westinen's (2014) doctoral research exploring the construction of scalar frames of reference and of an 'ideological topography' of Finland in Finnish Hip Hop. This topography includes references to geographical, social and cultural margins and centres and stereotypes of people and places, among other aspects. Such an ideological topography also emerges in the data we present in this chapter, in which the participants build scalar frames of understandability in their discourse and use these scalar references to evoke normative frames of expectation about their interlocutors. These expectations in turn become questioned in the unfolding talk as they are faced with contrasting evidence.

Introducing the Site in Catalonia

The secondary school level Global StoryBridges site in Catalonia is based in a municipality in the Barcelona Metropolitan Area where approximately 13,000 inhabitants live in an area of less than one square kilometre. Visually the town is characterised by rows of public housing tower blocks built in the 1970s (towards the end of the Franco dictatorship) to provide accommodation mainly for workers migrating from other parts of Spain. There is also a significant population of Catalan and Spanish gypsies and of more recent migrants from other parts of the globe. From an aerial view, the town represents the map of the Iberian Peninsula and the Balearic Islands, and the street names refer to different Spanish toponyms and geographic features. The municipality is bounded by two major highways. In terms of educational facilities, there are four primary schools, two secondary schools, a school for vocational training, a school for adults, two day-care centres, a library and a civic centre. Disposable household income is below the Catalan average, while unemployment in general, and youth unemployment in particular, are quite a lot higher. The town is located less than a kilometre – walking distance – from a large public university and within kilometres of innovative business and technological hubs with international projection.

Global StoryBridges in our context is one of several initiatives implemented as part of a larger consortium-led project that began in 2016. The steering group of the larger project is led by a university outreach office and is made up of head teachers and English teachers from the town's two secondary schools, members of the local council, the Catalan Education Department and university-based researchers – the latter group including the authors of this chapter. The project is aimed at boosting educational and professional outcomes generally, and English language competences in particular, of youth in the municipality (see Masats & Guerrero, 2018). Young people's educational outcomes in the town are among the poorest in Catalonia. Indeed, the results of the Basic Competences tests taken by all fourth year ESO (compulsory secondary education) students in Catalonia reveal enormous differences in educational results between youth in more and less affluent places. Students are assessed in Science and Technology, Mathematics, Catalan, Spanish and English, and socioeconomic differences are most accentuated in students' results for English. According to the data, approximately half of the students at the two secondary schools in the municipality do not achieve minimum competence in English. The consortium-led project sets out from a first premise that investigating and taking action to improve the competences in English of the youth in this municipality is a meaningful contribution towards more socially-just educational outcomes for them.

The consortium-led project also proceeds on the supposition that impacting on the English language competences of the youth targeted will contribute to more equitable professional outlooks for them. It is no secret that the concentration in recent history of military and socioeconomic power in English-speaking nations and English-dominated multinational corporations has made English central to globalised international relations, higher education, media and business, among other fields. The European Commission (e.g. 2013), among other official bodies, has repeatedly issued recommendations linking competences in foreign languages to domestic and international employability of youth, while Spain continues to lag behind European targets in this regard.

Finally, we are guided by a third conviction that young people learn not only in schools but also in the myriad of interactions across space and time that they encounter beyond the classroom. Research has demonstrated that educational opportunities and practices beyond school hours are decisive in youth's educational trajectories, at the same time as access to out-of-school learning opportunities, including out-of-school English activities, is often obstructed by socioeconomic factors. Non-formal education has the potential to either counter or enhance socioeconomic and educational inequalities, depending on who can or cannot afford access.

The 10 youth participants in our Global StoryBridges site were approximately 14 years old at the time the data presented in this chapter was collected (2018–19 academic year) and had a variety of cultural and linguistic backgrounds. The site was facilitated by four researchers – all of whom author this chapter – and one student volunteer. Both the student volunteer and one of the researchers (a PhD student) were from China and had been in Catalonia/Spain for a short time, while the other three researchers were originally from other parts of the world (Chile, Menorca and Australia) and had lived for many years in the region. Sessions were held in the municipality's Youth Centre once a week for two hours.

Interaction 'Behind the Scenes' at Our Site

In this section of the chapter we analyse two extracts of interaction from the same weekly project session at our site. In the day-to-day flow of the sessions, different overlapping and complementary activities take place. Some of these activities are more directly related to the project's vertebral tasks of producing digital stories for sharing and engaging in commentary on the digital stories with the youth at sites in other parts of the globe. Other activities, which are a necessary foundation for the former, are more closely related to establishing and upholding constructive relationships among the participants and negotiating roles and responsibilities.

The sequences of interaction represented in the transcripts below emerge as part of the main activity being carried out during the session, while also deviating from it. The adults facilitating the session – Claudia, Emilee and Miaomiao – are guiding the youth to generate and type up a list of the places in their town where they would like to do some filming for future digital stories (the fourth project researcher/facilitator was not present). The young people struggle to agree on interesting places in the town and propose going to Barcelona or to the nearby university instead. Some of the young participants have an avid interest in 'all things Asia', including K-pop, Chinese cinema and Japanese manga, as well as novels, food, fashion and languages. Miaomiao's participation as facilitator/PhD researcher in the sessions (as well as the participation of another Chinese student volunteer who was not present in this session) regularly prompts curiosity about and enquiries from the young people about her tastes, her languages, her schooling and life experiences and her familiarity with different Asian cultural products with which the youth are acquainted. The youth are much less interested in the backgrounds and interests of the other (older) adult facilitators, who, as mentioned earlier, also hail from other parts of the world.

The participants named[1] in the transcriptions and who are visible in the screenshot from the video recording (Figure 2.1) are: NAN: Nanyamka (youth participant, previously schooled in Ghana); NAI: Naiara (youth participant); SAR: Sara (youth participant); JUL: Julian (youth participant) and MIA: Miaomiao (facilitator/PhD student from China). EMI: Emilee (facilitator/researcher) and CLA: Claudia (facilitator/researcher) also participate in the two extracts but are not in the view of the camera. Another significant participant in the interaction is a laptop computer (COM) handled by Nanyamka and Naiara in order to use the Google Translate tool and which is oriented to by all of the participants taking part in the interaction at different times. The transcription conventions are included in the Appendix to the chapter.

We now present a first short extract that is representative of the interactional dynamics, and the transidiomatic practices involving the

Figure 2.1 Distribution of participants in camera view

computer in particular, as they initially emerge and then endure for the remainder of the project session. During the activity of brainstorming places to film in the municipality, the students re-signify the role of the laptop computer from a simple note-taking tool to conversational participant and linguistic mediator. In line 1 of the transcription Nanyamka types a statement into the Google Translate tool on the laptop computer to be translated into Chinese for Miaomiao and read aloud by the same application. It is not clear from the video recording, nor were the authors able to see as participants in the interaction, which language she uses to type into the computer. We can assume, however, based on her later comment in line 64 of the second extract – 'estamos en español' (we are in Spanish) – and on other comments made in the recording, that the computer was set to translate from Spanish to Chinese. In any case, the use of the translation tool to mediate communication between Miaomiao and the young people – and in particular between Miaomiao and Nanyamka in this case – is significant. Miaomiao knows little Spanish but is quite fluent in English, as is Nanyamka, having been previously educated at an English-medium school in Ghana. Communication between them usually flows with little obstruction. While it is not the main focus of this chapter, Nanyamka often takes on the role of linguistic mediator in the project sessions between Spanish and English herself. Furthermore, while the other young people's English language proficiency is below that of Nanyamka, at other times in the project sessions they draw on Nanyamka, the other adult facilitators or their collective competence in English to achieve communication. Thus, we can only explain the participation of the computer in this session as linguistic mediator in terms of the youths' critical cosmopolitanism – their curiosity for listening to the Chinese language and their desire to use a digital tool at their disposal for connecting with Miaomiao through this language. The choice to include Chinese through the computer could also be interpreted as a way to generate complicity with Miaomiao.

1. NAN: (typing on computer keyboard)

2. NAI: (reading from computer screen) wǒmen xiǎng jìlù (name of
     town omitted)[(name of town omitted)

3. NAN. [dónde está?
     translation: where is it

4. NAI: (pointing to computer screen) aquí está.
     translation: it's here

5. NAN: sí pero dónde es (.) para que se escuche?
     translation: yes but where is it to listen to it

6. (NAN points to the computer screen, NAN presses play, all the young participants look at MIA, NAI points at MIA, see Figure 2.2))

7. C: wǒmen xiǎng jìlù (name of town omitted) de hǎi'àn
     translation: we want to record the coast of (name of town omitted)

8. (NAN presses play again, others still looking at MIA))

9. COM: wǒmen xiǎng jìlù (name of town omitted) de hǎi'àn

10. MIA: ah (..) that it's not correct.

11. NAN: ah! (.) [(pretending to hit the computer) me has fallado!
      translation: ah you let me down

12. (laughter from all participants)

Once Nanyamka has typed the statement into the computer, Naiara reads the translation as it appears on the screen (line 2). Nanyamka then seeks Naiara's help to find the button allowing the translation to be read aloud by the computer tool (lines 3–5). Having located the button, Nanyamka presses play and all of the young people orient their gaze and bodies towards Miaomiao (line 6 and Figure 2.2) as they listen to the computer speak Chinese. The English version of the statement read by the computer is roughly 'we want to record the coast of (name of town

Figure 2.2 Screenshot taken at line 6

omitted)'. The students are referring to the town where the Global StoryBridges site is located, which is approximately 20 km inland from the coast, thus the comment is meant to be ironic. As mentioned already, the students had been struggling to identify places of interest to film in the municipality. Thus, the statement is interesting in terms of transidiomatic practices in the way that its vocalisation crosses languages and is mediated by the computer, as we observe throughout the interaction. It is also interesting because of what it tells us about how the young people ideologically construct their town as an uninteresting place lacking attractions of interest to youth at other sites, such as a beach.

Interestingly, in response to the statement, and similar to elsewhere in the recording, Miaomiao focuses on the accuracy of the Chinese version rather than on the message itself, thus further diverting from the task of deciding where to film (line 10). Miaomiao mistakenly hears 'jìnrù' (come into) rather than 'jìlù' (record), while the translation 'hǎi'àn' to refer to coast is unusual. She seems to interpret the young people's use of Chinese through the computer in terms of their interest in learning the language and positions herself as language teacher in response. Reacting to Miaomiao's response, Nanyamka reproaches the translation tool in line 11, as she does elsewhere in the recording, thereby positioning it not only as a tool facilitating transidiomatic communication, but also as an accountable interactional participant.

The second extract takes place a few minutes after the first. Previous to the second extract, as we have seen in the first one, Nanyamka writes a question into the translation tool to be translated and read aloud in Chinese for Miaomiao. We are again unable to say which language Nanyamka employs to type the question, but can make the reasonable guess that the tool continued to be set to translate from Spanish to

Chinese. Given that Nanyamka and most of the young people know enough English to formulate the question asked at the beginning of this extract – 'what do you like about Spain?' – and to collectively understand the answers given by Miaomiao in the following lines, we again explain their recourse to the computer as linguistic mediator in terms of their interest in hearing Chinese and using it with Miaomiao.

1. MIA: you want to ask me? (.) what-
2. NAN: do you like about Spain?
3. MIA: [what do I like of Spain?
4. NAN: [(to COM) traductor nos has fallado varias veces.
   translation: translator you have failed us several times
5. NAI: mmh
6. MIA: aaah (.) weather
7. (.)
8. EMI: weather. (laughs)
9. (general laughter)
10. NAN: weather is beautiful.
11. MIA: not today not today. weather food and ah the church.
12. NAN: (stroking her right hand, see Figure 2.3) la iglesia.
    translation: the church
13. NAI: (moving gaze from NAN – see Figure 3 – to MIA – see Figure 2.4) la iglesia?
    translation: the church
14. (NAN and SAR make eye contact – NAN seems unenthusiastic and SAR smiles confused, see Figure 2.4)
15. NAN: (to MIA) church right?
16. MIA: yes church.
17. NAN: (to NAI) lo que escuchas. [iglesia.
    translation: what you hear church
18. CLA: [ask her Naiara (.) ask her (.) why

19. NAI: why?

20. SAR: (laughs)

21. MIA: why?

22. NAI: why?

23. JUL: te sorprende?
           translation: does it surprise you

24. NAI: no.

25. MIA: because is beautiful. the weather's beautiful.

26. NAN: but here or [in Barcelona?

27. MIA: [ee-

28. NAI: [you are (.) Christian? or- (looks to NAN for assistance)

29. MIA: both (.) Christian?

30. NAN: are you Christian? or-

31. MIA: no I'm not Christian but is beautiful is beautiful.

32. NAN: ella creo que es buda.
           translation: I think she is Buddha

33. SAR: but in (.) in China? [you have xxx? eh-

34. NAI: [y por qué va a ir a la iglesia?
           translation: and why is she going to go to church

35. NAN: [y?
           translation: and

36. NAI: [la iglesia es de Dios.
           translation: the church is of God

37. SAR: [como se dice iglesia?
           translation: how do you say church

38. NAN: [pero iglesia no es para los-
           translation: but church is not for the

39. CLA: church.

40. SAR: church?

41. NAN: [la iglesia no es para los budos.
    translation: church is not for the Buddhas

42. MIA: [oh no we have no church. we only have temples.

43. NAI: los bud?- ya por eso pero los- pero le gusta-
    translation: the Budd yeah that's why but the but she likes it

44. NAN: dice que le gusta porque es bonito y que allí-
    translation: she says she likes it because it's beautiful and that there

45. SAR: y que allí no hay iglesia.
    translation: and that there is no church there

46. NAN: por eso. que allí no hay-
    translation: that's it that there they aren't

47. NAI: hay templos.
    translation: there are temples

48. NAN: sí.
    translation: yes

49. NAI: espera. (typing on computer keyboard)
    translation: wait

50. NAN: [you have temples in your country?

51. JUL: [xxxx llevan a la iglesia.
    translation: they take them to the church

52. MIA: a lot of temples.

53. NAN: when they are young they prepare them to go to the temple and dress with a yellow:?

54. MIA: ee:

55. NAI: (presses key on keyboard)

56. COM: sìmiào
    translation: temple

57. NAI: sìmiào
    translation: temple

58. NAN: xx

59. MIA: yes to learn kung fu yes?

60. NAN: yes. and they- they- ay- (reaches for keyboard then changes her mind and places hand to her head)

61. MIA: they don't have hair.

62. NAN: yes.

63. MIA: yes it's a tradition in my province.

64. SAR: (writes on computer keyboard)

65. MIA: the city is Kaifeng near my city. the [kids]

66. NAI: [no no estamos en español.]
    translation: no no we're in Spanish

67. MIA: learn kung fu when they are very young.

68. NAN: yes. I read a book about it

Miaomiao's question in line 1 – 'you want to ask me? what?' – and Nanyamka's scolding of the computer in line 4, similar to what was observed in the previous extract – 'translator you have failed us several times' – suggest that Miaomiao does not understand the question as it is posed to her by Nanyamka through the computer. This prompts Nanyamka to ask the question in English through her own voice in line 2 and after line 4 the computer is not brought into the interaction again until line 49. The question – 'what do you like about Spain?' – establishes the nation-state (as opposed to a city or a region) as the 'benchmark scale' in Blommaert *et al.*'s (2015: 120) terms, or the scale offering the young people and Miaomiao the greatest scope of understandability. In response to the question, Miaomiao explains that she likes 'weather' – generating laughter and commentary as this particular day it was raining and miserable – 'food' and 'church' (lines 6–11).

Miaomiao's reference to the church is met by surprise on behalf of her young interlocutors. In line 12, Nanyamka strokes her right hand (Figure 2.3) as she translates Miaomiao's response into Spanish, possibly to stress that particular piece of information for her peers, while her gesture and falling intonation also express her incredulity at the response given by Miaomiao. Nanyamka's gaze is focused on Miaomiao at this point (Figure 2.3). Naiara looks with disbelief at Nanyamka as she translates the response in line 12 (Figure 2.3), before turning to look at Miaomiao and seeking confirmation of her answer in Spanish with rising confirmation – 'la iglesia?' – in line 13. Interestingly, at this point Nanyamka and Sara, one of the young participants who has so far been quiet, make eye contact; as they do, Nanyamka's expression suggests she is unenthusiastic about Miaomiao's interest in church, while Sara smiles in a way that suggests she

Figure 2.3 Screenshot taken at line 12

is also confused (Figure 2.4). Indeed, the young people's frames of reference – they are asking someone from China about Spain – evoke stereotypical understandings both of Miaomiao (for example, that she would not attend church) and of Spain (including that all Spanish churches are Christian ones, as emerges in the following lines).

In line 15, Nanyamka again takes on the role of linguistic mediator, translating Naiara's question from line 13 into English for Miaomiao – 'church right?'. Miaomiao, who seems quite unaware of the young people's surprise, confirms that she likes church in line 16. In line 17, using Spanish – 'lo que escuchas, iglesia' (what you hear, church) – Nanyamka ratifies

Figure 2.4 Screenshot taken at line 13

Naiara's understanding of Miaomiao's response. Claudia, one of the other adult facilitators participating in the session, prompts Naiara to ask Miaomiao to expand her answer in line 18, which Naiara does in line 19 ('why?'), prompting laughter from Sara. Miaomiao also seems slightly surprised by the interrogation in line 21 as she repeats Naiara's question, seeking confirmation of it. Julian, who until now has watched on silently, asks Naiara if she is surprised by Miaomiao's liking for church ('te sorprende?', are you surprised?). Still looking at Miaomiao, Naiara responds with a 'no'. Miaomiao then justifies herself and simultaneously shows that she has not picked up on the reason for the young people's confusion, explaining that 'the weather's beautiful' (line 25). At this point, Nanyamka poses her own clarification question to Miaomiao – 'but here or in Barcelona?' – which scales down the frame of reference from the nation-state to either the capital city of the region (Barcelona, where Miaomiao lives) or to the municipality where the project takes place. Indeed, while Barcelona is known as a tourist destination in part due to its churches and other famous buildings, in which case Miaomiao's interest in them might be conceivable, in generating their list of places to film for the project the young people had discarded the church in their own town as a place of relevance or interest to them and to other young participants in the Global StoryBridges project.

In overlap with Nanyamka's question, Naiara formulates a different one which prompts further enquiries. She asks in line 28, 'you are Christian or?'. Both Nanyamka's and Naiara's questions receive responses in line 29. Miaomiao says she likes the churches in both Barcelona and the municipality, and repeats Naiara's mention of Christianity with rising intonation, seeking clarification of the question. Naiara looks to Nanyamka for language assistance in line 28 (Figure 2.5). Nanyamka

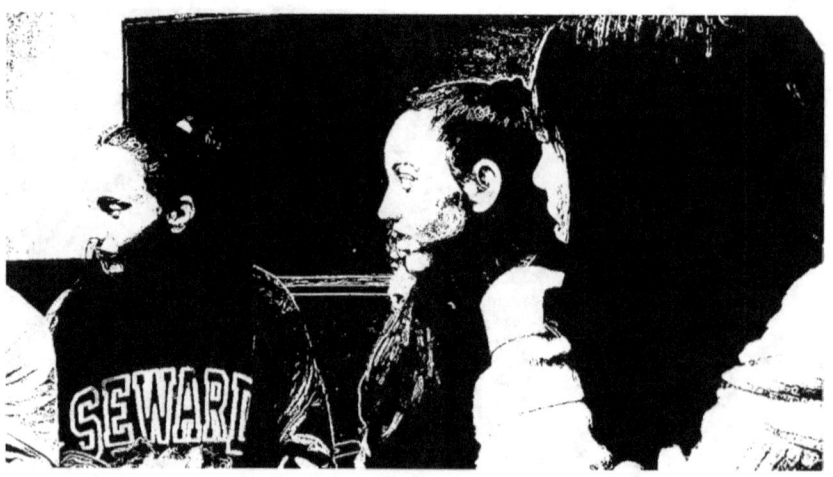

Figure 2.5 Screenshot at line 28

repeats Naiara's question for Miaomiao in line 30, implicitly correcting her peer's English grammar as she does so. Miaomiao responds that she is not Christian, but she finds the churches beautiful (line 31).

The discussion about Miaomiao's religion and about churches is expanded from line 32 in two parallel conversations; her responses continue to contradict the young people's stereotypical understandings of China and being Chinese. Speaking with Naiara, Nanyamka puts forward the hypothesis, based on her knowledge of 'all things Asia', that Miaomiao is Buddhist. This prompts Naiara to ask why Miaomiao would go to the church then if the church is for worshipping the Christian God (lines 34 and 36). Nanyamka agrees in lines 38 and 41 that church is not for Buddhist people. It is interesting that neither of the pair use the correct word for Buddhist (i.e. budista) in Spanish, suggesting that they are not terribly familiar with this religion. Meanwhile, in overlap with Nanyamka's and Naiara's conversation, Sara speaks with Miaomiao, with language assistance from Claudia, asking her whether there are churches in China (lines 33, 37, 40). Miaomiao responds that there are no churches in China, only temples. Of course, there are indeed Christian churches in China, however Miaomiao deploys her own topographical ideologies about China in making this claim. From line 43 to 48, Sara, Nanyamka and Naiara bring their information together, reaching the consensus that despite being Buddhist in their imagination (which has neither been confirmed nor refuted in the interaction), Miaomiao likes churches because they are beautiful and that in China there are no churches, only temples.

In line 49, Naiara asks to halt the conversation – 'espera' (wait) – as she takes the laptop computer and types into the translation tool, presumably 'templo' (temple) in Spanish, engaging in the same type of transidiomatic practice as Nanyamka elsewhere in the extracts. The computer translates the word into Chinese and says it out loud when cued to do so by Naiara (lines 55 and 56). Naiara repeats the word, however she does not succeed in getting the group's full attention, with her peers' and Miaomiao's attention divided between this activity and a parallel conversation between Nanyamka and Miaomiao. Nanyamka is asking Miaomiao about the temples in China, drawing again on her knowledge of Asian cultures from global popular culture in probing into whether children attend the temples dressed in yellow (line 53) with shaved heads (lines 60–62). It is actually Miaomiao who helps Nanyamka to verbalise this enquiry, which Nanyamka first expresses with gestures (putting her hand to her head). It is interesting here that Nanyamka does not resort to the use of the translator tool, thus showing the many modalities at play. Miaomiao confirms this feature of the temples in China, including in her own province of origin. The extract closes in line 68 with Nanyamka explaining that she knows this information as she read a book about it.

We now turn to the implications of this analysis.

Discussion and Conclusions

In the previous section we have offered a glance into youth-led interactional practices at one particular Global StoryBridges site. In doing so, we aimed to shed light on how scalar frames of understandability are built and the multimodal ways in which the youth engage in meaningful exchanges. As pointed out in the introduction to this volume, one of the main aims of the project is to develop critical cosmopolitanism among participants in very different sites through transnational and transmodal asynchronous encounters. The frame of reference in these asynchronous communication exchanges, as shown in other chapters in this volume, necessarily includes not only the worldview of the digital story youth producers but also of the addressees. In synchronous face-to-face encounters such as those analysed in this chapter we observe how similar understandings of people and places are built, confirmed or questioned in real-time. Thus, as clear as it is that our globalised lives require that youth experience transnational and transmodal encounters framed by criticality and collaboration to prompt openness and empathy with global others, the ethnographic observation of the inner dynamics at our site show that encounters that promote critical cosmopolitanism can also become relevant in local interactions.

In the extracts, we have seen young site participants from diverse backgrounds engaging with a Chinese facilitator/PhD researcher, drawing on and enriching their keen interest in Asian cultures. What strikes us as interesting is that while the Global StoryBridges project has a more or less established protocol to trigger engagement with global 'others' on a transnational scale through producing and exchanging audiovisual narratives and questions-answers with peers at other sites, this particular face-to-face interaction can be seen to accomplish similar objectives, while being initiated by the site youth as a deviation from the planned activity. This is doubly significant as at our site we have experienced irregular success in engaging young participants in meaningful encounters with their peers from other global sites. Against this backdrop, a somehow unexpected factor (the Chinese origin of an adult participant) opened a space for transcultural and translinguistic communication 'within' the site, where youth actively deploy their full linguistic repertoires, knowledge, curiosity and skills, while displaying and negotiating different roles in interaction. A clear example of this negotiated agency in the extracts is displayed by Nanyamka, a girl with a migrant background who had learned English as the medium of instruction at school in Ghana and who offers a lot of insight on Asian cultural and religious traditions, regularly self-adopting or being assigned the roles of language and/or cultural mediator between her peers and Miaomiao.

We clearly see sociolinguistic scales or frames of understanding intersecting in these encounters: the youths' interest and knowledge about 'all things

Asia', which somehow shape their local interactions with Miaomiao, are informed by the global circulation of and access to Asian popular culture (music, fashion, etc.) through digital technologies and global social networks of communication and information. Miaomiao is positioned by the youth as a Chinese person in Spain, which indexes different stereotypical assumptions including that she is not a Christian. Miaomiao's assertion that she likes church in response to their enquiry about her favourite things about Spain challenges the young people's 'pop-culture' informed imaginations and expectations about Chinese people, complexifying their frames of reference. Her unexpected response prompts a great number of interactional turns during which an ideological topography emerges and is confronted with unanticipated evidence which needs reconciling in the youths' worldviews. A translocal scalar frame of 'what it is to be Chinese' encounters a local scalar frame of 'who goes to the church'. At the same time, Miaomiao also tries to make sense of the youths' reaction to her answer. Meanwhile, Miaomiao's mention of Spanish weather and food as likeable aspects of the country fit well within the young people's normative frame of reference for a Chinese person in Spain and are accepted without further discussion.

The extracts also show how the young participants' curiosity and eagerness to know more about Miaomiao and Chinese language and culture relate to their strategic assemblage of multiple, digital and embodied modes, including artefacts such as the computer's translator tool and other people. (Note that we use the singular for language and culture here as we do not see hegemonic understandings of China and being Chinese questioned in the interaction, suggesting that some opportunities remain for the development of critical cosmopolitanism.) By deploying expanded communicative repertoires and resources, the youth try to make sense of the scalar frames of understandability they use in their discourse. This resonates with Jacquemet's (2005, 2016) notion of transidiomatic practices. We would like to discuss the transidiomatic practices involving the role of the laptop computer a little further. Laptops are a regular feature of Global StoryBridges sites globally and usually serve a key function in the project's aim of editing the digital stories and facilitating transnational exchanges. However, as we have seen in the extracts, the relevance of the computer – and of the Google Translate tool in particular – in the site interaction studied here differs, as the youth attribute to it the status of non-human participant and linguistic mediator, whom they incorporate, set aside and even scold according to the needs of the communicative situation.

In line with this, Jacquemet suggests that transidiomatic practices conceive digital communication technologies as much more than facilitators of interaction and mobility, understanding them as:

> altering the very nature of this interactivity, confronting people with expanded rules and resources for the construction of social identity and transforming people's sense of place, cultural belonging, and social relations. The integration of communication technologies into late modern

communicative practices has resulted in the emergence of a telemediated cultural field, occupying a space in everyday experience that is distinct from yet integrated with face-to-face interactions of physical proximity. This field is transforming human experience in all its dimensions. (2016: 4)

Indeed, as the transcripts presented in this chapter show, the role of digital technologies in this interaction cannot be defined solely in terms of being a tool for communication or disconnected from the social relations at play. As we explained in introducing the first extract, both the youth and Miaomiao were able to communicate through multilingual and multimodal resources without the Google Translate tool. The choice of recurring default to the computer as linguistic mediator has more to do with their willingness to hear and use Chinese with Miaomiao than with overcoming communicative obstacles. This language choice could also be interpreted as a way to create complicity by attempting to involve Miaomiao, for example, with their humorous proposal to record their town's non-existent coast.

The fact that the youth participants can creatively choose tools and strategies for communicating without strict adherence to specific languages or modes enhances the non-formal educational settings' potential to promote co-learning dynamics (Li, 2014) where students can engage in creative and meaningful ways and actively display skills that do not usually find a place in mainstream educational settings. Along with promoting flexible expert-learner role arrangements, and fluid language, cultural and multimodal uses, such settings can challenge still pervasive monolingual, monocultural and monomodal approaches to teaching and learning. Considering that one of the main rationales of Global StoryBridges is to boost participants' foreign language competence in English, it is indeed relevant to document how local practices such as the ones presented in this chapter promote opportunities for learning English and learning about others, along with other languages and digital resources, in contexts of meaningful, critical cosmopolitan exchanges.

In this sense, and as a final reflection, we would like to reiterate the contribution of an ethnographic approach to the understanding not only of processes of transmodal and transnational meaning making and language learning across sites, but also of the many other local and translocal practices where multilingualism, critical cosmopolitan curiosity and openness can be boosted by the program.

Acknowledgements

This research was supported by the Spanish Ministry of Science, Innovation and Universities project entitled 'IEP! Inclusive epistemologies and practices of out-of-school English learning' (Ref: PRPPGC 2018-099071-A-I00).

Note

(1) The names of people used in this chapter are pseudonyms in order to protect participants' anonymity, with the exception of the adult facilitators/authors who agree to their real names being used.

References

Appiah, K.A. (2005) *The Ethics of Identity*. Princeton, NJ: Princeton University Press.
Blommaert, J. (2005) *Discourse: A Critical Introduction*. Cambridge: Cambridge University Press.
Blommaert, J. (2007) Sociolinguistic scales. *Intercultural Pragmatics* 4 (1), 1–19.
Blommaert, J. and Backus, A. (2013) Superdiverse repertoires and the individual. In I. de Saint-Georges and J. Weber (eds) *Multilingualism and Multimodality: Current Challenges for Educational Studies*. Rotterdam: Sense Publishing.
Blommaert, J., Westinen, E. and Leppänen, S. (2015) Further notes on sociolinguistic scales. *Intercultural Pragmatics* 12 (1), 119 – 27.
Consell Superior d'Avaluació del Sistema Educatiu (2018) L'avaluació de quart d'ESO 2018. *Quaderns d'Avaluació* 40. Departament d'Ensenyament, Generalitat de Catalunya.
Delanty, G. (2006) The cosmopolitan imagination: Critical cosmopolitanism and social theory. *The British Journal of Sociology* 57 (1), 25–47.
European Commission (2013) *Education and Training Monitor 2013*. See https://op.europa.eu/en/publication-detail/-/publication/25626e01-1bb8-403c-95da-718c3cfcdf19/language-en (accessed April 2021).
García, O. and Li, W. (2014) *Translanguaging: Language, Bilingualism and Education*. Basingstoke: Palgrave Macmillan.
Gumperz, J.J. (1964) Linguistic and social interaction in two communities. *American Anthropologist* 66 (6), 137–53.
Hansen, D.T. (2010) Cosmopolitanism and education: A view from the ground. *Teachers College Record* 112, 1–30.
Hansen, D.T. (2014) Cosmopolitanism as cultural creativity: New modes of educational practice in globalizing times. *Curriculum Inquiry* 44 (1), 1–14.
Hawkins, M. (2014) Ontologies of place, creative meaning making and critical cosmopolitan education. *Curriculum Inquiry* 44, 90–112.
Hawkins, M. (2018) Transmodalities and transnational encounters: Fostering critical cosmopolitan relations. *Applied Linguistics* 39 (1), 55–77.
Jacquemet, M. (2005) Transidiomatic practices: Language and power in the age of globalization. *Language and Communication* 25, 257–77.
Jacquemet, M. (2016) Sociolinguistic superdiversity and asylum. *Tilburg Papers in Cultural Studies* 171. See https://pure.uvt.nl/ws/portalfiles/portal/32303298/TPCS_171_Jacquemet.pdf (accessed April 2021).
Jewitt, C. (ed.) (2017) *The Routledge Handbook of Multimodal Analysis*. London: Routledge.
Li, W. (2014) Who's teaching whom? Co-learning in multilingual classrooms. In S. May (ed.) *The Multilingual Turn: Implications for SLA, TESOL and Bilingual Education* (pp. 167–90). New York: Routledge.
Masats, D. and Guerrero, P. (2018) The ins and outs of teamworking: When university teachers, in-service secondary teachers and pre-service teachers collaborate to transform learning. *European Journal of Social Science Education and Research* 5 (3), 188–96.
Rymes, B. (2014) *Communicating Beyond Language: Everyday Encounters with Diversity*. New York: Routledge.

Vallejo, C. and Dooly, M. (2020) Plurilingualism and translanguaging: Emergent approaches and shared concerns. Introduction to the special issue. *International Journal of Bilingual Education and Bilingualism* 23 (1), 1–16.

Vallejo, C., Moore, E., Llompart, J. and Hawkins, M. (2020) Semiosis y cosmopolitismo crítico: un análisis transmodal de un dilema ético en comunicación transnacional entre jóvenes. *Profesorado, Revista de Currículum y Formación del Profesorado* 24 (1), 304–25.

Westinen, E. (2014) The discursive construction of authenticity: Resources, scales and polycentricity in Finnish hip hop culture. PhD dissertation, University of Jyväskylä. See http://urn.fi/URN:ISBN:978-951-39-5728-5 (accessed April 2021).

Appendix

Transcription conventions

1. Intonation:
    a. Falling: .
    b. Rising ?
2. Pauses: (.)
3. Overlapping: [text
4. Interruption: text-
5. Lengthening of a sound: text:
6. Transcriber's comments: (text)
7. Incomprehensible fragment: xxxx
8: Translation on non-English text: *translation: italics below original*

3 Cosmopolitan Aims/ Cosmopolitan Realities: How Immigrant Youth Negotiate Languaging and Identity in One After-School Program

Anneliese Cannon and Sarah J. Turner

Introduction

In the United States, many educators, researchers, activists and concerned citizens have united in concern about anti-immigrant and often anti-Muslim rhetoric that has now become common in politics, the media and legislation (Gadsen & Levine, 2017). With serious talks of travel bans or punitive actions for immigrants and/or asylum seekers, the situation for immigrants in this country is tenuous at best.

Not surprisingly, with the current emphasis on the basic question of whether immigrants and refugees are even safe to *be* in the United States, we fear the loss of attention to the nuances of the experience of being an immigrant – and, for our purpose, a young person – in the United States, learning to live and communicate in a new land. For example, we may forget the multi-faceted process of learning to language in new environments – a highly social undertaking that involves, among other things, learning the multiple forms of language that enables a person to communicate in a variety of settings (Hawkins, 2004).

In this chapter we describe our work at one Global StoryBridges (GSB) site located in the Intermountain West of the United States with the aim of keeping such social issues as power and identity central to our discussion of what it means to establish new understandings and identities. During 2017–18, we co-facilitated sessions of GSB with a diverse group of five female participants who were originally from Burma, Afghanistan,

Somalia and Nepal (although, as will be explained, had all lived in different countries as refugees) at the Harmony Center, a community-based after-school program. The overarching question that guided our work was: What affordances did engagement in GSB offer for fostering communication and critical cosmopolitan interactions and understandings for participating youth? In this discussion, we focus on the interactions among the youth participants at the Harmony Center and those with other GSB sites, paying explicit attention to the process of how the participants navigated their social worlds both on and offline, which together illuminated fascinating perspectives on identity, negotiation of meaning, and the role of place in creating stories.

We use the concepts of transmodalities and critical cosmopolitanism as key ideas to frame our discussion of how participants in our study communicated with, interpreted, and created and negotiated narratives about their lives with other GSB participants. While these theoretical ideas will be discussed in greater detail in the following section, transmodalities underscores not only that there are multiple modes of communication, including movement, gesture and online interactions, but that there are junctures where these modes of communication meet and intertwine, often in messy and unpredictable ways (Hawkins, 2018), conveying complex messages. Critical cosmopolitanism also guides this analysis conceptually. We follow its tenet that there is value in building understanding of and curiosity for global peers; the *critical* descriptor denotes that we should be mindful of how differences in resources and power can shape and influence interactions among diverse groups of people (Hawkins, 2014).

Significance and Roadmap

As discussed throughout this volume, one of the aims of the larger, multi-site GSB project is to facilitate language learning and intercultural/global communication among global children and youth. As stated, we looked closely at the communication at our particular site, as well as online communication (through the creation of videos and participation in the online chat platform) and to what extent this communication fostered and reflected attitudes of critical cosmopolitanism.

By researching the processes and outcomes of the youth and children's communications on and off-line, we aim to contribute to the literature on multimodality and youth, as well as to the literature on immigrant learning in after-school or community-based spaces. As Lee and Hawkins (2009) point out, given that children in the US spend only 20% of their time in school, it is important that researchers also examine the influence of other environments on language use and social integration (Miller, 2003). A significant proportion of immigrant youth from low-income families, such as those in our project site, attend after-school and community programs, which, as Halpern (1999) notes, are tasked with numerous responsibilities (often with little or unreliable financial support), such as providing a safe space for recreation, places where youth can get homework help, work on academic skills, eat and, when possible, gain exposure to enrichment activities like the arts, drama and dance.

In the following section, we describe the theories and empirical investigations that informed us as we made sense of our participants' language use, storytelling and interactions among each other and with the various other project sites. We then give a brief description of the research site and methods used to analyze the fieldnotes, video stories, online chat entries and interviews that made up our data. Next, we offer a discussion of key themes illustrated empirically, namely, how our young adolescent participants perceived, negotiated and presented their lives as new Americans and forged relationships with other global youth. Finally, we focus on the implications and further directions for the study.

Theoretical Framework and Literature Review

With Norton Peirce (1995), we believe that language acquisition and use is inextricably linked to issues of power and identity. As researchers, we must remain aware of how dynamic factors such as self-perception, relationships and power affect languaging (Norton Peirce, 1995). Drawing from Hawkins (2018), we recognize that applied linguistics is an interdisciplinary field, from which we draw several theoretical tools to decode how immigrant youth make sense of and leverage new semiotic representations, and novel values and cultural understandings. As we analyzed artifacts and interactions, we used concepts from several theories to interpret the data and to sometimes challenge any preconceived or simplistic notions of what was unfolding as the participants made videos and engaged in dialogue with other global youth translocally and transglobally. Therefore, while our focus is primarily on the sense- and meaning-making of the youth in our site, we also discuss language-in-use as multimodal in nature and show its effects. Multiple forms of representation, including language and the content of the students' presentations of self, were extremely significant, particularly as study participants curated their digital stories, often in response to videos they viewed from sites in East Africa, to highlight their prosperity and ease of life in America. Participants' choices about storytelling dovetail with Hawkins' (2014) assertions about the contextual details of place, and their 'directive force in shaping the thoughts and interactions of those who inhabit it' (2014: 94).

Multimodality and transmodalities

Kress (2000) defines modes to include not only written or spoken words, but also gestures, drawings, and other embodied forms of communication. Further, Kress (2000), Van Leeuween (2015) and others state that when literacy is viewed strictly from an academic or cognitive perspective of what English learners can read or write, we gain a diminished sense of their meaning-making. Multimodality denotes the social nature of literacy and meaning-making (Lam & Warriner, 2012). In the words of Lam and Warriner (2012), 'the rhetorical styles, interpretive strategies, and semiotic systems that are involved in any act of reading or writing are predicated on, and in turn, give meaning to, the beliefs, practices, and social relationships of particular social groups' (2012: 192). Therefore, as we examined the language learning and interactions of our adolescent participants, we looked closely at spoken and written language, and also embodied modes of communication and artistic artifacts. We also took into consideration pop culture artifacts, such as music and songs that the participants talked about, wrote and even sang about, which played a key role in the participants' friendships.

Our research builds on the body of empirical studies about multimodality among English learners/plurilingual youth. For example, Toohey *et al.* (2015) studied video-making about the topic of social justice and sustainability with 9- and 10-year-olds in a linguistically diverse urban Canadian classroom. The authors found that the multimodal practices accompanying video-making were highly inclusive of English learners and drew from the repertoires of knowledge that all students in the class had experience with, such as documentaries and newscasts. Ajayi's (2008) investigation looks at the possibilities for using multimodal texts to engender more socioculturally, social justice-based lessons with English-learning teens in high schools.

Lastly, although not specifically focusing on English learners, Hull and Katz (2006) examine how the creation of multimodal texts (digital stories) can unlock youth's sense of agency and narrative freedom. Each of these studies give support to the validity of teaching and learning with multimodal representations, confirming that when students are able to deploy more modes to demonstrate their learning, they often, in Hull and Katz's (2006) words 'create authoritative texts which embodied their agentive selves' (2006: 36). Together these theoretical and empirical perspectives help to shed light on the laden process of youth creating stories that go beyond words and transcend borders.

The focus on multiple modes of literacy gave us insight into the social and literate practices that the participants engaged in as they made sense of their place in US society as newcomer immigrants and English-speakers. A transmodalities perspective added yet another dimension to this analysis. Speaking about translanguaging, Canagarajah (2017) argues that the trans- prefix can move our attention to the interrelated dimensions and modes of language to 'transcend' (2017: 32) beyond words and to 'transform [...] and challenge our understandings of language as regulated or determined by existing contexts of power relations' (2017: 32).

Hawkins (2018) advances the idea of transmodalities, which highlights (among other things):

> the simultaneous co-presence and co-reliance of language and other semiotic resources in meaning-making [...]; the complexity of modes and the entanglements and relationships between them that shape meaning in multimodal artifacts and communications [...] within trajectories of time and space, continuously shifting and re-shaping in their contexts and mobility. (2018: 64)

These theoretical guideposts helped us as we interpreted relationships between and across the participants' various modes of communication – and across time and space. For example, we were often curious about how the youth in our study would watch a video (from one of the various international sites), converse with each other about the video in real time, and then compress these interactions, often losing ideas and content in the process, as they struggled to formulate valid English questions and then type them into the computer. This interplay among languages and modes of communication seemed to exemplify what Hawkins (2018) calls the 'complexity of modes and the entanglements and relationships between them that shape meaning in multimodal artifacts and communications' (2018: 63).

Multiple cosmopolitan ideas

As others in this volume have described, the concept of cosmopolitanism is at the foundation of the GSB project. Hawkins (2014) states that one of the goals of this online global conversation is to 'create citizens of the world: those with the proclivities and abilities to shift across boundaries – geographically, disciplinarily, professionally, and in engagement with others – with a moral and ethical imperative to engage in and sustain equitable and just relations' (2014: 97). Because global communication is central to this project, we were curious how, if at all, this project helped our participants cultivate 'an openness to strangers and strangerhood or difference' (Werbner, 1999: 26), particularly because our research participants – although living in the United States – came from disparate countries across Africa and Asia, and a key part of many of their experiences was spending large portions of their lives in refugee camps outside of their natal lands. These participants were transnationals in the truest sense. And, as transnational communities proliferate around the world, there is increased interest in making sense of their interactions across real and imagined nations (Lam & Warriner, 2012). Youth such as those in our study often stand at the forefront of the transnational experience. As they engage in online communications like sending email messages and participating in chat spaces, they give us insight into their multilingual practices, language learning, interpretation of world events (Lam, 2011), and significant here, feelings about their position and belonging in the larger society.

Like other scholars (Hall, 2006; Hawkins, 2014; Werbner, 1999), we were concerned by elite notions of cosmopolitanism, as reflected by Werbner (1999: 17): 'Eurocentric and class bias: transnational cultures are most often centered in the north and manned by high status professionals'. These affluent individuals, maintain critics, have the *privilege* to be curious about and open to others. Out of this concern for the elitist implications of cosmopolitanism, scholars have coined new terms to describe the various forms of cosmopolitanism as they develop in circles of under-resourced yet globally-minded people. In particular, postcolonial scholars have been interested in how less affluent people cultivate cosmopolitan sensibilities, such as awareness of other languages and cultural practices. Calling these subaltern forms of cosmopolitanism *working class cosmopolitanism* (Werbner, 1999) or *vernacular cosmopolitanism* (Werbner, 2006), or *cosmopolitanism from below* (Hall, 2006), these ideas underscore how postcolonial people – often refugees, displaced by force (rather than voluntary travelers) – also embody cosmopolitan proclivities of linguistic and cultural knowledge that extend beyond their own homelands.

While much of the writing referenced above is focused on adults, we sought to understand how cosmopolitanism played a role in youths' lives. One key empirical study, Kromidas' (2011) investigation of 9–11-year-olds' development of their racial awareness, employs the term *elementary cosmopolitanism* to describe how children in 'super diverse' (Sanjek, 1998, as cited in Kromidas, 2011: 586) communities in New York City make sense of difference and overcome stereotypes regarding ethnicity, language and national origin. She writes: 'Friendships were not a "natural" result of being amongst diversity; rather, they were a result of the kids' work to overcome the baggage they inherited, baggage that they took on unexpected journeys' (2011: 586). As we will discuss in a later section, we found study participants working to overcome this kind of 'inherited baggage' and developing surprising affinities based on their friendships with diverse others.

Finally, Hawkins' (2014) work on place and critical cosmopolitanism guided us as we pondered the kind of 'processes, interactions, and understandings' (2014: 109) at play when the youth at our site watched, interpreted and created videos. As we will discuss, each of these perspectives on cosmopolitanism helped us to make sense of our diverse participants' behavior as they both forged new friendships and gained linguistic and cultural knowledge, as well as voiced biases and preconceptions. In the next section, we will describe the research site and our positions as co-researchers in the project.

Site Description and Positionality

The study took place in a community-based after-school program called the Harmony Center[1] in an Intermountain western city in the

United States during the 2017–18 school year and the following summer. The Harmony Center, an after-school program for students in grades 6 to 12, was, at the time of the study, part of a larger city-wide initiative that implements programs and services to meet the needs of the diverse community's children and youth. Almost all of the students who attended the program are recent immigrants or refugees who are learning English and live in a nearby apartment complex.

The study participants included a group of five 11- and 12-year-old girls who regularly attended programing at the Harmony Center, as well as their after-school teachers. The girls were close friends and neighbors who spoke a variety of languages and came from different backgrounds. The group included: Dorje and Pema, twin sisters originally from Nepal who had lived in refugee camps in India prior to moving to the United States; Nin, whose family was from Burma but had previously lived in Thailand and identified as Thai; Anisa, who was originally from Afghanistan and who had arrived in America from a refugee camp in Pakistan seven months before joining the study (and whose family was celebrated in the local newspaper as the last Afghani family to arrive before bans or quotas took effect); and finally, Bashira, who was from a family of Somali refugees who had lived in a refugee camp in Kenya before moving to the US. Bashira and Anisa were both Muslim and wore a head scarf – a detail that has key implications in this discussion. All of the girls were in sixth grade at the local elementary school at the start of the study and were preparing to transition to junior high the following year. The group walked together to the Harmony Center almost every weekday after school and attended the various programs at the center, including our GSB project, from mid-afternoon until the evening.

The staff of the Harmony Center staff were also a diverse group. They included Stephanie, the program coordinator and leader of the staff, and Leah, the wheelchair-using program manager. Both were white, middle-class women who had strong backgrounds in working with children and youth. Other staff included Than and Nitika, two Asian immigrants who spoke English as an additional language; Carlos, a university student DREAMer, who also used a wheelchair; and Amy, a white middle-class college student from the same college where we taught and studied.

At the time of the study, we were an education professor at a small liberal arts college (first author) and undergraduate pre-service teacher (second author). We are both white, female and middle class. These details are significant because we are very typical of the adults our students come into contact with and view as authority figures, both in their schools and after-school programs (because in the US the majority of teachers are white, female and from middle-class backgrounds). It is also noteworthy that we did not share the same cultural, religious or linguistic background as the youth participants or most of the program staff. As we will discuss in our findings, we were often puzzled, if not troubled, by the participants' reactions to videos and to others. We recognize that our reactions were shaped by our own privilege, race and education. Clearly, we had not shared the same lived experiences as the participants of our study – young refugee youth who had immigrated, lived in refugee camps, and, in the US, still lived in relative poverty.

We have provided these descriptions of the Harmony Center staff and children and ourselves to underscore the diversity and uniqueness of the participants (both the youth and adult staff members), as well as our positionality within this mix of people. We were often intrigued about how students not only negotiated language but also complex social issues, such as etiquette around pushing a staff member's wheelchair or a willingness or resistance to interacting with a staff member of a different gender or minority group. We wish to underscore again that our race, class, gender, education and (dis)ability gave us status and privilege in this space, as well as a unique interpretive lens.

Methods

To research questions related to language use and interaction surrounding GSB, we selected a variety of qualitative research methods to understand the unfolding interactions between participants at the Harmony Center, their adult instructors and the other global participants of GSB (who were located in Uganda, Wisconsin and Kenya). This case study (Yin, 2002) sought to define both the phenomena of multi- and transmodal language use in our research site and across others, taking into account the often-blurry boundaries between 'phenomenon and context' (Yin, 2002, as cited in Yazan, 2015: 137). Data was gathered using participant observation; group interviews with the students; individual interviews with the staff; and video and chat texts drawn from the GSB website. We co-facilitated a weekly GSB meeting at the Harmony Center throughout the school year and summer, paying close attention to how the students interacted with the project, the teachers and staff, and each other during the meetings. Immediately after each session, we recorded the happenings of the day (fieldnotes) in a shared file.

Facilitating the sessions and interacting with students on a weekly basis allowed us to build strong relationships with the students. Although the participants seemed initially very guarded, the duration and high level of engagement allowed us to build rapport so that we could ask and learn about the participants' experiences. We conducted two semi-structured group interviews with them – once in the middle of the school year and once at the end of the summer as they were transitioning to a new school and after-school program. The group interview was focused on the students' learning and their perceptions of the project. We also conducted individual semi-structured interviews with the Harmony Center staff, focusing on their teaching background and thoughts on the project's value and implementation. Finally, we analyzed the videos and comments the students created and posted to the GSB website as part of the project.

To analyze the data, we used an iterative process of in vivo coding (Saldaña, 2015), wherein we generated codes, categories and larger themes. We also wrote and exchanged lengthy analytical memos (Saldaña, 2015) and read and commented on each other's work to enhance reliability with a process of member checking, asking clarifying questions or reading fieldnotes and interpretations among the two researchers, the staff at the center and the youth participants (Creswell & Miller, 2000). For example, after visiting a local museum, we wrote fieldnotes about the experience of accompanying the youth as they were closely followed by a security officer. In this particular day's findings, codes like 'surveillance' and 'hijabs' (worn by two members of the group) emerged. These codes were verified and discussed among the research team and the other Harmony Center staff members that had been present, as a way to member check the alignment of experience among stakeholders.

To analyze the video footage, we watched the videos several times, using codes to describe what we were seeing and hearing. We took screenshots of particularly salient frames of the story and wrote analytic memos (Saldaña, 2015) based on these frames. Because we often engaged students in creative pre-writing and drawing activities to spark their interest in the pre-video production stage, we also closely looked these artifacts, such as the community map that we will describe in a later section, looking for similarities and differences between what participants chose to highlight on their maps.

Next, we turn our attention to discussing key findings from our data – visual, written, drawn and spoken – to illustrate how multimodal data enriched our interpretations of the study participants using English and creating stories to reflect their realities as new Americans forging cosmopolitan identities.

Findings

Presentation of community: 'Our community'

Ethnographic data can be likened to a kaleidoscope. Each turn or new angle offers a new perspective (Dye *et al.*, 2000). We take this visual metaphor to heart as we examine data that on the surface might strike the viewer as fairly simplistic. The video discussed here was the final video students made after a year of working on GSB. As educators, we often suppressed our urge to be overly didactic; however, in this instance, we worked with students to create a video that went beyond their initial impulse to record their friendships through a series of selfies adorned with captions reading 'best friends forever'. That is, while self-representation did play a role in the GSB project, a larger goal is to create videos that represent the participants' lives and communities so that these videos can be springboards for questions and discussions among global peers and increased global understanding for all. Further, these representations arguably did offer valid characterizations of their emerging identities and friendships, but, based on an earlier prewriting/drawing exercise of community map-making (wherein they drew pictures of their neighborhoods, emphasizing buildings that were important to them), the participants rallied behind the suggestion to create a video about places they all knew in their neighborhood.

Figure 3.1 shows how participant Bashira included such images as the local mosque, Walmart (a large chain store) and the park. While students made positive representations of their neighborhoods, we also heard many students explaining that the park in their neighborhood was for 'poor people' (9 March 2018) or that where they lived was 'dirty' and had 'too many African people' (fieldnotes, 9 March 2018), an attitude that took on significance in shooting their video.

When it came time to make the final video, the participants made choices to represent another reality from that in which they lived, namely, one that was more prosperous. In the introduction of the video, Nin describes that that they will be presenting about food; during this portion, the participants walk us through a local supermarket, highlighting the abundance of chips, cakes, candy and ready-to-eat snack foods, pictured

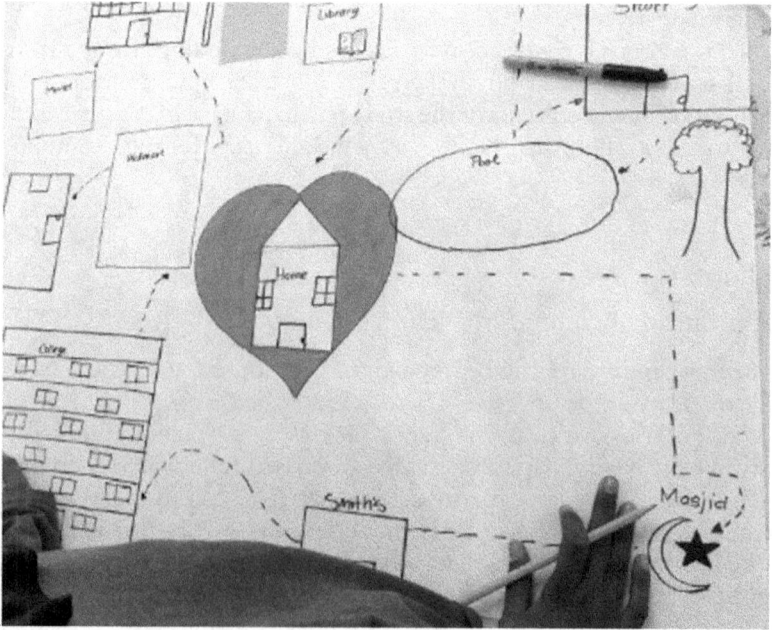

Figure 3.1 Bashira's drawing of her community

Figure 3.2 The girls showing snack foods while stating, 'We have lots of chips.'

in screen shots taken from the video (Figures 3.2 and 3.3). This particular grocery store was not the closest store to where the students lived, but it is noteworthy that the participants had a particular aim in visiting this store and that was, as Nin, a sixth-grade Burmese student who grew up in Thailand, states, to show food that 'English people' (videotape, 2 August 2018) eat. While we do not know what exactly the participants bought

Figure 3.3 Anisa shows the different kinds of cakes. The caption reads: 'I'm talking about cake. There are many types.'

when they shopped at such stores (though food was often a prominent topic of conversation among the girls, who were often hungry after the long school day), the objective seemed to focus on curating a presentation of American ('English') food and the sheer plethora of it. For example, the students added captions to the videos such as 'We have lots of chips' (videotape, 2 August 2018), or focused their commentary on listing the many kinds of cakes, such as 'Nutella', 'Strawberry' and 'Happy Birthday' (videotape, 2 August 2018). Even in the presentation of the produce section, there seems to be a focus on the presentation of the vegetables – one of sanitized presentation and abundance that is typical of grocery stores in the United States.

While the video clearly shows the unique ways of packaging and consuming food in the United States, it also speaks to participants' new collective reality, their presentation of self and audience awareness. As we mentioned, the excerpts from the grocery store primarily focus on abundance and junk food. We trace a potential reason for this choice back to the girls' reactions to a video created by our Ugandan partners and the ensuing conversation about food in Africa. In this particular video, the Ugandan youth show an involved, multi-step process of harvesting potatoes by hand, building their own fire and cooking the potatoes (videotape, 31 January 2017). As we watched the video, several of the participants from sub-Saharan Africa voiced an awareness and familiarity with these ways of cooking and finding food from their own past experiences (fieldnotes, 17 November 2017). Despite this familiarity, we noted that during the viewing of the video, while watching the food preparation, the girls were unwilling to engage, and '… talked to each other about how they'd never eat the food in the video because it looked "disgusting"' (fieldnotes, 2 March 2018). Further, as the video played, the participants continued to make negative comments about what they expressed as the backwardness of the youth.

We then engaged in a brainstorming discussion about what kind of video we would make. While the ideas presented below were never included in the final community video we have thus far discussed, the conversation, as recorded in our field notes, is significant.

> They wanted to show our different ways of life […] We voted and decided on the topic of food. We would show the students in Africa a stove because these students say that their African counterparts don't have one […] We decided to show the ease of American life by bringing in a camp stove and cooking spaghetti and sauce from a jar. (fieldnotes, 17 November 2017)

The reaction to the video coupled with the conversation above give key context that presenting life in America meant showing having things, foods and conveniences. Further, while we witnessed the children in the after-school program talking fondly about foods from their home country (often to complain about the pre-packaged dinners served in the program), the participants seemed to agree that the best way to present their lives was by showing the ease of US life with its abundance of convenience and prepared junk foods. This particular issue of food as an assimilating force dovetails with Karrebæk's (2012) study of how immigrants to Denmark are re-educated about their notions of food and health, belonging and difference: 'There seems to be a perceived relation between national and cultural belonging, on the one side, and food practices, on the other. By eating something different than the majority population, immigrants index different understandings of belonging and of self' (Karrebæk, 2012: 1–2).

While Karrebæk's study focuses on how immigrant children assimilate into Danish school food culture, our data suggest that the immigrant youth in this study were committed to showing American foods and highlighting their convenience and easy access, as a way to suggest that they had moved beyond more basic ways to prepare food.

As with the presentation of food, the participants made several editorial choices to make their lives seem more prosperous than they really were. When it came time, for example, to film the local park (featured prominently in each of the girls' community map drawings), participants explicitly stated that they did not want to film their neighborhood parks that were, in Dorje's words, 'for poor people' (fieldnotes, 9 March 2018). Additionally, although the girls agreed to film the simply constructed housing development that they called home, they did not want to share much of the footage in their final video.

In sum, through analyzing the artifacts like the community map and processing conversations and video together, we gain a compellingly layered portrait of the participants as they altered their stories to show the prosperity of American life. As stated, while food and assimilation may seem peripheral to language use and learning, the notion of transmodalities enabled us to track the participants' various overlapping modes of verbal, gestural, written and online communication as they progressed from reacting to the Ugandan video to creating maps of their neighborhood and selectively presenting their lived realities, and were the media through which their representations of self were negotiated together and portrayed to their peers. More poignant still is the idea that the participants, who by US standards lived in poverty, created a story that portrays more prosperous, if unhealthy, versions of their diets, play spaces and themselves – seemingly in the name of being American and having American things.

The 'concept' of Africa

A second theme that emerged was how the participants framed the notion of Africa in their discussions of the videos from fellow GSB participants in Uganda and Kenya. These data give us interesting insights into how cosmopolitan orientations are forged, albeit in slow, non-linear, and even messy ways.

In one of our earlier sessions with the group, the participants were working on a video about things they learned in school by making a list of what they remembered learning in history classes. The following excerpt from our field notes illustrates what transpired next. 'After listing 9/11 and the Civil War [...] one girl then suggested that "people starving and dying in Africa" be added to our list of historical events, and whether this was a valid historical event was debated' (fieldnotes, 1 December 2017). From what we gathered, the participants had internalized Africa as a problematic entity (Ferguson, 2006) or a 'single story' (Adichie, 2009) of war, famine and poverty. We found this view – which reduces a rich, varied continent to a stereotype – troubling, even more so because two of the participants in our group (and many more in the larger after-school program) were themselves from Africa. As we continued our work with the participants, we discovered similar troubling attitudes related to Africa. Through time and a concerted effort to engage in dialogue, we were able to unpack some of the context for how these kinds of negative feelings arose, and the trajectory of how they were navigated in our site.

A few months into our work, the participants began to insist that we stop watching videos from Africa. It was common for a member of our group (usually Dorje from Nepal) to complain that the participants 'hate[d] watching African videos' (fieldnotes, 19 January 2018). We often tried to clarify that the videos were Ugandan or Kenyan, as if to humanize and be more specific about where the other GSB participants came from, but the group continued to call the videos 'African' with disdainful tones. Meanwhile, we felt concerned about how the sole African group member, Bashira from Somalia, internalized these comments as her Asian and Middle Eastern counterparts loudly complained about the 'African videos'.

Troubled by these attitudes, we strove to strike a balance between intervening (to stop any derogatory comments) and investigating the beliefs underlying these dismissive, prejudicial attitudes. One possible explanation – aside from perhaps the educational messages from school that Africa was a place where only *bad* things happened – came from the experiences the girls had in the neighborhood.

During the community mapping discussion, Dorje told us that one thing she didn't like about her neighborhood was that there were 'too many *African* people' (fieldnotes, 9 March 2018). After Dorje's proclamation, Nin and Thein (who were, to recall, ethnically Burmese but had grown up in Thailand) chimed in, pointing out that Africans in their neighborhood seemingly flouted rules and would 'walk in the road instead of on the sidewalk' (fieldnotes, 9 March 2018).

Beyond refusing to conform to norms, we also discovered that the females in our group had an antagonistic relationship with a few of the young African males who occasionally attended the after-school program. We draw from fieldnotes that describe an incident that occurred on the way to film one of the videos:

> As we waited for the bus to come, we were approached by a group of young African boys. They stayed at a distance but shouted profanities and yelled that the girls in our group were 'a bunch of whores'. Dorje flipped off the boys and then told our group to ignore them. Bashira [from Somalia] ran at the group of boys and they disappeared. (fieldnotes, 20 April 2018)

Perhaps the confluence of these experiences, from negative educational messages presenting Africa as a problem to hostile relationships with African neighbors and pre-teen males, significantly shaped our participants' reactions toward Africa and the Ugandan videos. These attitudes, while they show how place shapes ideologies and lived realities, however, ran contrary to our goals of helping to engender cosmopolitan proclivities, specifically good-willed curiosity toward global others. At the same time, we also are hopeful that some of our work – often taking the backseat in the conversations and listening – helped the study participants work through these feelings.

To illustrate, toward the end of our study, the following interaction between Dorje from Tibet and Bashira from Somalia occurred. During a class session, the Asian girls in the group were discussing why they thought Asia was better than Africa, while Bashira listened to them, looking, by our assessment, uncomfortable (fieldnotes, 9 March 2018). Carlos, a staff member, intervened and 'explained to Dorje that Bashira was from Africa and might have her feelings hurt' (fieldnotes, 9 March 2018). Dorje corrected the staff member, telling him that Bashira was from *Somalia*, not Africa, and was surprised to learn that Somalia was indeed in *Africa* (fieldnotes, 9 March 2018).

Dorje's surprise might have indicated that she considered Bashira to be a friend first and a Somali second. Moreover, Dorje also seemed to think that Somalia and Africa were separate places. After this realization, Dorje reflected 'about how sad she feels when people say hurtful things about Nepal' (fieldnotes, 9 March 2018). This kind of processing showed Dorje's initial steps to making a connection between the feelings of prejudice she had experienced and those that Bashira might feel when her home country was negatively portrayed. Further, because Dorje herself had lived in multiple countries (Nepal, India and the US), she started to question her own national origins and, according to the fieldnotes, 'seemed confused and talked about how she lived in many different countries and thought maybe she might have lived in Africa at some point, saying "Maybe I'm from Africa too"' (fieldnotes, 9 March 2018).

While Dorje's realization and turn to empathy represents preliminary steps to dismantling prejudicial attitudes, this interaction shows the power of cross-national friendships in eliminating bias and creating new understandings. After connecting Africa – a place she had previously showed disgust and dislike for – to a friend who she cared about, Dorje was able to empathize with the concept of Africa so much that she considered identifying herself as 'from Africa'. This point echoes findings by Kromidas' (2011) work on elementary cosmopolitanism. Her 9- to 11-year-old participants, regardless of their true origins, would often take on or borrow the nationalities of their friends, evincing that the 'obstacles of blood, birth and bodies' (2011: 583) were outweighed by the youth loyalties and interest in their friends. These findings seem to suggest that friendships (as well as conflicted relationships, such as that with the neighborhood African males) carry great weight in youth's perceptions of global others, which in turn influence their multicultural awareness and openness.

Moreover, had we only observed and collected data about the participants' dismissive attitudes toward the videos, we would not have been able to understand how they were making sense of the diversity that they encountered in their daily lives. Instead, our prolonged engagement with the participants doing such activities as taking the bus, walking the neighborhood and listening closely to their conversations as they made and responded to videos gave us a more complex portrait of their lives and community. As Appadurai (1996: 60) reminds us, 'The world on the move affects even small geographical and cultural spaces'. We submit that this data also illustrates how one small 'cultural space' – the Harmony Center and surrounding neighborhood and its inhabitants – becomes a *translocality*, a 'de-territorialized' (1996: 196) community where novel identities, relationships (both friendly and adversarial) and a sense of belonging are being formed and cultivated. In the next section, we discuss the significance and limitations of this constellation of multimodal data points and provide suggestions for further research.

Significance: The Messiness of Cosmopolitan Teaching and Learning among Transnational Youth

Thus far, we have focused on how different modes of data – from videos, written artifacts and conversations among our participants – greatly deepened our understanding of how the youth reacted to and participated in Global StoryBridges. Second, we have examined the interesting process and transmodal negotiation of making a video about a community that did not entirely accurately reflect the subjects' lives, but instead showed greater affluence and access to food, and a community that was more reflective of a certain idea of the United States that seemed desirable to the youth participants. Third, we have discussed the multiple conversations surrounding participants' reactions to the African videos, which to us demonstrate the experience and importance of forging translocal relationships and identities. We argue that these themes underscore the critical roles of context and place for educators who wish to facilitate cosmopolitan encounters among linguistically diverse youth.

Multiculturalism and cosmopolitanism

One key takeaway for us has to do with multicultural and cosmopolitan education. As white, female educators and researchers, we felt surprise and shock in instances where participants shied away from presenting their cultures, languages and customs in favor of an Americanized, or more white-washed version of their lives. While our discussion has focused on the presentation of affluent city parks and American grocery stores, we would be remiss not to mention that the two Muslim participants in our group were often reluctant to respond to, and were even offended by, questions posed by other GSB members about their religion, specifically, their wearing of the veil (fieldnotes, 18 January 2018).

As white educators versed in discourses celebrating multiculturalism and youth's funds of knowledge (González *et al.*, 2005) and as people genuinely interested in languages and cultures, we believe that our surprised reaction reflects our privilege of not facing discrimination (based on religious or other grounds) ourselves. Further we, unlike our participants, did not share in the daily experience of leaving our homelands, living in transitional camps or in a super-diverse housing development, or, for that matter, experiencing the sexist heckling of the neighborhood preteen boys. These contextual details underscore the often difficult reality of our participants' lives and remind us how power and privilege play a central role in multicultural work. Kromidas (2011: 582) reminds us that 'mainstream multiculturalism's seemingly neutral surface' can easily ignore or gloss over 'histories of oppression'.

However, as we listened in and participated in conversations, we were able to more fully comprehend the lived experiences of our participants, an understanding that allowed us to appreciate that their perspectives were often marked with ambivalence stemming from being in liminal positions, as adolescents, immigrants and new Americans. This awareness has implications for educators who may, with the noblest of intentions, try to get their students to share details about their pasts, languages and cultures in educational contexts. Multicultural experts caution educators about beads and feathers or static versions of multiculturalism (e.g. Howard, 2010). We too urge educators, as well as researchers working with linguistically and culturally diverse groups, to be more vigilant than ever of privilege and power, and to adopt a stance of openness and inquiry (to embody critical cosmopolitanism) rather than push for textbook examples of multicultural sharing.

Arguably, our attempts to engender students' cosmopolitan attitudes and care for the global peers that the students interacted with on the computer were often met with resistance, and, by that measure, were less than successful. However, we maintain that participants in the study were developing burgeoning cosmopolitan identities outside of and in conjunction with the GSB experience. The girls exhibited many instances of cultural and linguistic crossing (Rampton, 2017), whether through their shared affinity for Korean pop music, which they studied diligently, or taste for each other's snack foods, like Takis (from Mexico) or dried mango from Southeast Asia.

It was this friendship among the participants, and newly-found shared affinities, that helped students question their attitudes and preconceptions, namely here of *Africa*. That is, as Dorje wrestled with Bashira's nationality and confusion about her own origins, her loyalty and care for her friends helped her build a bridge of empathy in place of misunderstanding and prejudice. The process of working on videos, responding to others', and conversing about these topics, while messy and even offensive, constituted important grappling for the participants as they made sense of their new place in the world and among diverse others. Again, this dovetails with Kromidas' claim (2011) that informal conversations and friendships have greater power than formal 'teacher-led' attempts to engender cosmopolitan stances, and that these interactions can transgress 'traditional understandings of difference and their circumscribed possibilities for enacting social relations – a living curriculum … [of] elementary cosmopolitanism' (2011: 583).

This finding is interesting for the larger project of Global StoryBridges, or for other researchers doing multi-site research with global youth, because it highlights that much of the cosmopolitan work will not be done by watching or participating in the online discussion boards alone, but also in the many face-to-face conversations that occur locally off camera or screen. Further, it underscores the importance of the transmodal (Hawkins, 2018: 61) perspective that takes into account what Hawkins calls 'context and culture' and puts into focus these 'entanglements and relationships […] that shape meaning in multimodal artifacts and communications' (2018: 64). Understanding these 'entanglements and relationships' across participants' various modes of communication gave us intriguing insights into data, but, more importantly, allowed us to have richer relationships *with* our participants – a caring relationship between researcher and researched that was, at its very heart, critically cosmopolitan.

Conclusion

While the multi- and transmodal focus of our study, combined with our extended engagement with our participants, helped us to have more egalitarian dialogues, a future direction for this work is to bolster the participatory nature of GSB. While facilitators are directed to let youth drive the process of gathering ideas and creating videos, we also felt a responsibility to help our female participants develop audience awareness and to present their lives in ways that were comprehensible and also educative to fellow GSB members in places like Vietnam and Uganda. As we move forward, we believe that a place-based curriculum (Demarest, 2014) combined with Critical Participatory Action Research (Cammarota & Fine, 2010) may be used to help both participants and facilitators gain more ownership of the process, while experiencing the creative latitude that derives from the project being an after- rather than in-school activity.

A second direction for future research that we see is to pursue more cross-site research about the multi- and transmodal work that goes into participating in GSB. In this chapter, we have focused on our participants' reactions to African videos. Because the data on the online forum is truncated and often reflects students who are just learning to read and write in English, and even use the keyboard, we often wish that we could be flies on the wall across the world to overhear the conversations occurring as youth in other sites negotiate their questions and comments. Because we are currently developing a robust relationship and exchange of ideas in our transnational research team, we are even more hopeful about the possibility of a multi-site study to illuminate even more facets and affordances of the GSB project, some of which are represented in other chapters in this volume.

In this chapter, we have presented data relating to one unique site and time. As researchers, we are cognizant that our ethnographic footprint is as ephemeral as a mark in the sand. We know that the female participants in our study, though frozen in time here, continued to develop more complex understandings of culture, language and belonging. In this way, our representation shows that the youth lived a highly dynamic, situational and ambivalent version of cosmopolitan life as demonstrated through their languaging and communication practices. We hope that this portrait informs future researchers and teachers as they work with and interpret the complex languages and lived worlds of global transnational youth.

Note

(1) All names of people and locations involved in the study are pseudonyms.

References

Adichie, C.N. (2009) The danger of the single story. See https://www.ted.com/talks/chimamanda_adichie_the_danger_of_a_single_story (accessed April 2021)/

Ajayi, L. (2008) Meaning-making, multimodal representation, and transformative pedagogy: An exploration of meaning construction instructional practices in an ESL high school classroom. *Journal of Language, Identity, and Education* 7 (3–4), 206–29.

Appadurai, A. (1996) *Modernity at Large: Cultural Dimensions of Globalization.* Minneapolis: University of Minnesota Press.

Cammarota, J. and Fine, M. (eds) (2010) *Revolutionizing Education: Youth Participatory Action Research in Motion.* New York: Routledge.

Canagarajah, S. (2017) Translingual practice as spatial repertoires: Expanding the paradigm beyond structuralist orientations. *Applied Linguistics* 39 (1), 31–54.

Creswell, J.W. and Miller, D.L. (2000) Determining validity in qualitative inquiry. *Theory into Practice* 39 (3), 124–30.

Demarest, A.B. (2014) *Place-based Curriculum Design: Exceeding Standards through Local Investigations*. New York: Routledge.

Dye, J.F., Schatz, I.M., Rosenberg, B.A. and Coleman, S.T. (2000) Constant comparison method: A kaleidoscope of data. *The Qualitative Report* 4 (1), 1–10.

Ferguson, J. (2006) *Global Shadows: Africa in the Neoliberal World Order*. Durham: Duke University Press.

Gadsden, V. and Levine, F. (2017) Statement by AERA President Vivian L. Gadsden and Executive Director Felice J. Levine on the White House Executive Order on Visas and Immigration. See https://www.aera.net/Newsroom/News-Releases-and-Statements/Statement-by-AERA-President-Vivian-L-Gadsden-and-Executive-Director-Felice-J-Levine-on-the-White-House-Executive-Order-on-Visas-and-Immigration (accessed April 2021).

González, N., Moll, L. and Amanti, C. (2005) *Funds of Knowledge: Theorizing Practices in Households, Communities and Classrooms*. Mahway, NJ: Lawrence Erlbaum Associates.

Hall, S. (2006) On the limits and possibilities of cosmopolitanism. See https://blackatlanticresource.wordpress.com/2012/03/19/video-stuart-hall-on-the-limits-and-possibilities-of-cosmopolitanism/ (accessed April 2021).

Halpern, R. (1999) After-school programs for low-income children: Promise and challenges. *Future of Children* 9 (2), 81–5.

Hawkins, M.R. (2004) Researching English language and literacy development in schools. *Educational Researcher* 33 (3), 14–25. https://doi.org/10.3102/0013189X033003014

Hawkins, M.R. (2014) Ontologies of place, creative meaning making and critical cosmopolitan education. *Curriculum Inquiry* 44 (1), 90–112.

Hawkins, M.R. (2018) Transmodalities and transnational encounters: Fostering critical cosmopolitan relations. *Applied Linguistics* 39, 55–77.

Howard, T. (2010) *Why Race and Class Matter in Schools: Closing the Achievement Gap in America's Classrooms*. New York: Teachers College Press.

Hull, G.A. and Katz, M.L. (2006) Crafting an agentive self: Case studies of digital storytelling. *Research in the Teaching of English* 41 (1), 43.

Karrebæk, M.S. (2012) "What's in Your Lunch Box Today?": Health, respectability, and ethnicity in the primary classroom. *Journal of Linguistic Anthropology* 22 (1), 1–22.

Kress, G. (2000) Multimodality: Challenges to thinking about language, *TESOL Quarterly* 34 (2), 337–340. See http://www.jstor.org/stable/3587959 (accessed April 2021).

Kromidas, M. (2011) Elementary forms of cosmopolitanism: Blood, birth, and bodies in immigrant New York City. *Harvard Educational Review* 81 (3), 581–606.

Lam, W.S.E. and Warriner, D.S. (2012) Transnationalism and literacy: Investigating the mobility of people, languages, texts, and practices in contexts of migration. *Reading Research Quarterly* 47 (2), 191–215.

Lee, S.J. and Hawkins, M.R. (2008) 'Family is here': Learning in community-based after-school programs. *Theory into Practice* 47 (1), 51–58.

Leeuween, T.V. (2015) Multimodality in education: Some directions and some questions. *TESOL Quarterly* 49 (3), 582–589.

Miller, B. (2003) *Critical Hours: After School Programs and Educational Success*. Quincy, MA: Nellie Mae Education Foundation. See http://www.nmefdn.org/uploads/ Critical_Hours.pdf (accessed 11 October 2006).

Norton Peirce, B. (1995) Social identity, investment, and language learning. *TESOL Quarterly* 29 (1), 9.

Rampton, B. (2017) *Crossing: Language and Ethnicity among Adolescents*. New York: Routledge.
Saldaña, J. (2015) *The Coding Manual for Qualitative Researchers*. Thousand Oaks, CA: SAGE.
Sanjek, D. (1998) "I Ain't Afraid of No Kids!" Douglas Rushkoff and the Ascendance of the Digital Sublime. *The Review of Education/Pedagogy/Cultural Studies* 20 (2), 173–187.
Toohey, K., Dagenais, D., Fodor, A., Hof, L., Nuñez, O., Singh, A. and Schulze, L. (2015) 'That sounds so cooool': Entanglements of children, digital tools, and literacy practices. *TESOL Quarterly* 49 (3), 461–485.
Werbner, P. (1999) Global pathways. Working class cosmopolitans and the creation of transnational ethnic worlds. *Social Anthropology* 7 (1), 17–35.
Werbner, P. (2006) Vernacular cosmopolitanism. *Theory, Culture & Society* 23 (2–3), 496–498.
Yazan, B. (2015) Three approaches to case study methods in education: Yin, Merriam, and Stake. *The Qualitative Report* 20 (2), 134–152.
Yin, R.K. (2002) *Case Study Research: Design and Methods*. Thousand Oaks, CA: Sage Publications.

4 A Place-Based Critical Transmodal Analysis of Chinese Youth's Digital Storytelling

Rui Li and Jiayu Feng

Introduction

This chapter investigates how the power of the educational administrative system in China has impacted Chinese youth's digital storytelling processes and transnational engagements in the Global StoryBridges project. Data are drawn from a project site located in northwestern China. Framed by Hawkins' (2014, 2018) notions of *transmodalities* and *place*, this study offers a critical lens on youth's digitally-mediated transmodal production and communication in a global digital storytelling project, with consideration of the hidden power relationships between the young participants and their school administrators. Findings show that within the social and educational structure of the Chinese site, youth, despite participating in a project in which they are supposed to be decision-makers, had limited opportunities to control the design processes of their transglobal participation when it occurred in their school, and they had more agency in out-of-school spaces.

In- and Out-of-School Learning

Considering the features of the 21st century in global and digital contexts, learning and educating is no longer about teaching textbooks to a group of well-seated, immobile students in classrooms (Hawkins, 2014, 2018; Li & Hawkins, 2021; Mills, 2010). The spaces where learning takes place are expanding from in-school towards out-of-school settings, from physical spaces to digital platforms, and from local to global contexts, all of which interweave together for a more complicated educational landscape (Bezemer & Kress, 2016; Choi & Yi, 2016; Jewitt, 2008; Lam & Rosario-Ramos, 2009). As Hawkins (2018) has argued in her transnational research, we are now facing a '*trans-turn*' (see also Hawkins & Mori, 2018) in education and communication, which urges educators and educational scholars to prepare learners to become 'citizens of the world' (Hawkins, 2014: 97), global citizens (Appiah, 2008; Truong-White & McLean, 2015), digital citizens (Hull & Stornaiuolo, 2014) and cultural citizens (Hull *et al.*, 2010). Modes of learning and educating are no longer limited to fixed ensembles but have been expanded to include multimodal and transmodal complexes across people, places, spaces, time, cultures, and technologies (Jacobs, 2012).

The Global StoryBridges project (GSB) is designed to prepare participants to be citizens of the changing world. Through creating videos about their lives and communities, and sharing and discussing them with youth in other parts of the world through a dedicated website, it is meant to enhance transmodal transnational learning opportunities, to encourage learners to walk outside of their classrooms to revisit and showcase their own community life using digital resources, and to watch and respond to worlds unknown to them, represented by global others. Although each site has an adult facilitator, GSB is created as a youth-owned space, in which youth who participate are supposed to collaboratively make all decisions themselves on all processes of the project, including their video topics, storyline, editing, and where and how to videotape, as well as how to respond to videos from global peers.

However, when conducting this project, we find that the design of learning, in its shift from traditional classrooms towards community, or to spaces outside of school, challenged the educational systems and school administrative policies in China. For example, because of administrative intervention following government educational policies with extremely high levels of attention and stress on safety issues (The People's Republic of China General Office of State Council, 2017), most of the GSB project activities had to be conducted in physical areas within the school, because taking students outside of the school was considered by the Board of Education as risking students' safety, and accountability rests on the principal. Therefore, under such pressure from the educational system, societies, and parents of students to guarantee the safety of students, school administrators often have to make a series of difficult administrative decisions, such as whether or not they can give permission to teachers to take students outside of school for other activities (Lao, 2004). On the other hand, the time allowed by the school for conducting this project during school time was limited because more time was expected to be given to formal instruction in school, with a focus on assessment. The following excerpts by the school administrator and project teacher facilitator who were involved in the Chinese site confirm the challenge:

> Personally, my own child is also attending an elementary school, and I do think it is very important to let children go outside to participate in some out-of-school activities. I think this is good. However, I can take my own

child outside but I will become very cautious and concerned to make the decision to allow and organize a large number of my students, or even part of the students, outside of school. (Interview, Administrator,[1] 18 September 2019)

Our Chinese students are having too much pressure on exams, so we can't have students work for longer time on this. (Interview, Teacher Facilitator #1, 18 September 2019)

The above statements show a typical tension for out-of-school projects taking place in a Chinese school. To clarify, this doesn't mean that the neighborhood is dangerous. Rather, it is a result of previous negative news reposted by national and local newspapers about some accidents or injuries (for instance, students were hurt by cars outside of school) that have warned school administrators to restrict teachers from organizing students outside of school in order to avoid the risk. Therefore, students in the Chinese site had less opportunity to videotape stories outside of their school. Even though there were a few out-of-school videos produced by the Chinese site, the majority of these videos (during the time of our study) were not made collaboratively involving all youth participants but individually by one or two children with their parents' supervision and help.

In a study by Lao (2004) of injury accidents of Chinese elementary and middle school students and resulting imputation of responsibility, it is claimed that the current family structure of only one child in China has led to 'parents' rigorous attitude on school' (2004: 15) to be responsible for any potential risks to children's safety. According to Lao, parents' 'overprotective attitude' is 'impolitic' (2004: 15) and problematic, which might constrain learning. In order to solve this educational problem, Lao suggests that we should start from critical reflection and rethink our traditional way of thinking about education, accepting the new goal of educating our children in the new age to empower them to be engaged from a home orientation towards the community and society.

In this study, we recognize the complicated sociocultural contexts, for instance student safety issues, that were embedded in the Chinese project site activities, particularly the digital story producing process, and its subsequent effects on a series of social decisions on the place where video recording occurred, theme selection and technological participation. We aim to reexamine the affordances and constraints of the 'mediational nature of place' (Hawkins, 2014: 91) – in in-school spaces versus out-of-school spaces – on youth's digitally mediated transmodal production in this project, attending to the potential power relations between youth and adults. In this study, 'adults' refers to the school administrator and teacher facilitators who were involved in the project working with these youth. We provide descriptions of how the power flow from top-to-bottom affected decisions from the school administrator to the teacher facilitators, and from the teacher facilitators to youth participants.

Considering Transmodalities in Place

In Hawkins' (2018) conceptualization of *transmodalities*, she provides five complexities for analyzing youth's transnational transmodal engagements in digital settings. In her analysis, it is underscored that we must shift from simply analyzing the 'modes' of communication towards 'a view of semiotic resources' (2018: 64) and modal movement, and the reshaping of these resources across local and global, people and places, physical and digital spaces, and time. Hawkins' definition and framework of transmodalities is helpful for us to rethink the resources – for instance, place – that shaped the youth and adult participants in the Chinese site. Hawkins (2014: 94) defines *place* as 'more than a geographically bounded entity, it has directive force in shaping the thoughts and interactions of those who inhabit it, while also being shaped and defined by them'. According to Hawkins, place is a mediational tool to help us understand transmodal meaning-making in globalized educational contexts. However, few empirical studies have been done to investigate the power relations embedded in place among people who are co-inhabiting and co-positioning themselves within a particular place. In her words:

> Failure to attend to these issues leads to discourses and practices that exacerbate misunderstandings and inequities between people and groups of people, and serves as a barrier to educational initiatives that promote open and equitable engagement. (2014: 91)

In this study, we consider place as a significant resource and concept for us to gain understandings of transmodalities, representations and relations. Through situating our study in the local Chinese site, we investigate not only the digital stories that were transmodally produced and posted on the project website, but also the social stories behind the digital stories that reconstructed and reshaped transmodalities through a lens of place. It leads us to question: What kinds of social relations were built among the Chinese students and their global peers, among the youth and adults, and the participants and researchers? How did the sociocultural, sociopolitical, hierarchical context impact the processes and products of the GSB project in the Chinese site? In order to answer these questions, we identify two different sets of spaces in the lives of youth in this study – in-school and out-of-school spaces – to investigate the potential power relations and social effects hidden behind these spaces mirrored by youth's digital participation with their global peers.

Research Contexts

This is a qualitative case study focusing on the Chinese site of the larger GSB project. This local site involved seven youth participants from low-income families, facilitators, and an administrator in an elementary school in northwest China. Both of the facilitators were English language teachers and were selected by the same administrator. In the rest of this chapter, we call them teacher facilitators to indicate their complicated, perceived roles as both teachers in school and facilitators in the project. There was also technical support from professors and graduate students from a local university to help in technology training for participants. Youth participants in this site were fourth to sixth graders (sixth grade is the highest grade in Chinese elementary schools). It is worthwhile to explain that youth participants in the project site were selected based on a policy of 'outstanding-student' and 'student willingness', as explained by the teacher facilitator:

> Most of our students' parents are working class from other places so their living conditions are not very good. When selecting GSB students in the school, we mainly consider students of outstanding character and academic scholarship from lower-income family, firstly based on students' willingness and voluntariness and their English language skills. (Interview, Teacher Facilitator #2, 18 September 2019)

The excerpt above shows that the selection of students in this site privileged some of the 'better' students, who had better English language skills and academic records, which embedded inequities from the start. Despite discussions about selecting youth participants that took place when the project director set up this site, in which it was clear that the primary criterion (other than socioeconomic status) to be considered was that less-recognized and less academically accomplished youth could benefit most, these 'better' students, in administrators' eyes, can better represent the school in a privileged mode of languaging, English, to global peers.

However, we question: If the goal of the project is to create equal opportunities for global learners who are living in under-resourced communities, how might we address the potential inequities when project criteria conflict with societal norms around inclusion and opportunity? We believe it is important for us to recognize the issue of privilege even among students considered less privileged from a socioeconomic perspective.

Additionally, being part of such a program initiated by a professor from a prestigious US university, and supported by professors from a well-known local Chinese university, also served to distinguish participants as more privileged, and those not selected as less privileged, as the administrator acknowledged:

> This international project is very meaningful. We feel the sense of honor that our school is determined by Professor Hawkins as the only research site in the whole nation. This is a recognition of us so we will make complete effort to coordinate in the project. (p.c., 10 December 2016)

Here, again, potential power relations are manifested, mediated by the relations between elementary schools and universities, and between domestic and international influences. Revisiting such contextual background is helpful for us to gain in-depth understanding of the mediational functions of place in the following analytical sections situated within this broader context.

Data Sources and Analyses

With the awareness of the place-based administrative decisions on video production and the selection of GSB participants, given the administrator's concerns of student safety and school reputation directed by the broader educational and administrative system that we have discussed above, we aimed to study how such decision-making led to different social effects on video production. In order to achieve this objective, we conducted in-depth interviews, collected GSB project website data, and carried out field observations (in the Chinese site), to study our participants' participatory experience and their perceptions of their roles, gains, challenges, and reflections as they took part in this out-of-school project under the directive educational and social contexts.

Semi-structured interviews were conducted with the school administrator and relevant teacher facilitators. Because of the challenge of doing transnational research, especially given that the two authors/researchers (Li and Feng) are located in different places (USA and China respectively), we decided to conduct WeChat[2] audio interviews with the adult participants to enable both of us to participate. Each interview, lasting approximately one to two hours, was conducted individually to avoid cross-intervention among participants; we were particularly aware of the potential power relations between the administrator and teachers. Before interviewing the administrator, we were asked to send her the questions because she wanted to be better prepared for answering our questions. All interviews were conducted in Mandarin Chinese, were audio recorded and were transcribed and translated into English.

We also collected video data from the GSB website. Particularly, from the interview data, we were able to identify *transmodal moments* and *critical incidents* (Li & Hawkins, 2021; Newfield, 2014) from two specific videos made by the Chinese site – one is an in-school video, and the other is an out-of-school video – as all adult participants frequently mentioned the two videos and their roles in producing them. Therefore, we collected, transcribed and analyzed the two videos.

In order to understand how videos were actually produced in the local site and how youth participants perceived their experience in the project, we employed an ethnographic approach as participant-observer in the Chinese site. One of the authors (Feng) conducted on-site observations and collected field notes (including personal communications with youth and adult participants) in this site.

The combination of ethnographic approach and transmodal analyses of online data enabled us to provide a more detailed *place-based critical transmodal analysis* in this study by situating the social moments and incidents in specific, complicated contexts (Flewitt, 2011; Hawkins, 2018; Li & Hawkins, 2021). In Hawkins' words, such methods 'offer insights into not only the moment of production but also the entire process of meaning construction and negotiation across place and space' (2018: 61).

In- and Out-of-School Video Production

In the following section, we showcase two of the videos made by the Chinese students. The first video was entitled *School Culture*. The second video, entitled *City³ Attractions*, showed their city views and places where they liked to visit. We chose these two videos because the first one was taken in school and the second one was taken outside of the school. During the interviews with the adult participants, we learned that the in-school video was decided on due to the school administrator's suggestion, or demand, and the out-of-school one was proposed by a student's question, 'Can I video something by myself?' (Interview, Teacher Facilitator #1, 18 September 2018). Both videos were frequently mentioned and discussed by the teacher facilitators, which compelled us to conduct an in-depth comparative analysis on the production processes of the two videos mediated in different spaces.

Through analyzing and comparing these two videos and the stories behind them, we aimed to study how the videotaping space had impact on the Chinese youth's video design and production and how each space mirrored different levels of administrative or adult intervention on youth participation digitally and transmodally. By showcasing one of the school-related videos, we are not claiming that all school-based videos were like this. Rather, we chose this video because it explicitly manifested the existing power relations between the administrator and the teacher facilitator and students. It is worthwhile to mention that there were other school-based videos produced by the Chinese students that embraced more of students' interests. Table 4.1 provides the comparative analytical fieldnotes, codes, video screen shots and participant quotes.

In-school video: *School Culture*

This 5-minute-5-second school video first shows a male student orally introducing the school gate with a subtitle mirroring his words, 'Hi everyone. This is our school gate. It looks like eyes. It watches us and witnesses our growth every day.' (Video transcription,[4] 19 September 2018). Then the scenery switches to a female student showing a 3-meter-high stone with the Chinese characters 德 (morality, virtue) on one side and 责 (responsibility) on the other side (see the figures in Table 4.1). The stone is named 德石 (translated as 'Moral Stone' on the screen). At the bottom of the stone, it shows a sign saying 明德守责 (translated by the teacher facilitator as 'To disseminate virtue and stick to responsibility'). Then, the screen switched to the school Heart Hall, Ceremony Well (礼井), Music Garden and calligraphy performance. It ended with students singing a Chinese song together, 'Plant the Sun', at the music garden.

It was notable from the video that the female student who was introducing the school moral stone was holding a piece of paper from which she read the script; she then quickly put it into her pocket while the

Table 4.1 Place-based critical transmodal analytical fieldnotes and codes

	School Culture Video	*City Attractions* Video

Place	In school	Outside of school, downtown
Decisions	School administrator	Youth
Script	Teacher facilitator wrote, youth recited	Youth created
Recorder	Teacher facilitator	Youth/Parents
Video Editing	Youth with better technology skills, adults supported	Youth with better technology skills, adults supported
Themes	Place, morality, politeness, responsibility, school/place were the focus of the video	Names of students, downtown view, places of interest; images of youth were centralized on the screen
Administrator Quotes	'We suggest that students should prioritize themes that reflect the school culture when they make decisions on the video topics, which is a very good propaganda for the school. *School Culture* is also part of students' daily life and it meets the requirements of the project.' (p.c., Administrator, 17 April 2018)	'Personally, my own child is also attending an elementary school and I do think it is very important to let children go outside to participant some out-of-school activities. I think this is good. However, I can take my own child outside but I will become very cautious and concerned to make the decision to allow and organize large number of my students, or even part of the students, outside of school.' (Administrator Interview, 18 September 2019)

camera switched from the front of the stone to the back, where it shows the Chinese character referring to 'responsibility'. At that point she seemed to forget what to say, so she used her hands to cover her face to try to remember the English script and then spoke, 'We know that it is in print for us to behave on ourselves in school' (Video transcription, 19 September 2018). The following statements by the teacher facilitator who helped with this video production provides us with a more detailed picture:

> We have a visitor coming to the school so our administrator asked if we can make a school video in English. We had a video in Chinese version for the previous Russian student visitors so we were able to translate the video scripts into English for our students because they could not do it in a short time. Then, we sent the translation to the children and asked them to recite in ten days. After children were familiar with the language, we started videoing and I was helping holding the camera for a better video quality because students could not handle it. (Interview, Teacher Facilitator #1, 18 September 2019)

The excerpt above shows that this in-school video production was predominantly directed by adults (also see administrator quotes in Table 4.1), namely the school administrator and the teacher facilitator. Students were not the designers of the scripts but were recipients and reciters, which limited youth's opportunities to engage with transmodalities, or even creativity.

In Choi and Yi's (2016) study of two teachers' employment of multimodality in teaching with English language learners, they suggest that teachers can also benefit from employing multimodality in their teaching practice and personal development, but for them the goal was to engage students to be the multimodal producers. In their words:

> Teachers should help students become producers, not just consumers, of multimodal messages. Only when students create texts multimodally can they achieve more nuanced and layered understandings of content knowledge through deeper engagement with learning (Jacobs, 2012). (Choi & Yi, 2016: 323)

However, even though students were presented on the digital screen, neither they nor their own voices were positioned as the center of the video; instead, the whole video was highly focused on the different spaces of the school with a highlight on morality and virtues. Meanwhile, because the administrator expected the GSB videos to be high quality, the teacher facilitator, instead of the youth, was holding the camera and shooting the video in order to ensure that the video quality met the administrator's expectation. Therefore, we can see that place, and policies, relations and politics within specific places, were central in the production of this video. The youth participants who were shown in the video seemed to be positioned as English script reciters and followers of adults' decisions. The video was posted on the project website and watched by youth from other sites. However, although it was supposed to be a youth-centered project, youth were decentered, which contradicts the concepts of transmodal design that underscore learners' agency and interests, and the goals of GSB.

We also noticed that all students were not involved in the video. One of the youth participants stated:

> We all participated in the group discussion. However, only some of the students were chosen as the representatives to be shown in the video because their English is very good. Our teachers think that they, compared to others stammering, can say the scripts more fluently and can represent and win the honor for our school. (fieldnotes, p.c., 24 April 2018)

Given the levels of English proficiency and academic achievement of the GSB students privileged over others in the school, this student's statement, particularly, shows that within the project, students were selectively chosen to be shown and to talk in the video as they were considered to represent the school image in public, particularly among the global school sites in the project. This video was produced in (and by) the school, where youth activities were directed by adults. However, the video was posted later on the GSB site as a 'youth-produced' video though it was actually not, which was unnoticed by the other sites. In contrast, the following section showcases an out-of-school video production.

Out-of-school video: *City Attractions*

In this 55-second video, two male students in sequence each introduced their names, then introduced their city attractions. The first student introduced the city bell tower:

> Hello, good afternoon. My name is Han Xiaoxue.[5] Today, I talk about Tang tower building. Follow me. This is Tang tower building. (Subtitle shows 'Bell Tower' on the upper right.) It was built in 1384. It has three floors. Second floor has the biggest clock in the world. (Subtitle: 'This is the biggest clock in the world') Wow, Tang tower building is very beautiful! (video transcription, 19 September 2018)

The second student introduced the city Muslim quarter where many of the local Muslims sell varieties of food, drink and clothes. The street was shown with the students standing in the front while the students were talking in English. 'This is City Muslim Streets. There are many famous nuts. Let's go. Follow me. This is yogurt. It's very sweet.' This is accompanied by the subtitles: 'This is Muslim Quarter' (see figure in Table 4.1). 'This is Yogurt. It's very sweet' (video transcription, 19 September 2018).

In this video, we find that students felt more fluent and confident in using the language they themselves created as video scripts, which is conveyed in their facial expressions, which are more animated than in the previously-discussed video. They included their personal names, emotional and directive phrases, such as, 'Wow!', 'Let's go. Follow me!' (video transcription, 19 September 2018) to invite their audiences to join them in their digital tour of their city. Comparing the screen shots of the two videos in Table 4.1, students' images were more centralized on the screen in this video, with more highlights on people than places. Although this video was cut into less than one minute, it reflects that the *youth* designed this digital story, orchestrating their interests and knowledge about the place where they live, their preference of what to say and show, their creative ways of editing the video, and their personal information and emotions, through which they show authorship and ownership of the video representation. Because of the absence of the adults – the school administrator and the teacher facilitator – youth were able to take more responsibility in their digital storytelling, but also have more power and voice on a range of transmodal design decisions in out-of-school spaces.

However, given the challenge of taking the youth as a group outside of school for project activities, only two of the students were involved in this video, leading to less participation and collaboration. This was confirmed by one of the teacher facilitators:

> It becomes more troublesome to organize so many students to be involved in out-of-school activities, which lead to more serious concern of student safety issues, particularly in our city, a tourism city with so many people during the weekend. It was hard to have other teachers to help because it is out-of-school time and no one can be responsible for any risks of accident as an organization teacher. To be honest, this is also my personal concern. On the other hand, asking the parents to take their own child is unrealistic, either, because parents have their own thing and they can't gather all students, either. However, if we ask students to do the project individually, it might not meet the project goal to facilitate group cooperation. Our school has repeatedly stressed to us not to take students out in group. Students' safety is the most important concern. The regulations of the Board of Education also don't allow this without application in advance, and the application process is very complicated but it is thoughtful for students' safety. (p.c., Teacher Facilitator #1, 9 June 2017)

Revisiting Adult Roles: From a Directive toward a Reflective Stance

Through analyzing the two videos as they were mediated by different spaces, with consideration of the hierarchical flows of power from the administration to the staff to the students, we find that youth in this Chinese site had less power to become creative performers and producers when conducting the project activities in school under adult intervention, and more when performing outside of a formal school space. The in-school video was mainly directed by the school administrators for propagandizing the school, while the out-of-school video, on the other hand, drew on youth's funds of knowledge and interests as they exercised more independence and responsibilities in decision-making. Therefore, the social role of the youth participants shifted from that of 'follower' toward that of 'director', co-constructed by all of the social, political and cultural factors we have discussed thus far. In both videos, similar modalities, or transmodal assemblages (e.g. image, speech, subtitles, screen transitions, body gestures, facial expression, sounds), were used for the digital representations. However, they reflected different social effects considering the stories behind the stories, and different learning potentials.

Despite the primary design and goal of the project being to empower youth to become collaborative decision-makers, we found when situating the transmodal digital storytelling process in this specific site that youth had limited opportunities to control the design processes. For example, the decision as to whether video could be captured in or outside of school was made by adults. On the other hand, without adult participation, the collaboration goal became challenging to achieve. Considering these challenges, what kinds of adult support should be provided in such a project to support, rather than constrain, youth learning and production? How did the adult participants perceive their roles over time? When asked what kinds of support their school administrators had provided to them to conduct the GSB project, both teacher facilitators expressed their appreciation of the administrator's presence in some of the group meetings and her advice on project activities. One of them stated:

> When we had time conflicts with class time, our principal helped us to coordinate with other teachers and told us to well accomplish the project tasks. The principal often came to our project activities, for example, when we were watching some videos. After watching the first video, she noticed the image quality was not very satisfied, so she suggested us to improve the image quality. She also suggested us to videotape more about the school. Because of the principal's suggestion of the image quality, I was the one who held the camera for videotaping. (Interview, Teacher Facilitator #1, 18 September 2019)

The quote above mirrored the teacher facilitator's perception of the administrator's role as a supporter who was willing to help them negotiate with other teachers to do the project during school time. It also reflected the hidden power relations between the teacher and the administrator. However, although the educational system, hierarchical structure and power relations (as shown in this specific local site) mediated these project processes and products, the project also opened up spaces for critical reflection that could potentially lead to educational change. For example, when we asked the administrator to discuss her understanding of her role in the project, she said:

> Sometimes when I spoke too much, it might affect the project. Now I just listen and summarize, not too much, some of my opinions. Though I think I want to help, but sometimes they might think that I as the principal want them to do what I think. (Interview, Administrator, 18 September 2019)

The administrator's statement shows her awareness of the potential power relations that might affect how the teacher facilitator conducted the project with the children and how the project took place in the local site with her supervision. It was interesting to us that the teacher facilitator also reflected on her roles in a similar way:

> I wanted to have them to do things by themselves, but they didn't know most of the words. Therefore, I had to write for them for more than sixty percent of the scripts. I wanted to let them do, but I couldn't maybe because I had a high standard. ... Later I wondered if my understanding about this project was inaccurate. Maybe because my standard was too high. (Interview, Teacher Facilitator #1, 18 September 2019)

The reflective statements above show the adult participants' ongoing, dynamic understanding of their social roles in working with youth participants. Both the administrator and the teacher facilitator seemed to be aware of the potential power relations between themselves and the youth participants. However, due to the traditional Chinese ways of schooling with specific standards designed by adults, it was challenging for them to find the balance point between providing 'not too much' and 'not too little' guidance in the project. As the administrator herself realized, too much administrative involvement might have challenged the student-centered philosophy of the project. On the other hand, when asked how she worked in the project, the administrator claimed:

> In this project, we mainly respect students' decision on the themes they wanted to video record. Sometimes students' ideas and thoughts can surprise us because we teachers might have never thought about it. The teacher facilitator later told me that the project methods inspired her to ask students' opinion when designing her teaching. For example, our students wanted to video their rope jumping activity. At an earlier time, we had the School Culture video to highlight our culture and featured activity for students abroad. Therefore, we, from teacher's perspective, thought rope jumping might be too common to video. However, from students' perspective, it was special and important because it is part of their daily life, so later we let students make it for their interests. Students gained happiness from the project, which urges us to rethink our education. We should start from students' life and maximize students' interests and value. (Interview, Administrator, 18 September 2019)

The administrator's statement above manifests her honest reflection on how they negotiated the teacher's perspective and student interests across the time axis. During personal communication with her and the teacher facilitator, we were frequently asked if they were conducting the project in a 'correct way'. As researchers, we were challenged to rethink what we mean by student-centered methods in a 'right' or 'wrong way', considering the complicated contexts in which the project takes place across global places and spaces, people, societies and cultures. It seems to us that there was a blurred and potentially hierarchical construction of the youth-centered methods as the Chinese adults were negotiating their roles in a project brought from a Western university, as the statement by the administrator suggests: 'When our teachers are communicating with the university professors, particularly the professors from abroad, they felt unconfident, and I would encourage them and support them' (Interview, Administrator, 18 September 2019).

The statement of the administrator above leads us to reflect on issues of a 'correct' way for engagement in the project, as offered by the Western professor who designed the project, or even by the researchers of this paper. Here, again, we see how place, and domestic/abroad and elementary school/university divided and reshaped the adults' perception of themselves and others, which in turn affected their collaboration with the youth. Through situating the transmodal engagement in the domain of place, we argue that understandings of social (inter)action – for example, adults' intervention and student-centered methods – cannot be considered as a fixed or one-size-fits-all concept, because we all live in different places, which are infused with different understandings and perspectives.

Particularly, in considering the two authors of this paper, one is trained as a researcher in a US research university and one in a Chinese institution. Our perspectives and understandings on the extent to which the students were centralized, and on the extent to which intervention constrained learning in the project, have also been constructed in different ways. Therefore, in this study, we are not making judgements. Instead, we hope to illustrate that we should be very cautious in positioning any one construct over another, for example, a Western concept over the Chinese setting, or a researcher perspective over that of participants. It is our intent to showcase the complexities embedded in transmodal global storytelling processes and their situated nature.

We question: If we situate adults' roles in each site of the project across the multiple diverse cultures and societies in which sites exist, where is the line between support, intervention, and constraints? Particularly in the Chinese site, given the high level of responsibility inherent in organizing students to make videos outside of school, how can the adults achieve the goal of taking students outside of the school, which they clearly considered as positive for students, but without having to bear the risks to students' safety? How can they let students digitally represent their community life if they are unable to take students outside of the school? How can students work collaboratively to represent their lives and communities if they are not allowed to be taken by the teacher as a group outside of school for GSB activities? These dilemmas are worth future empirical study across sites, conducted with researchers' eyes critically on national educational policies, particularly those that impact youth's participation in out-of-school programs.

Conclusion

Through analyzing and comparing the two videos that were taken in different spaces and settings in one GSB site, we have discussed how place and space reshaped youth's transmodal global storytelling process with adult involvement. There were also other school-based videos from the Chinese site, for example, *Daily School Life*, that showed a high level of student engagement and interaction, and was based on children's interests. In choosing the *School Culture* video, we did not intend to conclude that all school-based videos produced by the Chinese site were controlled by the school administrators, with limited student agency. Instead, we selected this video to demonstrate the potential, not absolute, power relations that might disrupt child-centered learning and digital participation in out-of-school projects. While this video doesn't represent all of the videos produced by the Chinese students within the space of school, it shows us potential disruption from the hierarchical relations between adults and youth and provides an analytical lens.

We found that simply analyzing the online video production was inadequate for us to gain in-depth understandings of youth's digitally-mediated transnational digital storytelling processes, until we zoomed in to analyze the stories behind the stories through a critical lens of place and space. We recognize that one limitation of this study is that we were unable to conduct interviews with the project youth to gain their perspectives, because most of the youth participants involved in the videos we analyzed had graduated by the time of our investigation. Although we missed the opportunity to directly talk with them, we were able to learn from our fieldnotes taken during meetings and interactions with them to include their voices in our study.

Last but not least, as we analyzed the adults' interventions in this study, we recognized that under the current educational system and structure, they were struggling to make the same decisions on their students' learning as they do for their own children. The top-down power structure mediated and facilitated their negotiation of how to conduct such an out-of-school project in their school. Therefore, we call on policymakers to make more open and flexible policies for school administrators and teachers, so that they can feel more comfortable engaging with their students outside of school – just as they do for their own children – without fear of being punished by the policies. In that way, we advocate for more transnational transmodal programs to build bridges across nationalities, schools and universities, and for practitioners and researchers to embrace the changing educational landscape in the current global and digital context to explore answers for the universal question: What can education do to prepare students for 21st-century citizenship and social relations so that they can become successful and confident living in this increasingly transmodal transnational age? Meanwhile, in order to prepare future learners for digital and global citizenship, educational policymakers, school administrators and teachers must become digital, global, transmodal, and critical citizens so that they are able to better prepare their learners to 'become producers, not just consumers' (Choi & Yi, 2016: 323) of digital and global knowledge.

Notes

(1) This and all quotes from interviews and personal communication (p.c.) presented in this study were translated verbatim from Mandarin Chinese into English.
(2) WeChat is a popular Chinese multi-purpose app for messaging, audio/video chatting and social media.
(3) City name is avoided purposefully to protect participants' privacy.
(4) This and all quotes from video and online chats are represented verbatim in the text and table. We have not edited the originals.
(5) All names are pseudonyms to protect the privacy of the participants.

References

Appiah, K.A. (2008) Education for global citizenship. *Yearbook of the National Society for the Study of Education* 107 (1), 83–99.
Bezemer, J. and Kress, G.R. (2016) *Multimodality, Learning and Communication: A Social Semiotic Frame.* London: Routledge.
Choi, J. and Yi, Y. (2016) Teachers' integration of multimodality into classroom practices for English language learners. *TESOL Journal* 7 (2), 304–327. doi:10.1002/tesj.204
Flewitt, R. (2011) Bringing ethnography to a multimodal investigation of early literacy in a digital age. *Qualitative Research* 11 (3), 293–310. http://doi.org/10.1177/1468794111399838
Hawkins, M.R. (2014) Ontologies of place, creative meaning making and critical cosmopolitan education. *Curriculum Inquiry* 44 (1), 90–112. https://doi.org/10.1111/curi.12036
Hawkins, M.R. (2018) Transmodalities and transnational encounters: Fostering critical cosmopolitan relations. *Applied Linguistics* 39 (1), 55–77. https://doi.org/10.1093/applin/amx048
Hawkins, M.R. and Mori, J. (2018) Considering 'trans-' perspectives in language theories and practices. *Applied Linguistics* 39 (1), 1–8. https://doi.org/10.1093/applin/amx056
Hull, G.A. and Stornaiuolo, A. (2014) Cosmopolitan literacies, social networks, and 'proper distance': Striving to understand in a global world. *Curriculum Inquiry* 44 (1), 15–44. https://doi.org/10.1111/curi.12035
Hull, G.A., Stornaiuolo, A. and Sahni, U. (2010) Cultural citizenship and cosmopolitan practice: Global youth communicate online. *English Education* 42 (4), 331–367. https://doi.org/10.2307/23018017
Jacobs, G.E. (2012) The proverbial rock and hard place: The realities and risks of teaching in a world of multiliteracies, participatory culture, and mandates. *Journal of Adolescent and Adult Literacy* 56, 98–102. doi:10.1002/JAAL.00109
Jewitt, C. (2008) Multimodality and literacy in school classrooms. *Review of Research in Education* 32, 241–267. https://doi.org/10.3102/0091732X07310586
Lao, K. (2004) Responsibility for injured accidents in primary and secondary schools. *Journal of Beijing Normal University (Social Science Edition)* 2, 13–23.
Lam, W.S.E. and Rosario-Ramos, E. (2009) Multilingual literacies in transnational digitally mediated contexts: An exploratory study of immigrant teens in the United States. *Language and Education* 23 (2), 171–190. https://doi.org/10.1080/09500780802152929
Li, R. and Hawkins, M.R. (2021) Figured worlds in transnational transmodal communications. *TESOL Quarterly* 55 (1), 5–28. DOI:10.1002/tesq.569
Mills, K.A. (2010) 'Filming in progress': New spaces for multimodal designing. *Linguistics and Education* 21 (1), 14–28. https://doi.org/10.1016/j.linged.2009.12.003
Newfield, D. (2014) Transformation, transduction and the transmodal moment. In C. Jewitt (ed.) *The Routledge Handbook of Multimodal Analysis* (pp. 189–204). New York: Routledge.
The People's Republic of China General office of the State Council (2017) Opinions on strengthening construction of students' safety risk prevention and control system. No. 35. http://www.gov.cn/zhengce/content/2017-04/28/content_5189574.htm
Truong-White, H. and McLean, L. (2015) Digital storytelling for transformative global citizenship education. *Canadian Journal of Education/Revue Canadienne De L'éducation* 38 (2), 1–28. doi:10.2307/canajeducrevucan.38.2.11

5 Navigating Transnational Transmodal Terrain: Perspectives from Ugandan Lugbara Youth

Willy Ngaka

> It has become something of a truism that we are functioning in a world fundamentally characterized by objects in motion. The objects include ideas and ideologies, people and goods, images and messages; and technologies and techniques. (Appadurai, 2000, cited in Newfield, 2015: 269)

Introduction

A careful look at the above quotation depicts a scenario in which emerging Information and Communication Technologies (ICTs), networks and globalization have increasingly made it inappropriate to continue relying on monolingualism and monomodality in communication and different terrains of study. This is evident in the current globalized world in which communication practices are now crossing local, national and modal boundaries as a result of advances in technology, which offers the ability to connect and expand into realms of communication formerly considered inconceivable (Hawkins, 2018). This ushers in the need to search for new ways of approaching and negotiating sociocultural norms and differences which allow interactions and learning to be pluralistic, translocal, transnational and transmodal – thereby making it possible to traverse between and among different cultures, perspectives and modes of thinking. This possibly explains why present literacy scholars and educationists are now trying to emphasize the acquisition of 21st-century skills, dubbed the 4Cs – critical thinking and problem-solving; communication; collaboration; and creativity and innovation – necessary for coping with the challenges of globalization, which appears to align well with the idea of critical cosmopolitanism (Hawkins, 2018). Hawkins uses the term critical cosmopolitanism to refer to:

> how all people encounter one another within global flows of mobility, whether the encounter takes place through people who move, or materials and resources, or messages, understanding that the semiotic modes that

mediate encounters – face-to-face or virtual – embody, reflect, and shape meanings derived and constructed. (2018: 66)

This chapter draws on the lived experiences of participants in a project – Global StoryBridges (GSB) – in rural Uganda to analyze how new modalities afforded by digital interactions on an online platform allow these youth in the Global South to negotiate their sense of place (as discussed in Hawkins, 2014) and sociocultural identities while working toward developing critical cosmopolitanism and global citizenship (Birk, 2014; Hawkins, 2018). It begins with a review of conceptual and theoretical perspectives that inform the ideas being presented herein – New Literacy Studies, the New Literacies Studies (multiliteracies), transliteracies, multimodality, transmodalities, and critical cosmopolitanism. Thereafter, I describe the setting of the site that is the focus of this study, and the methodological dimensions that guided the collection and analysis of the data which focused on establishing how the Ugandan youth engaged in and reacted to technologically-mediated engagements with their global peers in the other sites, what particular things they encountered during their interactions and challenges they faced in their transnational and transmodal communications. I then describe a video created by the youth, offer the chat texts that resulted between the sites, and identify key themes resulting from the analysis. Before making concluding remarks, I apply the five complexities associated with transmodalities (as discussed in Hawkins, 2018) to the data and findings, showing their explanatory power for understanding transnational transmodal communications. Hence, the chapter aims to enhance an understanding of the experiences, feelings and learning of youth in the Global South as they negotiate their sense of place and their sociocultural identities through participation in GSB, in the face of the complexities inherent in a rural site where technologically-mediated communications are not the norm.

GSB and Globalization

As detailed in Chapter 1, GSB is an initiative whose main purpose is to connect youth across the globe through digitally-mediated communication. The project, which has several sites across the world, comes at a time when we are now living in an environment that is rapidly globalizing and is characterized by widespread migrations, emergence of new technologies and structural changes in the global economy that put on the global community a demand for unique skill sets and new approaches to learning and communication. As discussed in Burke and Hughes (2018), recent developments have led to many initiatives in classrooms to adapt to the learning potential of new technologies. For example, some schools have now introduced laptops, tablets, iPads, or students' own devices to foster inclusive learning and literacy education. This is important because through a lens of cosmopolitanism, learners across geographies are using technology and different modes of communication that enable them to gain an understanding of what Appiah (2005: 151) calls 'universality plus difference' and to forge relationships that value the ways in which people see one another as one as well as the ways in which they differ (Hawkins, 2018). As Hawkins (2014, 2016) argues, critical cosmopolitanism integrates a focus on creating and sustaining just, equitable, and affirming relations with global as well as local others in global engagements and interactions, through attending to the workings of status, privilege, and power between people and groups of people.

However, it should be noted here that contexts for local, transnational and transmodal engagements vary. For example, the GSB site in northwestern Uganda that is the focus of this chapter is unique in many ways as compared to other sites. It is located in a rural village in northern Uganda, where residents have few economic resources. Schools here have no hydroelectricity and limited access to modern learning technologies like desktop computers, iPads, tablets and laptops. Internet connectivity, too, is erratic and expensive. One main idea behind GSB is that through the power of video, youth in globally diverse sites will be able to explore their worlds through stories, sharing images, information, comments, and questions as they create and negotiate digital texts and technologies in the process of learning English and technology skills. Yet all youth do not have equal access to and experience with digital communications and resources, or even prior communications and interactions with transnational others.

This chapter focuses on communications between youth in the Uganda Rural Literacy and Community Development Association (URLCODA) site – the Ugandan site that is the focus of this chapter – and youth from Spain and Vietnam, elucidating the affordances and challenges as the Ugandan youth navigate their identities, belongings and understandings of selves and others through new forms of communication and engagement. Figure 5.1 below depicts selected GSB student participants from the URLCODA site engaged in their weekly meeting in which they create their own videos, watch and discuss videos posted by global youth from other GSB sites, and agree on questions they need to raise and responses they need to provide to questions asked about their videos by youth from other sites across the globe.

Figure 5.1 clearly demonstrates the engagement of URLCODA youth as they collaboratively engage in transnational communication using multiple modes. Participants in the URLCODA site are working to enhance their language, literacy and technology skills and gain increased awareness and understanding of other people's cultures in different parts of the world. To me, this is in line with Shipka's (2016) idea that learning about and working across different languages, cultural conventions, multiple modes, and digital as well as analog communicative technologies greatly helps to highlight processes of meaning-making, engaging, remixing and transforming – which in turn provides enriched points of entry for experiencing and appreciating dynamic, distributed, translingual, multimodal

Figure 5.1 URLCODA youth working on their videos

and embedded communicative practices. In the section that follows, I provide an overview of the different theoretical perspectives that can enhance an understanding of the complexities in translocal, transnational and transmodal communication settings.

Overview of Theoretical Orientations

In the current globalizing world, characterized by the emergence of new and diverse ICT tools and the resulting structural changes in the global economy requiring new skill sets, people are being forced to seek non-traditional ways and multimodal approaches to learn and communicate across borders. As Hawkins (2018) suggests, the 'trans- turn' in language (and literacy) studies is in part a response to new and rapidly changing contexts of mobility, and new global configurations of people, resources, and communications. Hence, this chapter draws on a number of slightly different but seemingly related theoretical approaches and perspectives to better understand the complexities involved in transnational and transmodal communication settings, namely: (i) New Literacy Studies (Gee, 2015; Heath, 1983; Scollon & Scollon, 1981; Street, 1984), (ii) the New Literacies Studies (Multiliteracies) (Alvermann *et al.*, 1999; Gee, 2004, 2013; Knobel & Lankshear, 2007; The New London Group, 1996), (iii) transliteracies (Stornaiuolo *et al.*, 2017), (iv) multimodality (Hawkins, 2018; Jewitt, 2013, 2017; Jewitt & Kress, 2003; Kress, 2000, 2010; Murray,

2013; Van Leeuwen, 2015); and (v) transmodalities and critical cosmopolitanism (Hawkins, 2018).

The New Literacy Studies (NLS), the New Literacies Studies (Multiliteracies) and Transliteracies

The New Literacy Studies

The New Literacy Studies (NLS) is commonly associated with Scollon and Scollon (1981), Heath (1983) and Street (1984), whose works from the outset blended the study of culture, discourse, language, literacy, and often history and politics. The NLS opposes the then traditional psychological approach to literacy, which views literacy as a 'mental' or 'cognitive' phenomenon and defines literacy in terms of mental states and mental processing. In this case, reading and writing are treated as things people do inside their heads. Unlike the traditional psychological approach, the NLS argues that literacy is something people do in the world and in society, not just inside their heads, and should be studied as such. According to its proponents, literacy is primarily a sociocultural phenomenon, rather than a mental phenomenon. It is a social and cultural achievement centered in social and cultural practices. It is about distinctive ways of participating in social and cultural groups. The NLS further argues that written language is a technology for giving and getting meaning. In turn, what written language means is a matter determined by the social, cultural, historical, and institutional practices of different groups of people. Thus, literacy should be studied in an integrated way in its full range of contexts and practices, not just cognitive, but social, cultural, historical, and institutional, as well. Unlike psychology, which saw readers and writers as primarily engaged in mental processes like decoding, retrieving information, comprehension, inferencing, and so forth, the NLS sees readers and writers as primarily engaged in social or cultural practices. Written language, according to NLS, is used differently in different practices and used in different ways by different social and cultural groups. In these practices, written language never sits all by itself and it is rarely if ever fully cut off from oral language and action. Rather, within different practices, it is integrated with different ways of (1) using oral language; (2) acting and interacting; (3) knowing, valuing, and believing; and often (4) using various sorts of tools and technologies (Gee, 2015).

The New Literacies Studies

In a related development, a similar but slightly different school of thought, the New Literacies Studies emerged from and carries over the NLS argument about written language, shifting it to new digital technologies. It is construed grammatically differently than the NLS in that, whereas the NLS is about studying literacy in a new way, the New Literacies Studies is about studying new types of literacy beyond print literacy, especially 'digital literacies' and literacy practices embedded in popular culture. As seen in Alvermann *et al.* (1999), Gee (2004, 2013), Knobel and Lankshear (2007) and the New London Group (1996), the New Literacies Studies view different digital tools as technologies for giving and getting meaning, just like (and in tandem with) language. Like the NLS, the New Literacies Studies further argue that the meanings to which these technologies give rise are determined by the social, cultural, historical, and institutional practices of different groups of people and that these practices almost always involve more than just using a digital tool. In fact, they involve ways of acting, interacting, valuing, believing, and knowing, as well as often using other sorts of tools and technologies, including very often oral and written language (Gee, 2015). Like NLS, the New Literacies Studies talk about different literacies in plural but extend this to take up discussion of different 'digital literacies' – that is, different ways of using digital tools within different sorts of sociocultural practices. In this sense, the New Literacies Studies is a natural offshoot of the NLS (with some overlapping scholars). The emphasis the two approaches put on multiplicity is in line with what Hawkins (2018) refers to as the 'trans'-turn, which makes them appealing in trying to understand the issues discussed in this chapter and then takes us to the notion of transliteracy, as in Sukovic (2016), discussed below.

Transliteracies

The term transliteracy, according to Sukovic (2016), refers to an ability to use diverse analogue and digital technologies, techniques, modes and protocols to: (a) search for and work with a variety of resources, (b) collaborate and participate in social networks and (c) communicate meanings and new knowledge by using different tones, genres, modalities and media. This means transliteracy consists of skills, knowledge, thinking and acting, which enable a fluid 'movement across' in a way that is defined by situational, social, cultural and technological contexts. This is possibly why some scholars interested in a transliteracies framework talk of literacies on the move. The term transliteracy comes to the fore in information and technology rich environments, so it is based on information and ICT capabilities which encompass 21st-century skills, namely, 'critical thinking and problem-solving, communication, collaboration; and creativity and innovation' (Levin-Goldberg, 2012: 59). A transliteracies framework, as discussed in Stornaiuolo *et al.* (2017), functions as a flexible heuristic for attending to how meaning-making and power are intertwined in and distributed across social and material relationships. It not only builds on and extends the work of scholars in the New Literacy Studies and multiliteracies scholars that examine the situated, contingent, and ideologically-rooted nature of meaning-making across modes, but it also deliberately attends to how meanings are made across interactions among people, things, texts, contexts, modes, and media and possibly across borders. A transliteracies framework also foregrounds how people and things are mobilized and paralyzed, facilitated and restricted, in different measure and in relation to institutions and systems with long histories. The notion of transliteracies is relevant in discussing the experiences of GSB participants because its tools, as stated in Stornaiuolo *et al.* (2017: 68):

> facilitate an inquiry stance that positions researchers to attend to people's emic meaning-making processes, work to balance multiple perspectives, account for privilege and position, question normative assumptions and beliefs, and engage in and value multiple ways of knowing.

Hence, the importance of a transliteracies framework in what Appadurai (2000, in Newfield, 2015: 269) describes as a 'world fundamentally characterized by objects in motion' is that it encompasses two primary dimensions of mobile literacy practices, which according to Stornaiuolo *et al.* (2017: 68), are: '(a) the everyday activity of creating, maintaining, and disassembling associations across movements of people and things (indicated by the prefix trans) and (b) the dynamic and material nature of meaning-making in activity (indicated by the plural root word literacies)'. The framework is therefore relevant in understanding the context of youth participants in GSB engaged in transnational and transmodal communications.

Multimodality, Transmodalities and Critical Cosmopolitanism

Multimodality

Multimodality is a theory that looks at how people communicate and interact with each other, not just through writing (which is one mode) but also through many different modes such as speaking, gesture, gaze, and visual forms. It considers the many different modes that people use to communicate with each other and to express themselves (Kress, 2010). The relevance of the theory is related to the increase in technological tools and associated access to multimedia composing software, which has led to people being able to easily use many modes in art, writing, music, and dance in everyday interactions with each other. A mode is generally defined as a communication channel that a culture recognizes such as writing, gesture, posture, gaze, font choice and color, images, video, and even the interactions between them (Anstey & Bull, 2010). Kress (2000) and Jewitt and Kress (2003) maintain that whereas many such modes have always existed, they have not always been recognized as a legitimate or culturally accepted form of communication or expression. Advocates of multimodality emphasize that people communicate in a variety of ways and that in order to completely understand someone the many modes they use to communicate must be observed and recognized. It is also important to note that whereas much of the existing work considers modes as 'co-present' and 'co-dependent' (as in Murphy, 2012, cited in Hawkins, 2018), communication in the 21st century is often digitally or electronically mediated and may be across distances and asynchronous (Hawkins, 2018).

Hence, in its most basic sense, multimodality is a theory of communication and social semiotics. It describes communication practices in terms of the various semiotic systems, namely: textual, aural, linguistic, spatial, and visual resources – or modes – used to compose messages (Murray, 2013). According to Murray, where media are concerned, multimodality is the use of several modes (media) to create a single artifact. The collection of these modes, or elements, contributes to how multimodality affects different rhetorical situations, or opportunities for increasing an audience's reception of an idea or concept. This includes everything from the placement of images to the organization of the content that creates meaning.

Kress (2010) observes that discussions about multimodality involve medium and mode, which are not synonymous. To him multimodality is canonical in writing studies, and he defines mode in two ways, the first being that a mode 'is a socially and culturally shaped resource for making meaning where image, writing, layout, speech, moving images are examples of different modes', and the second being 'semiotic modes, [which] … are shaped by both the intrinsic characteristics and potentialities of the medium and by the requirements, histories and values of societies and their cultures' (2010: 79). Accordingly, every mode has a different modal resource, which is historically and culturally situated and which breaks it down into its parts, because 'each has distinct potentials [and limitations] for meaning' (2010: 1). We can therefore say that in Kress's theory, 'mode is meaningful: it is shaped by and carries the "deep" ontological and historical/social orientations of a society and its cultures with it into every sign. Mode names the material resources shaped in often long histories of social endeavor' (2010: 1).

Transmodalities

As indicated in my introduction to this chapter, we are now experiencing a trans- turn in communication practices, as evidenced by the emergence of certain terms such as translingualism, transnationalism, transliteracies and transmodalities. For example, Stornaiuolo *et al.* (2016) talk about a transliteracies framework to conceptually account for the contingency and instability of literacy practices on the move and to offer a set of methodological tools for investigating these mobilities. According to them, phenomena not only move and intersect as separate entities, but also intermingle, interpenetrate and assemble in emergent configurations. In her article 'Traveling Literacies: Multilingual Writing on the Move', Leonard (2013) explores the lived literacy experiences of four multilingual immigrant writers in the USA, showing, first, how they have moved their literacy practices among multiple languages and locations in the world, and, second, how these practices have been destabilized and redefined by the social contexts they have met along the way. The importance of the trans- turn in communication practices is seen in Hawkins (2018: 64), in which she says:

> What 'trans-' offers to conceptualizations of modalities is comparable to affordances it offers to applied linguistics. [...] Transmodalities index the simultaneous co-presence and co-reliance of language and other semiotic resources in meaning-making, affording each equal weight. It highlights the complexity of modes and the entanglements and relationships between them that shape meaning in multimodal artifacts and communications.

To Hawkins, transmodalities 'highlights the need to destabilize and move beyond named categories of "modes", to a view of semiotic resources as embedded and given meaning within the specific assemblage, and within trajectories of time and space, continuously shifting and re-shaping in their contexts and mobility' (2018: 64). Murphy (2012) adds that from a transmodal point of view, modes such as speech, drawing and gestures not only supplement each other in relationships of mutual support, but also sequentially perforate and interpenetrate each other. Although these standpoints offer a more complex view of semiotic resources in action, we also know very well that transmodalities are more than just localized multimodal interactions (Hawkins, 2018). In fact, Brandt and Clinton (2002) and Hawkins (2014) also point to the movements and trajectories of flows of semiosis across local, translocal, and transnational borders as well as across diverse contexts and communities. They maintain that the movements of semiotic resources and artifacts across time and space, and across and among different groups of people, are an integral aspect of the meaning-making they afford. Hawkins (2018: 65) stresses the point that:

> transmodalities attends to meaning-making across the arc of transmodal communications, such that, while production and assemblage may be the starting point, the spaces and timescales traversed, as well as the contexts and processes of reception and negotiation, are given equal weight.

From the above we can clearly see that modes shape and are shaped by the systems and cultures in which they are located. Hence, 'transmodalities references transcendence and transgression, where inequitable relations of power can be dismantled and reconfigured, affording equal access, value, and representation to all participants in transmodal interactions' (Hawkins, 2018: 65). It can be said here that just as is the case with the notion of transliteracies (Stornaiuolo et al., 2017; Sukovic, 2016), Hawkins' concept of transmodalities 'has much to contribute to language and literacy studies, and to understandings of semiotic resources in meaning making' (2018: 65) in translocal and transnational engagements and interactions.

Critical cosmopolitanism

Drawing from ideas of Appiah (2005, 1996) and Kleingeld and Brown (2019), one can conceptualize the term cosmopolitanism to refer to the idea that all human beings are or could or should be members of a single community – which may be small relatively personal ties or large group affiliations such as national, international or virtual communities – meaning that anyone who adheres to the idea of cosmopolitanism in any of its forms is a cosmopolitan or cosmopolite. Hawkins (2018) uses cosmopolitanism to reference how all people encounter one another within global flows of mobility, whether the encounter takes place through people who move, or materials and resources, or messages, understanding that the semiotic modes that mediate encounters – face-to-face or virtual – embody, reflect, and shape meanings they make. In this case is it possible to talk of a cosmopolitan community, which, according to Appiah (1996), may be a community in which individuals from varying locations (physical, economic, etc.) enter relationships of mutual respect regardless of their differing beliefs. Kleingeld and Brown (2019) take this a step further and note that different views of what constitutes a community may include a focus on moral standards, economic practices, political structures, and/or cultural forms. These differing opinions indicate there are complexities in communication processes due to the multiple beliefs and allegiances people have, and the multiple modes people use in transnational and multi/transcultural settings. This has led Hawkins (2018: 65) to offer critical cosmopolitanism, which addresses communication across differences, and to raise an important question:

> If modes are defined as shaped by and recognizable to members of a culture or community, how can we think about global communications between members of different cultures and communities, who may not share common understandings of codes or modes or messages?

She then argues that: 'understandings constructed through transnational engagements matter – they shape how we view others in the world, the relationships we forge with them, and how we understand ourselves in relation to these others' (2018: 65). To her in the current geopolitical climate, forging relations of goodwill, responsiveness, and caring seems an important goal, and she suggests that achieving this requires deep understandings of transmodalities – of 'semiosis across time and space' – such that we can account for and attend to how representations carry meaning across diversity, but also conceptualizations attending to the relational dimension of such communication. She uses the lens of critical cosmopolitanism for ethical consideration of dispositions, understandings, and interactions in situated human encounters and engagements, following Appiah (2005) in stressing the importance of developing dispositions of openness, inquiry, and care to cater for ethical considerations in encounters with global others, and to the outcomes of such engagements, as is the case with GSB youth participants discussed in this book. To this effect, Canagarajah (2013) emphasizes the idea that we must seriously pay attention to the ways in which meanings are negotiated and constructed with (global) others so as to re-organize, re-source, and re-distribute knowledge, privilege, and resources, which will in turn lead to critical personal and societal transformations and the cultivation of open and equitable relationships. It is on this basis that that I consider transmodalities and critical cosmopolitanism very important in discussions about how youth in a rural Uganda GSB site negotiate their places and identities in the rapidly globalizing world in which communication involves engagement with multiple modes.

Methods and Setting

Setting

The GSB site in northwestern Uganda was established in 2016. Its first group of youth participants started interacting with their global peers in early 2017. Hosted by an indigenous nongovernmental organization – URLCODA – the site has to date attracted a total of 36 students of lower secondary classes, with approximately 12 in the group in any given term (with ages ranging from 14 to 16). All attend a rural secondary school that has no hydroelectricity and limited access to the internet and modern teaching and learning technologies such as laptops, desktop computers, iPads and tablets. This means the participants live in communities of poverty and are all English learners (as schooling in Uganda is in English after Primary Three, and they speak the local vernacular at home and in their communities). All the participants are products of Uganda's Universal Primary Education (UPE) programme which emphasizes the use of pupils' mother tongue in their initial years of schooling. Generally, the local community detests the UPE programme because they consider English as a language of power that will enable their children in future to get good jobs, and therefore want English instruction to start in pre-school. This is attributed to the fact that UPE graduates come out with low literacy abilities, academic achievement and English language proficiency. It was on this basis that GSB was established in the area to help the youth learn about others' cultures and become global citizens, increase their English language and literacy skills, and develop their technology skills. In the project, the youth utilize a full range of modes to represent their unique culture through creating video stories in a transnational and transmodal communication setting, which they post to the project website for global peers to see and comment on. They work together to decide what to represent and how to tell their stories. They also watch and discuss videos from other sites and decide together what questions and comments to pose and how to respond to questions and comments they receive from others.

Methods

This section describes the approach, methods and tools that were used to collect data for writing this chapter. Since GSB is underpinned by a theoretical framework that is multimodal, transnational, and transmodal not familiar to the Ugandan youth, there was a need to adopt a multi-method research approach and an interpretivist paradigm to enhance an understanding of the initial reactions of the Ugandan youth in their transnational and transmodal encounters with their global peers; some particular issues they might have experienced while engaging with their global peers in other sites; and challenges they encountered in the course of their digitally-mediated cross-border interactions. Online data from global sites, including videos and chat texts, were drawn from the GSB website (www.globalstorybridges.com). Observation, especially participant observation, was used to collect data from 36 GSB youth (both previous and current) in the URLCODA site in the period 2017–19. Dewalt and Dewalt (1998) describe participant observation as a process that enables researchers to learn about the activities of the people under study in a natural setting through observing and participating in their activities. Erlandson *et al.* (1993) also add that using observation methods in qualitative studies enables the researcher to describe existing situations using the five senses, thereby providing a written photograph of the situation under study. Ethnographic and ethno-methodological lenses, video reflexivity, video content analysis (described in Collins & Makowsky, 1978; Collier & Wyer, 2016) and focus group discussions were used to complement participant observations. Morgan (1996) describes focus group discussions or interviews as a data collection method that consists of interviews in which groups of people are asked about their perceptions, opinions, beliefs, and attitudes towards a particular issue or phenomenon. In this case the GSB participants' opinions and views were sought about the project. Whiting *et al.* (2016) describe video content analysis as the analysis of all video materials not recorded by the researcher. Collier and Wyer (2016: 981) define video reflexivity as 'a process that involves the reviewing of video footage with participants to make sense of visual data that they have gathered or feature in themselves'. Thus I analyzed both the video made by the youth and posted on the website, and videos taken to record site meetings of the group. There were also monthly debriefs with the participants to solicit their reflections on their experience. This was followed by three focus group discussions conducted with participants to discuss their feelings, emerging issues and themes, and challenges faced in the course of their multimodal, transnational and transmodal engagements. Salmons (2017) maintains that mixing modes of data [and methods] provides an opportunity to understand the participants' lived experiences from multiple perspectives as well as the culture and environment of a community, group or organization.

Researcher Positionality

Throughout the observations of the interactions between the URLCODA youth and their peers in various global locales, I, as the researcher, was aware of my insider position in the community and hence chose to adopt a participant-as-observer stance in the course of the study. According to Gold (1958) and Kawulich (2005), in a participant observer stance, the researcher is closely associated with the group being studied, and the group is aware of his activities. I am from this same community where the site is located, and I brought the project to the community. Further, I work with the site facilitators to hone their facilitation skills and visit regularly. Being aware of this helps the researcher – me – to constantly address my personal biases so that they are accounted for in the final outcome of the study. It should be noted that data gathered with the aid of ethnographic methods and lenses, such as the participant observation and interviews here and their interpretation, are never neutral because of subjectivity involved in the process. As part of the global team of researchers involved in the ongoing research on GSB, I always seek to ensure that ethical principles are strictly adhered to while interacting with the youth. The participants were well informed about the purpose for being part of the research and the benefits of taking part in the study.

Data and Findings

This section presents the key findings from participant observations of the processes the Ugandan youth are involved in while making a video of their way of life on the one hand, and the examination of their back-and-forth communications with their global peers after sharing the videos, on the other. The findings from the digitally-mediated interactions between the youth in different sites were complemented by findings generated via focus group discussions which sought to establish the reactions of the Ugandan youth after interacting with their global peers, issues they found noteworthy while engaging with youth in other sites across the world, and some of the challenges they faced during their digitally-mediated cross-border interactions. A brief description of the first video the Ugandan youth shared with their global peers is given and the questions, responses and clarifications it generated are highlighted to depict some of the emerging issues in the course of their communications. The emerging issues and themes are analyzed using the complexities that characterize transglobal and transmodal communications.

The Video Posted by the Ugandan Youth and Subsequent Chat Text

The video entitled *How We Spend Our Holidays* is 4 minutes and 52 seconds long. In its first few seconds, a map of the world showing the different continents pops up on the screen. Then, the title of the video emerges from below the screen and flies away. After that, six youth who were reading different books of their choice in their community library began to introduce themselves one by one in English, each stating what they like to read. Inside the community library, one could see a bookshelf, sculptures of a man and some animals placed on the bookshelf, tables and plastic chairs. The majority of the youth wore T-shirts with different logos/badges inscribed on them. After introducing themselves, they went out to harvest sweet potatoes from a garden near the community library. They dug the potato mounds so as to get out the tubers. While the boys were digging the potato mounds, one could see isolated grass thatched houses behind them. The youth divided the work among themselves – with girls assigned the responsibility of collecting firewood and the boys creatively building a local oven out of blocks of solid soil to roast the potatoes.

When the boys were done building the oven, some of them started setting fire to heat the oven that would be used to roast the potatoes. As the fire continued to heat the oven, it began to turn red-hot, indicating that it had reached the expected maximum temperature required to roast the potatoes in the shortest possible time. As the other youth were waiting for the roasting to begin, two girls and one boy started playing a traditional game, which is locally known as *eli*. They kept laughing as they played. One of the youth playing the game invited some peers to join them (in English). After the oven became red-hot, the boys inserted all of the potatoes into it and dismantled it to ensure that the blocks of soil were broken into pieces to completely cover the potatoes in order to roast them. While doing this, some of the boys could be heard making jokes in Lugbarati, their home language. Ten minutes after the potatoes were buried under the hot broken soil, they became ready for consumption. The boys removed them from the hot soil and kept them in a yellow and blue basket made of plastic material, ready for eating. The youth, who were all actively involved in the preparation of their meal, gathered and sat around the basket to partake of the roasted potatoes. Some were seen sipping water from a blue plastic cup while others raised their thumbs up (as a gesture) to suggest that the roasted potatoes were really tasty. Although some were saying certain things in local vernacular, most of their communication was in English. The youth all looked happy and most of them were seen laughing while eating the potatoes. After eating, they posed together – holding each other in a sign of solidarity to verbally say good-bye. What they said while happily smiling and waving their hands was: 'Dear our friends, we are students from St. Andrew's Secondary School,[1] thanks for watching our movie. We look forward to seeing your questions, bye bye!' After this, the names of the students who made the video were printed in carefully chosen font type and size, and colour started flying from the bottom of the screen, vanishing upwards.

After the youth in different global locales watched the above video, they discussed it and generated questions, which were posted in the chat space below the video on the website. All chat data will be reported verbatim, remembering that all project participants are English learners. The questions below were compiled and sent by the youth from Barcelona, Spain. The Spanish youth said: 'Hello students from Uganda! We have seen your video and it was quite shocking for us, your lifestyle is very different to ours. Here we send you our question.' The questions and the responses that followed are shown in Table 5.1.

The Spanish youth ended their communication to the Ugandan youth with the words: 'We are waiting for your responds!' After receiving responses from the Ugandan youth, the Spanish youth gathered more questions and sent them back. The questions and responses that followed are shown in Table 5.2.

The youth from Spain ended their communication to their peers in Uganda with the statement: 'Lots of kisses, thanks, regards to all'. After receiving and internalizing the second round of questions from the Spanish youth, the Ugandan youth prepared and sent their responses and some questions of their own to the Spanish youth. They wrote: 'Hello our friends from Spain, we have got some more questions for you, here they are'. Questions from Ugandan youth and responses to them are shown in Table 5.3.

In the course of discussing the responses the Ugandan youth received from their peers in Spain, they identified some issues that needed to be clarified and decided to clarify them. They said to their friends in Spain:

> Hello friends, well be back from the Easter break, any way do you people also celebrate Easter? We hereby make some clarification on some of your concerns: (i) CRE – stands for Christian Religious Education, (ii) IRE – stands for Islamic Religious Education; (iii) Kiswahili is just a language like Catalan; and (iv) for the picture of our town you asked for, instead we took a video of the major parts of the town and busy areas of trading and we are looking forward to how we can upload it for you people.

Table 5.1 First round of questions from Spanish youth and the responses from Uganda

Questions from the Spanish youth	Responses from the Ugandan youth
1) What is your first language?	1) Our first language is Lugbarati
2) Why do you shave off your hair?	2) We consider it to be hygienic
3) Do you have lighters?	3) Yes we do.
4) Can the girls use pants?	4) Yes they do
5) Are there lions?	5) Many of them
6) Do you have phones?	6) We don't have
7) Are you in holidays?	7) Currently we are at school
8) Do you have big cities?	8) We don't have big cities
9) Do you have only one class?	9) We have several classes
10) What are you planning on doing your next video about?	10) How we help our parents in doing domestic work

Table 5.2 Second round of questions from Spanish youth and the responses from Uganda

Questions from the Spanish youth	Responses from the Ugandan youth
1) How many people talk your language? WHAT IS THE LONGEST WORD IN YOUR LANGUAGE?	1) There are quite many long words in Lugbarati but here is a sample 'onduparaka'
2) That is very interesting because here nobody shaves their hair because of hygiene, only for 'own choice' because for some people it looks good. What happens if somebody doesn't want to shave her/his hair?	2) You may be punished or they send you home to and save.
3) How do you control them [lions] from attacking you? Have you ever witnessed a lion attack?	3) Yes, they normally in the game parks and zoo.
4) Adults don't have phones neither? How do you keep in touch with others?	4) In case of any issue we communicate a week before.
5) We are doing little sketches with different dialogues and later we will put them together so you can see them	5) That's great and we love it.
6) When was your town created? Do you have a city hall? We would like to receive a picture of your town if possible	6) That will require research but very soon you will receive the pic of our great town. Arua.
7) Which currency do you use? we use the Europe and we have the same currency in most of the countries of Europe.	7) We use Ugandan shillings (UGX).
8) We are willing to seeing your videos	8) Soon we shall upload our next video because we have it already, the only problem is that the file is big it can't be uploaded

Table 5.3 Questions from the Ugandan youth to Spanish youth and their responses

Questions from the Ugandan youth	Responses from the Spanish youth
1) When do you people normally get your holidays?	1) We have holidays at Summer time, Christmas (winter) time and Easter week
2) Which co-curriculum activities do you people have at your school?	2) In our school we have Dance, Theater, Mountain
3) Do the teachers confiscate your phones in case you go with them to school?	3) Sometimes, depending on the teacher and the situation
4) Do students have their own PCs and laptops or you people use computer lab?	4) Yes, every student have their own laptop, we buy them by our own
5) Are you people examined by a national board or not?	5) Yes, the whole country have more or less the same education
6) Is your academic year also divided into three terms?	6) Year, is divided in 3 terms
7) Are you people also taught subjects like CRE, KISWAHILI and IRE?	7) What is CRE, KISWAHILI and IRE?
8) Your promotion to next, … is it termly or annually?	8) Every year
9) Do you have PTA meetings at school?	9) Yes

Interestingly, the Ugandan youth this time round switched languages and ended by mixing English and Kiswahili simultaneously. They said: 'Asante sana' (thanks a lot). As the discussions progressed, the Uganda youth started demonstrating interest in the way of life of their peers in Spain and sent them another set of questions. The questions sent and the responses received from the Spanish youth are depicted in Table 5.4.

After some time, youth from Vietnam watched the video posted by URLCODA and also raised some questions. They started their communication with the statement:

> Hi guys, we think it's a great video and there are some questions from Vietnam: (i) Do you yourselves grow sweet potatoes? (ii) What activities do you usually do on holiday beside those? (iii) What types of books did you read? (iv) How often do you grill the sweet potatoes? (v) What is the name of the game you were playing while your friends were setting up a fire? (vi) Where were you at the beginning of the video? (vii) Do you usually do these activities? (viii) Where do you usually read books?

They end their communication to the Ugandan youth with the statement: 'we are looking forward to hearing from you soon'. Unfortunately, for the Ugandan youth, the third term had come to an end, and since they were away for Christmas break, they could not respond to the queries posted by the Vietnamese youth, which came late. Although the questions from Vietnam were not very different from those from Spanish youth, it is possible that if the Ugandan youth provided responses, the Vietnamese youth could have raised more follow-up questions. Despite their failure to engage with the Ugandan youth, their questions serve as a proof of their desire to learn about the cultures of other people in different global locales.

Table 5.4 More questions from Ugandan youth and responses from Spain

Questions from Ugandan youth	Responses from Spanish youth
1) How do you greet a friend in Catalan or Spanish?	1) With two kisses one on each cheek and a hug.
2) Do you people still follow your tradition or not?	2) Not all of them. The younger people is very different than the older traditions
3) Are your teachers also transferred?	3) What do you mean by 'transferred'? We don't understand that question.
4) At what age does one become independent from his/her parents?	4) Legally at 18, but most of us still live with our parents until 25
5) Is your nation heterogeneous or homogeneous?	5) We are very heterogeneous. There is people from all around the word in Spain.
6) Do your schools organize cultural galas?	6) Yes. museum tours, historical tours, carnaval (we all get dressed with funny clothes), Sant Jordi (we give a book and a rose to our friends).
7) At what levels do you people sit for your final exams?	7) At the end of the high school at 16. Before the university at 18.
8) What is the name of your national examination board?	8) We call it 'Selectivitat'
9) Do men pay bride price to the girl's family when it comes to marriage?	9) Sometimes men pay the wedding's costs.

Preliminary Findings

The above information was generated through communications between the Ugandan youth and their peers in Spain. Analysis of this, and of information obtained through focus group discussions with 18 of the Ugandan youth involved in those exchanges, reveal the following key findings:

1. *Emotions*. The youth had different experiences while participating in GSB. They expressed such experiences using words like shocked, amazed, intimidated, happy, encouraged, inspired and empowered. For example from the focus groups, half of the youth felt happy, encouraged, and empowered, while the remaining half were shocked, amazed and intimidated by what they experienced in the course of these exchanges. The evidence of similar shock on the part of the Spanish youth is seen in the questions they asked about the video from Uganda in which they said: '*Hello students from Uganda! We have seen your video and it was quite shocking for us, your lifestyle is very different to ours*'. This message from the youth in Spain portrays both shock and amazement. The same was true with the Ugandan youth. As evidence of being intimidated while venturing to make their first video, a girl in one of the focus group discussions said:

> I realized that when we started making our first videos, it became clear to us that everything we wanted to pass across to our friend in our video could be said verbally. We noted that there were many ways we could express them. For example, we thought of the different objects, materials or things we were using to make the video and certain actions like blinking our eyes, shaking our heads, putting our thumbs up, kneeling down, bowing down, standing in a particular manner, etc. which one could use to understand what we were trying to put across. But my fear was that in the process of passing our message to our friends in different parts of the world, some of these bodily expressions or objects could mean different things in their custom. Also they were so many that I was not sure which ones would be okay and which ones were not. I felt intimidated and overwhelmed at the beginning. (Focus group discussion, 16 March 2019)

Another male participant who felt intimidated as well as inspired and empowered after participating in a GSB project expressed his feelings during one of the focus group discussions as follows:

> When I joined GSB, I listened to our facilitator and tried to get everything we were going to do in our group. I thought all the tasks we were expected to undertake involving the use of communication technologies like laptops and other equipment like cameras, all of which I had never used before were initially intimidating to me. But when I started fully participating, I paid a lot of attention to all the instructions and found the process of interacting with others in different parts of the globe using technology very inspiring and empowering. (Focus Group Discussion, 25 May 2019)

2. *Multiple modes.* The youth (especially those in Uganda) were stunned by the different modes they had to choose from to convey appropriate messages to their peers without leaving something very important out or offending their peers who are the target recipients of their messages. This was further compounded by their inadequate grasp of the complex relationship that exists between mode, language and material objects that all seem to play different roles in meaning-making. A girl in one of the focus group discussions expressed her frustrations as follows:

> I have seen that it is possible to send a message to another person using different ways and things like writing, facial expression, waving your hands, using certain objects or pictures, etc., but how can I be sure that someone far away from Uganda whom I do not know will understand me when I wave my hand like we were doing at the end of our video? I am saying this because someone told me that in India, nodding my head, which in our culture means approval, will mean the opposite. I feel it may not be good to assume that everybody will understand the different signs, pictures or bodily expressions we are using in communicating with others because we might end up offending some people, especially when any of the things, objects, symbols or signs we have used to express a meaning is taken to mean a different thing in their culture. I think we need help to understand how different people in different places and cultures use such objects, signs, images or body languages to express what they would like to say to other people. (1 August 2019)

3. *Critical cosmopolitanism.* The youth in all global locales exhibited great interest in learning and knowing the way of life of others in different parts of the world. This is clearly reflected in the nature of questions they asked each other on the GSB website. For example, the Spanish youth who watched the video their Ugandan peers posted asked: (a) What is your first language? (b) How many people talk your language? (c) WHAT IS THE LONGEST WORD IN YOUR LANGUAGE? (d) Why do you shave off your hair? (e) Your adults don't have phones neither, how do you keep in touch with others? (f) When was your town created? (g) Do you have a city hall? (h) Which currency do you use? The Ugandan youth on the other hand asked: (a) Do you people also celebrate Easter? (b) How do you greet a friend in Catalan or Spanish? (c) Do you people still follow your tradition or not? (d) At what age does one become independent from his/her parents? (e) Is your nation heterogeneous or homogeneous? (f) Do men pay bride price to the girl's family when it comes to marriage? (g) Do your schools organize cultural galas? As if to emphasize the intensity of the curiosity to learn about others, the third question from the Spanish youth was written all in caps.

4. *Context and culture.* Communication between the youth across global locales revealed that context and culture influence meaning, and as a result, a meaning given to something in one context and culture will not

always and necessarily be the same in another. Similarly, what is acceptable in one context and culture may be unacceptable in another. These were evident in some questions the youth asked: Can the girls use pants? Do you have big cities? Are you people also taught subjects like CRE, KISWAHILI and IRE? Are your teachers also transferred? For the youth in Spain, it was strange to see that none of the girls in the video posted by the Ugandan youth were wearing pants/trousers. They also expected every community to have big cities. On the other hand, the Ugandan youth were not aware that the youth in Spain may not know what is meant by 'transferring teachers', and subjects like Kiswahili and acronyms like CRE and IRE are not common in Spain. This is why the youth in Spain asked the Ugandan youth what they meant 'by transferring teachers?' In a focus group discussion, one boy did indicate that he was not comfortable with the use of the words 'kiss' and 'hug' because they are not acceptable in his rural setting. 'If you frequently use such words in my community, people will quickly associate you with prostitution', he said.

5. *Equity.* Transnational and transmodal communication are not neutral but inherently embedded in power, privilege and status. A number of questions asked by both the Ugandan youth and their peers in Spain attest to this finding. These questions are:

> Do you have phones? Adults don't have phones neither, how do you keep in touch with others? Do the teachers confiscate your phones in case you go with them to school? Do students have their own PCs and laptops or you people use computer lab?

These questions raise issues of power, privilege and status because having a phone in Uganda is associated with power and status. A teacher confiscating a student's phone also relates to power. Some people say information is power, so owning a phone enhances one's access to information, which many think is power. On the other hand, owning a personal computer or laptop may be a privilege and may also demonstrate status, while using a computer laboratory depicts a low-status community where people cannot afford personal computers or laptops.

Further Analysis and Discussion

This section analyzes and discusses the findings above in accordance with the five complexities associated with the transmodalities framework discussed in Hawkins (2018). The complexities include: (i) the multiplicity of modes in transnational, translingual and transmodal communications, (ii) the way modes intertwine and relate with language and material objects used for meaning-making, (iii) the way meanings are produced, received as they move, and negotiated, (iv) the role of context and culture in meaning-making and (v) issues of power, privilege and status.

Multiplicity of modes in transnationality, translinguality and transmodality

The youth participating in GSB reported feeling intimidated and shocked by the multiplicity of modes they were engaging with in the course of their transnational, translingual and transmodal communications. Anstey and Bull (2010) describe a mode as a communication channel that a culture recognizes such as writing, gesture, posture, gaze, font choice and colour, images, video, and even the interactions between them. The idea of interaction between different modes brings to the surface the notion of transmodalities in communication. According to Hawkins (2018), different modes are intertwined in transnational (and transmodal) communications. Some scholars in the field of literacy are now using the concept of multimodal literacy while discussing multimodal texts and digital resources in multiliterate classrooms (Anstey & Bull, 2009). This can truly be intimidating for youth who are not aware of new developments in literacy and applied linguistics. For example, the idea of multimodality in transnational and transmodal communications denotes integrating more than one semiotic mode to achieve communicative function (Kress & Van Leeuwen, 1996). In fact, looking at the video the Ugandan youth posted on the GSB website and watched by their global peers operating in different socioeconomic and cultural settings, it is clear that the youth were navigating a communication terrain that involves moving across languages (for example, Lugbarati, Kiswahili, English, Catalan), cultural conventions (both visible and implicit), and modes and communicative technologies (both digital as well as analog), which greatly overwhelmed them at the beginning.

It is important to note that each mode in any communication setting has its own specific task and function (Kress, 2010) in the meaning-making process, and it usually carries only a part of the message in a multimodal text. What this means for a group of youth not aware of the role each mode plays in transnational and transmodal communication is that the complexity of the relationships between the various meanings or semiotic systems in a text increases proportionately with the number of modes involved. For example, in the back-and-forth communications between the Ugandan and Spanish youth, one could see a dynamic combination of semiotic systems of moving image, audio, spoken language, written texts, space, and gesture – all used to convey different meanings, or components of the whole. In responding to some of the queries from the Spanish youth, the Ugandan youth, for instance, ended up crossing a linguistic border when they ended their communication to the youth in Spain with: 'Asante sana, thanks'. It can also be said that whereas the Ugandan youth living in a relatively remote and poor environment might have found GSB initially overwhelming, many have acknowledged that involving them in learning about other people in various global locales as well as working with a variety of languages, cultures, modes, and digital as well as analog communicative technologies has enormously helped them to appreciate what Anstey and Bull (2010) call 'the dynamic, highly distributed, translingual, multimodal, and embodied aspects of all communicative practices'. Anstey and Bull (2010) argue that modes are not only interactive but also integrative. This means they variously contribute to the construction of differing meanings and perspectives as they come together, evolve and move.

The nexus of modes, language, and objects

In communicative practices, modes, language and material objects exhibit interconnectedness in the process of meaning-making. For example, a careful look at the video posted by the Ugandan youth on the GSB website reveals the presence of different modes used together with languages and material objects to construct and convey meaning to their global peers. One of the focus group discussion participants indicated that in making their first video, they were stunned by the different modes they had to choose from to convey appropriate messages to their peers without leaving out things they considered very important aspects of their culture, or constructing and sending messages that could easily be taken to be offensive in the culture of their peers who are the target recipients of the messages. Their dilemma was further compounded by their inadequate grasp of the complex relationships that exist between mode, language and material objects that all seem to play different roles in meaning-making. For instance, during the back-and-forth communications between the youth in Uganda and Spain, they used three languages (Lugbarati (their mother tongue), English and Kiswahili) and mentioned at least two other languages (Spanish and Catalan). Instead of saying thanks after providing responses to the Spanish youth, the Ugandan youth used the Kiswahili phrase 'Asante sana' and then translated it into English: 'thanks'. This is interesting because multiple languages were used orally and in writing. Some of the modes included in their communications were written texts (on the screen, on the T-shirts the youth wore, on book covers and inside the books), postures, gazes, font sizes, font colours, different images, and sounds, while the material objects included the community library building, the different story and textbooks, bookshelves, clothes the youth were putting on – most of which had various institutional badges or logos inscribed on them – the reading tables and plastic chairs, a basket, hoes, cups, fire wood, potatoes, lighter, the little stones the youth were using to play their traditional game, and the bare background with isolated grass thatched houses. All of these carried meaning in conveying who they were and where they lived. The challenge the youth in Uganda reported was their inadequate knowledge of the roles and relationships between modes, language and objects. As Hawkins (2018: 160) notes, 'modes carry distinctive meanings in and of themselves, or entwined together even in the absence of spoken or written language'. The challenge the Ugandan youth face is further seen in Hawkins' (2018) view that, historically and currently, much of work on multimodality tends to privilege language, and consider modes as they relate to language. However, it is important to note that language is just one of the many resources used for making meaning. Such resources, according to Kress (2011), are available in one social group and its cultures at a particular moment and ought to be considered as constituting one coherent domain variously contributing meaning to a complex semiotic identity.

Production, reception and negotiations of meaning

The processes involved in the production of the video described above were youth-led, with serious negotiations between youth participants. This entailed discussions and agreements regarding the title of the video, selecting unique aspect of the lives of the youth and that of their community that they would like to share with their global peers, identifying places to shoot the video, allocating responsibilities during the production of the videos, determining the fonts (types, coulours and sizes) and written text they wanted to include, editing the video, uploading it, and receiving and discussing responses from their global peers. It is important to point out here that whereas the Ugandan youth might have intended to portray to the outside world positive aspects of their lives, it is possible that in negotiating among themselves what to share, they made choices within their own cultural understandings that may have been interpreted differently by youth in other locales who watched the video. This is because as modes begin to cross borders and cultures, the way that they portray meaning begins to change. In this way the reception by the outside world may not be the same. Hence, embracing a transmodalities perspective in communication is very important because what one mode fails to convey in a different sociocultural setting may possibly be effectively conveyed by another mode. For example, as the video described above was coming to an end, the Ugandan youth all came together and held their hands to wave as a sign of saying good-bye to their friends in Spain. Similarly, they wrote the names of the video producers in a slightly bolder and attractive colour and made it spread up the screen and fly away to capture the attention of their audience. This example demonstrates that the youth come to understand one another not solely from the production of the multimodal ensemble, but through the back-and-forth engagements via questions and responses in which they sometimes mixed languages to help them unpack, through dialogic engagement, the layered meanings as the messages fixed in the video pass through time and space, and come to be interpreted and then negotiated through transcultural lenses.

The deep reflection and dialog in transnational and transmodal engagements foster the process of forging relationships, through which the youth are able to gain an insider understanding of, and respect and care for, one another, which is very important in our current global village. This was evident in the following description one of the participants in a focus group discussion gave regarding her involvement in production and negotiations of meaning. She said:

> Whereas I had a lot of fear and anxiety at the initial stages of my participation in creating videos we later shared via GSB website because of my lack of knowledge and skills to operate the different communicative gadgets, after some time, I became relaxed and came to realize that giving a lot of time to contribute to the process of creating meaning through making videos not only helped me to learn new skills, but it also made me build useful relationships with others both within our group and with other youth in different sites we were communicating with. (17 August 2019)

The view of the youth presented in the above quotation suggests that the youth were able to gain awareness of their local environment and other people's ways of life beyond their national border, hence beginning to develop critical cosmopolitanism. According to Birk (2014), holding a cosmopolitan perspective means effectively extending one's identity, identifications, and ethical obligations beyond the bounds of what is familiar or proximate, to think and act with a strong concern for all humanity, thereby providing a complex, transformative, and socially relevant framework for global learning.

Contextual and cultural issues

Context and culture play important roles in cross-border, transmodal communications. This probably explains why some literacy scholars are now beginning to talk of literacies on the move and transliteracies (Stornaiuolo *et al.*, 2016; Sukovic, 2016). Hawkins (2018) observes that available literature on multimodality claims that modes are embedded in, and must be recognizable to, specific cultural groups. However, this assumption appears to leave hanging the question Hawkins raises regarding transmodal engagements across cultural groups, distances and spaces. She further points out that whereas cross-cultural encounters and exchanges are common, and necessary, both in light of globalization and for cultivating critical cosmopolitan relations, different modes, languages and material objects may not necessarily carry universal meaning in all contexts. For instance, when the Ugandan youth were asked to mention one thing they found peculiar in the course of their interactions with other youth in different global locales, one boy pointed out the use of the words 'kiss' and 'hug'. According to him, among the community he lives in, the two words are associated with prostitution and young people are advised to desist from using them. Another example was when the Ugandan youth expressed surprise at seeing that their peers from Spain were asking them why their girls were not wearing pants. It is possible that the Ugandan youth would ask the same question if they were communicating with youth from Scotland, where it is normal and acceptable for men to wear skirts.

This is why when questions the youth from other sites asked about the video posted by the Ugandan youth are critically analysed, they tend to demonstrate a strong desire to get to understand what is not familiar to them in their respective sites. Some of such questions the youth from Spain asked to their Ugandan friends included: What is your first language? Why do you shave off your hair? Can the girls use pants? Do you have big cities? These questions appear to be in line with the views of Agar (1994, cited in Hawkins, 2018), who asserts that things are not visible until they bump up against something unfamiliar. In this case, the youth who are watching the video tend to notice things as they relate to their own lives and contexts. Hence questions the youth from Spain and Vietnam asked were about things in the video which were not familiar to them. Responses to these questions by the Ugandan youth then try to help those asking the questions to connect what they are learning about their global peers to their own lives and understandings, and make meaning and connections from them. It can be said that what the youth from Spain failed to understand through watching the video became clear to them through the chain of semiosis; that is, through the unfolding sequence of transmodal interactions – the integration of visual, aural, oral, and textual semiotic systems – that enabled the negotiations and constructions of meanings. Hawkins (2018: 74) stresses the importance of context and culture as follows:

> Context and culture matter, not because they enable recognition of what is familiar within them, but because they have directive force in what is seen, thought, and represented across and through modes, and therefore what can be noticed, discussed, and learned. They are not only the 'background', or environment, for transmodal communication, they are fully engrained and entwined in assemblages and meaning-making, and cannot be separated from it. Thus transmodality enables the making and sharing of meanings through multiple means and modes within, across, through and as part of context and culture.

Power, privilege and status in global interactions

Issues related to power, privilege and status feature conspicuously in discussions about transmodalities and critical cosmopolitanism (Hawkins, 2018). Just like the argument in the concept of an ideological model of literacy, which views literacy as inherently political and deeply embedded in power relations (Street, 1984), both transmodalities and critical cosmopolitanism recognize differences at various levels, in terms of status, social, cultural and economic capital, and other resources among participants. For example, we continue to talk about the digital divide in our current context, meaning access to technology is not equal across the globe. As Hawkins (2018) reports, while some of the sites have computers, video cameras, and relatively good internet access, in others, community members have never seen or touched a computer or video camera, much less had internet experience prior to joining the project, and yet these are integral parts of the daily lives of other local youth. In fact, the questions exchanged between the Ugandan and Spanish youth after watching the video from Uganda clearly reflect issues of power, privilege and status. For example, the youth from Spain asked their colleagues in Uganda: 'Do you have phones?' Their response was: 'we don't have'. The Ugandan youth also asked their counterparts in Spain: 'Do your teachers confiscate your phones in case you go with them to school?' Their response was: 'sometimes, depending on the teacher and the situation'. The Ugandan youth also further asked their colleagues in Spain: 'Do students have their own PCs and laptops or you people use computer lab?' Their response was: 'yes, every student have their own laptop, we buy them by our own'. The question about having a phone and teachers confiscating students' phones seems to suggest that the youth in Uganda do not have the privilege of owning phones, much less the power to decide when, where and how to use them, while those in Spain do to a large extent. On the other hand, the question regarding students having their own computers or using a computer lab reflects issues of status, privilege and power as those students in Uganda can only use a computer lab and not their own personal PCs. This is also because they cannot afford a laptop, as the students in Spain can, as they made clear in their response to the Ugandan youth in saying that everybody has a personal computer and they buy it by themselves.

Conclusion

It is now clear that our current world is increasingly becoming mobile as evidenced by the global movement of people, commodities, cultures, and technologies, which in turn result in changes in the meanings of different things. This chapter explored the lived experiences of youth in rural Uganda participating in a project – GSB – to assess how new modalities afforded by digital stories and the online platform allow them to negotiate their sense of place and their sociocultural identities as they work toward developing a critical cosmopolitanism (Hawkins, 2014). Since Stornaiuolo *et al.* (2016) argue that phenomena not only move and intersect as separate entities, but also intermingle, interpenetrate and assemble in emergent configurations, the thesis this chapter advanced is that the digitally-mediated interactions between youth in various global locales support them to become critical cosmopolitan citizens. Critical cosmopolitanism, according to Hawkins (2018), references how all people encounter one another within global flows of mobility, whether the encounter takes place through people who move, or materials and resources, or messages. In GSB, the youth negotiate their sense of place and sociocultural identities by using the materiality of their local context to create videos and to construct meanings through a variety of modes, and by learning through others' videos and chat discussions, which are composed in the context of other localities and materialities.

Urry (2002) posits that the key feature of our current global world is mobility, where people, commodities, cultures, and technologies are all mobile and, as they move, meanings of different things continue to change. He further argues that issues of social inclusion and exclusion cannot be examined without identifying the complex, overlapping and contradictory mobilities necessarily involved in the patterning of an embodied social life. The new and rapidly changing contexts of mobility, and new global configurations of people, resources, and communications echoed by Appadurai (2000, cited in Newfield, 2015), now call for a critical examination of how language, culture, and community have historically been defined. Doing so through taking into account the complementarity of visual and verbal modes (Royce, 2007) will enhance our new understandings of semiotic assemblages and trajectories in which language is integrally intertwined with other 'things' to mediate meaning-making. As humans increasingly continue to interact with each other across the globe due to various reasons such as global trade, forced and voluntary migrations, educational interventions, etc., there is an urgent need to nurture what Hawkins (2018) calls a critical cosmopolitan ethics of care, openness, responsiveness, and equity in our relationships within the continuously emerging understandings of ourselves and others. As echoed in the multiliteracies approach, it is now inappropriate to use mono-lenses to view the multiple challenges facing us as a global community, and instead promote the dual frames of transmodalities and critical cosmopolitanism as guiding lenses in shaping and understanding the impact of dialogic engagements among global citizens.

Note

(1) For ethical reasons, St. Andrew's is used as pseudonym to replace the real name of the secondary school from which GBS participants are drawn.

References

Alvermann, D.E., Moon, J.S. and Hagood, M.C. (1999) *Popular Culture in the Classroom: Teaching and Researching Critical Media Literacy,* Mahwah, NJ: Erlbaum.

Anstey, M. and Bull, G. (2009) *Using Multimodal Texts and Digital Resources in a Multiliterate Classroom.* Sydney: Primary English Teaching Association.

Anstey, M. and Bull, G. (2010) *Evolving Pedagogies: Reading and Writing in a Multimodal World.* Sydney: Education Services Australia Limited.

Appiah, K.A. (1997) Cosmopolitan patriots. *Critical Inquiry* 23 (3), 617–39.

Appiah, K.A. (2005) *The Ethics of Identity.* Princeton, NJ: Princeton University Press.

Birk, T. (2014) Critical cosmopolitan teaching and learning: A new answer to the global imperative. *Diversity & Democracy* 17 (2). Online and retrieved December 5, 2018 from https://www.aacu.org/diversitydemocracy/2014/spring/birk

Brandt, D. and Clinton, K. (2002) Limits of the local: Expanding perspectives on literacy as a social practice. *Journal of Literacy Research* 34 (3), 337–356.
Burke, A. and Hughes, J. (2018) A shifting landscape: Using tablets to support learning in students with diverse abilities. *Technology, Pedagogy and Education* 27 (2), 183–198. DOI: 10.1080/1475939X.2017.1396492
Canagarajah, A.S. (2013) *Translingual Practice: Global Englishes and Cosmopolitan Relations.* New York: Routledge Press.
Collier, A. and Wyer, M. (2016) Researching reflexively with patients and families. *Qualitative Health Research* 26 (7), 979–993. DOI: 10.1177/1049732315618937.
Collins, R. and Makowsky, M. (1978) *The Discovery of Society.* London: Random House.
DeWalt, K.M. and DeWalt, B.R. (1998) Participant observation. In H. Russell Bernard (ed.) *Handbook of Methods in Cultural Anthropology* (pp. 259–300). Walnut Creek, CA: AltaMira Press.
Erlandson, D.A., Harris, E.L., Skipper, B.L. and Allen, S.D. (1993) *Doing Naturalistic Inquiry: A Guide to Methods.* Newbury Park, CA: SAGE.
Gee, J.P. (2004) *Situated Language and Learning: A Critique of Traditional Schooling.* London: Routledge.
Gee, J.P. (2013) *Good Video Games and Good Learning: Collected Essays on Video Games, Learning, and Literacy* (2nd edn). New York: Peter Lang.
Gee, J.P. (2015) The new literacy studies. In J. Rowsell and K. Pahl (eds) *The Routledge Handbook of Literacy Studies* (pp. 35–48). London: Routledge.
Gold, R.L. (1958) Roles in sociological field observations. *Social Forces* 36, 217–223.
Hawkins, M.R. (2014) Ontologies of place, creative meaning-making and critical cosmopolitan education. *Curriculum Inquiry* 44 (1), 90–113.
Hawkins, M.R. (2016) Mobility, language and critical cosmopolitan education. *AERA Second Language Special Interest Group Newsletter.* Spring, pp. 9–12.
Hawkins, M.R. (2018) Transmodalities and transnational encounters: Fostering critical cosmopolitan relations. *Applied Linguistics* 9 (1), 55–77.
Heath, S.B. (1983) *Ways with Words: Language, Life, and Work in Communities and Classrooms.* Cambridge: Cambridge University Press.
Jewitt, C. (2013) Multimodal methods for researching digital technologies. In S. Price, C. Jewitt and B. Brown (eds) *SAGE Handbook of Digital Technology Research* (pp. 250–265). London: SAGE.
Jewitt, C. (2017) An introduction to multimodality. In C. Jewitt (ed.) *The Routledge Handbook of Multimodal Analysis.* London: Routledge.
Jewitt, C. and Kress, G.R. (eds) (2003) *Multimodal Literacy.* New York: Lang.
Kawulich, B.B. (2005) Participant observation as a data collection method. *FORUM: Qualitative Social Research* 6 (2). See http://www.qualitative-research.net/index.php/fqs/article/view/466/996 (accessed September 2019).
Kleingeld, P. and Brown, E. (2019) Cosmopolitanism. In N. Zalta (ed.) *Stanford Encyclopedia of Philosophy.* Stanford, CA: Centre for the Study of Language and Information.
Knobel, M. and Lankshear, C. (eds) (2007) *A New Literacies Sampler.* New York: Peter Lang.
Kress, G. (2000) Multimodality. In B. Cope and M. Kalantzis (eds) *Multiliteracies: Literacy Learning and the Design of Social Futures* (pp. 182–202). London: Routledge.
Kress, G. (2010) *Multimodality: A Social Semiotic Approach to Contemporary Communication.* London: Routledge.
Kress, G. and Van Leeuwen, T. (1996) *Reading Images: The Grammar of Visual Design.* London: Routledge.
Leonard, R.L. (2013) Traveling literacies: Multilingual writing on the move. *Research in the Teaching of English* 48 (1), 13–39.
Levin-Goldberg, J. (2012) Teaching Generation TechX with the 4Cs: Using technology to integrate 21st century skills. *Journal of Instructional Research* 1, 59–66.

Morgan, L.D. (1996) Focus groups. *Annual Review of Sociology* 22, 29–152. doi.org/10.1146/annurev.soc.22.1.129

Murphy, K.M. (2012) Transmodality and temporality in design interactions. *Journal of Pragmatics* 44 (14), 1966–1981.

Murray, J. (2013) Composing multimodality. In L. Claire (ed.) *Multimodal Composition: A Critical Sourcebook*. Boston: Bedford/St. Martin's.

Newfield, D. (2015) The semiotic mobility of literacy: Four analytical approaches. In J. Rowsell and K. Pahl (eds) *The Routledge Handbook of Literacy Studies* (pp. 267–281). London: Routledge.

Royce, T.D. (2007) Intersemiotic complementarity: A framework for multimodal discourse analysis. *New Directions in the Analysis of Multimodal Discourse*. See https://forlingua.com/wp-content/uploads/2014/06/Chap02Royce-Erlbaum.pdf (accessed April 2021).

Salmons, J. (2017) Seeing and hearing the problem: Using video in qualitative research. See https://www.methodspace.com/seeing-hearing-problem-using-video-qualitative-research/ (accessed September 2019).

Scollon, R. and Scollon, S.W. (1981) *Narrative, Literacy, and Face in Interethnic Communication*. Norwood, NJ: Ablex.

Shipka, J. (2016) Transmodality in/and processes of making: Changing dispositions and practice. *College English* 78 (3), 250–257.

Stornaiuolo, A., Smith, A. and Phillips, C. (2016) Developing a transliteracies framework for a connected world. *Journal of Literacy Research* 49 (1), 68–91.

Street, B.V. (1984) *Literacy in Theory and Practice*. Cambridge: Cambridge University Press.

Sukovic, S. (2016) What exactly is transliteracy? See: http://scitechconnect.elsevier.com/what-exactly-is-transliteracy/ (accessed January 2020).

The New London Group (1996) A pedagogy of multiliteracies: Designing social futures. *Harvard Education Review* 66 (1), 60–92.

Urry, J. (2002) Mobility and proximity. *Sociology* 36 (2), 255–274.

Van Leeuwen, T. (2015) Multimodality in education: Some directions and some questions. *TESOL Quarterly* 49 (3), 582–589.

Whiting, R., Symon, G., Roby, H. and Chamakiotis, P. (2016) Who's behind the lens? A reflexive analysis of roles in participatory video research. *Organizational Research Methods*. DOI: 10.1177/1094428116669818.

6 Youth Transmodally Indexing Social Discourses: A Vietnam Video Narrative Analysis

Gordon B. West, Bingjie Zheng and Trang D. Tran

Introduction

This chapter presents a microanalysis of one online video narrative about the Tết holiday produced by a group of youth in Vietnam participating in the Global StoryBridges (GSB) project. GSB is a project that connects youth living around the world in under-resourced communities with each other through a digital platform where they create, share, and discuss videos about their lives. The youth in the focal site for this study are secondary students in Vietnam, and they meet regularly for the project after school in a martial arts center. This chapter aims to better understand the digital, transnational meaning-making that occurred through the video about Tết that they produced. Our guiding research questions were: (1) How do youth utilize affordances of the modes available through video to construct narratives? And (2) how do they (consciously or unconsciously) position themselves in relation to other groups of transnational youth?

We put forth a transmodal narrative analysis as one way of engaging with the complexity of analyzing transmodal online data by examining how the youth utilize affordances of the modes available to construct a narrative and position themselves, considering their imagined audience of global others. Using Bamberg's (1997, 2004) three-level analytical framework – the storyworld, the storytelling world, and relationship to broader discourses (e.g. national identity, cultural ideals, and consumerism in holidays) – we look at how the youth orchestrate semiotic modes (e.g. images, music, spoken narratives, and text) into a video narrative where they are positioned as cultural representatives, with the audience constructed as foreigners. Transmodal resources also index an imbricated set of social discourses around the youth.

Narrative and Identity

Narrative is a particularly useful way to understand identities and the ways that they can be crafted and negotiated in digital spaces. Humans tend to construct meaning from experiences and understand their world through narratives (Bruner, 1991, 1997; Somers, 1994). In this way, narrative is an epistemology, 'something we do, and in the process, we understand that experience' (Barkhuizen et al., 2013: 4). In this study, we define narratives not as individual and cognitive processes of meaning-making, but rather as interactionally constructed stories that are socio-materially situated. These stories may be either more rigid in structure, as the video narrative is, with a clear beginning, resolution, and coda, or they can be small stories, as in the comments youth post to others' videos, which are 'tellings of on-going events, future or hypothetical events, shared (known) events, but also allusions to tellings, deferrals of tellings, and refusals to tell' (Georgakopoulou, 2007: vii). In taking a narrative epistemology, we can look at the films the youth produce in GSB and the interactions around them to see how the youth themselves are making meaning through the narratives they construct and share.

Taking a narrative epistemology and doing narrative research also comes from a critical emphasis on making voices of participants, particularly those who are marginalized, be heard (Bernal et al., 2012; Cervantes-Soon, 2012, 2017). Through traditions in both Critical Race Theory (Delgado, 2000) and testimonio (Bernal et al., 2012; Cervantes-Soon, 2012), the voices of oppressed and marginalized people are used and amplified to speak against the systems of their oppression. Used in this way, narratives can also be a way through which tellers seek to transform broader deficit, or otherwise harmful, narratives and to 'resist and revise the scripting narratives of the culture and begin to compose their own' (Ritchie & Wilson, 2000: 7). We share this critical approach to narrative in seeking to lift and amplify the voices of the youth in this project.

We understand narratives as socially constructed and interactively achieved (Barkhuizen, 2009; Georgakopoulou, 2007; Vásquez, 2011). This fits with conceptions of identity as being situated within specific contexts and constantly negotiated in response to shifting contexts (Butler, 1990; Norton, 2013). In this regard, individuals do not always accept their assumed identities passively but take part in voicing their situated and multiple identities through agentive forms. Identity is fluid, multiple, and relational according to the audiences and purposes, where identity positioning involves the participants' understandings of their social realities, their own experiences and the social contexts in both a conscious and unconscious way (Weedon, 1987). This relational feature of identity positionality is not only revealed through face-to-face communication but is also reflected by how identity is imagined across scales of time and space. Identity positioning is formed, reinforced and negotiated through social participation in certain activities across time (Holland *et al.*, 2001) and through the social imagination of communities (Norton & Toohey, 2011). Aligned with identity theories, the identities of the youth in this project are embedded within several layers of both local and broader contexts, with multiple relationships being negotiated simultaneously (e.g. intergroup, martial arts center, national government, the Global StoryBridges project and the transnational communities it connects, etc.) (Bucholtz, 1999). Identity then is in a constant state of becoming within sociocultural, sociohistorical and institutional contexts (Armour, 2004; Duff & Uchida, 1997; Zembylas, 2003). Identities are also multisensory and multimodal, as van Lier has described:

> the source of the self is perceptual, through seeing, hearing, touching, tasting, moving about, usually in combinations of different sensory information and communication and therefore, perceptual action is typically multisensory and multimodal. (2008: 57)

Identities are then also negotiated multimodally, locally and in relation to broader discourses presented in audio, video, and print media.

One way to understand identities narratively as they are negotiated is through positioning (Bamberg, 1997, 2004). Narrative analysis allows us to look linguistically at how people position themselves interactionally with others in the construction of narratives (De Fina, 2009; Georgakopoulou, 2007). Studies of positioning in narrative analysis have largely been limited to face-to-face, real-time interactions. The tools used to examine this type of data do not work for many online interactions, and an adequate set of tools or an approach to analysis of online narratives has yet to be developed (De Fina & Perrino, 2017). One issue with looking at positioning in online data is that while it is achieved interactionally, the interactions are often asynchronous, as in the GSB project. Also, the multimodality of narratives and interactions is more salient in meaning-making than they might be in face-to-face interactions. To enhance the understanding of these characteristics of identities, this chapter advances transmodal narrative analysis as a way of addressing these gaps in methodology to look at how positioning and meaning-making are accomplished in online video and chat narratives.

Transmodalities and Narrative

We seek to bring to narrative analysis some of the tools of multimodal analysis. While there have been narrative analysis studies looking at various digital platforms, such as YouTube videos (Higgins *et al.*, 2016; Perrino, 2017), Facebook (Page *et al.*, 2013), and other digital spaces (see De Fina & Perrino, 2019), none have looked systematically at the ways in which other modes, beyond English language, are employed to construct narratives. Work in multimodality (Bezemer & Kress, 2016; Jewitt *et al.*,

2016) and, more recently, transmodalities (Hawkins, 2018), give us ways in which to more fully account for the complexity of multiple modes being orchestrated to create, interpret, and negotiate meanings.

From a multimodal perspective, meaning-making is accomplished beyond spoken or written language alone (Bezemer & Kress, 2016). In that frame, given that communication always relies on more than spoken or written language (i.e. gesture, images, sound, layout, color, etc.), it does not make sense to focus narrowly on a linguistic analysis, as most interactional narrative analysis has up to this point (De Fina & Perrino, 2017). We take up this focus on meaning-making from a narrative perspective wherein the meanings that are being constructed multimodally can be understood as narratives. In those narratives then we can read how the youth are using the various modes afforded to them by video production and the online environment to position themselves in different ways both to the other groups with whom they communicate in the project and in regard to broader discourses.

There have been several studies using a multimodal analysis to look at the way meanings are constructed in online and video data (Adami, 2009, 2015; O'Halloran *et al.*, 2015, 2016). These approaches, though, have largely focused on developing analysis for corpora of video data, looking to pull out patterns across large data sets and develop from those techniques for analysis. We hope to contribute to a more qualitative, microanalytic narrative analysis to examine in detail the complexities involved in digital communication and video production. There are two competing theories (i.e. Bateman & Schmidt, 2013; Burn, 2016) in multimodality for the analysis of film on a more micro level. Both seek to develop a grammar of the modalities of moving-image media from which analyses can be conducted, similar to and extending Halliday's (2014 [1985]) project from linguistic work to multimodality. Bateman and Schmidt (2013) take a more decompositional approach, teasing apart each mode to see the work it is doing to make meaning. Burn (2016), with his kinekonic mode, looks more holistically at the process of meaning-making in moving-image texts, taking filming and editing as the orchestrating modes which control the other contributory modes used. Both of these approaches have been developed looking mainly at cinematic, professionally produced films. While they provide some useful tools for analysis, they do not take into account the complexity of interactions around the films that show us how filmmaking and viewing is a social process. Using a narrative lens, we are able to broaden our micro-analysis to look beyond just the film itself and the meanings that are being produced, to see ways in which positioning and meaning-making are being crafted in relation to the audience. We can also look at the broader discourses, such as those found in the articulation of national identities, portrayal of holidays, and cultural ideals, that shape production and meaning in the narratives.

Understanding meaning-making in video and digital spaces requires us to consider the ways in which meaning-making is a socioculturally situated process. We also need to be conscious of the constraints that the youth face in designing their video narratives. Modes themselves, as Kress described them, are 'socially shaped and culturally given resources for meaning making' (Burn, 2016: 60). In this sense, for example, the affective meaning that a certain color might convey in the Mekong Delta region of Vietnam (i.e. red symbolizing luck, happiness, and joy) may not have the affective connotation for viewers at other sites in different parts of the world. The same could be said for music, words recorded in spoken language, and almost every other mode assembled in the construction of the video. These sorts of complexities are brought to the fore using transmodalities (Hawkins, 2018). Hawkins (2018) identifies five complexities that come when we look at multimodal communication, especially between groups from different cultures: the ways modes are intertwined, the way modes are connected to material objects, the arc of communication involving the production and reception of modes, context and culture, and relations of power. In this chapter, we hope to use a transmodal narrative analysis to draw out some of those complexities in our look at one video produced by youth in the GSB site in Vietnam.

Research Site and Participants

Riverbank[1] is the GSB site in the Mekong region of Vietnam. It started in November 2017. The 13 participating students (4 boys and 9 girls) are from seven different high schools in An Giang – one of the most economically disadvantaged and under resourced regions of the Mekong Delta. The participants come from low-income families and have limited proficiency in English. The project takes place within a martial arts center where youth learn Vovinam, the national martial art of Vietnam, during their out-of-school time. The master of the martial arts center offers lessons in Vovinam free of charge to youth who would not otherwise be able to afford lessons. This site was housed at the Vovinam center because it was the only site that was available for students to meet to work on the GSB project.

Data Sources and Analysis

Data for this chapter include: one 7-minute online video narrative posted by the Vietnamese youth on the GSB website; a transcript of one virtual interview between the first author and the third author (who is now US-based but was the original site facilitator) and some of the students; as well as the posted online chats between youth from different sites.

Our narrative analysis of the video was informed by Bamberg's (1997, 2004) positioning theory, meant to examine how tellers, or in this case filmmakers, position themselves through the narratives they tell at three levels. Since this framework was developed for analysis of spoken, interactional narratives, applying it to video data required adaptation and necessitated focusing our attention on how positioning was achieved transmodally in the narratives. Bamberg's first level is the storyworld that is created by the youth in their video. At this level, we considered how the youth themselves play the role of different characters in the film, both through their filmed speaking roles and through the still images and other modes they employed to communicate as characters in the film. We also looked at the setting as shown in video through both the filmed segments and the still images, and the sense of atmosphere set by the music to see how the setting of the storyworld was constructed. Finally, we looked at the sequence of events in the video, the plot, to see how actions are ordered (again through various modes including moving images, still images, audio, written text, and so on), and to give insight into the roles played by the characters (protagonists) in the story presented in the video.

Bamberg's (1997, 2004) second level looks at how the tellers position themselves in relation to their interlocutors. This presents challenges since the interactions here are asynchronous rather than in-person. Nonetheless, we see these video narratives as interactionally produced and understood. To analyze this level of the video narrative, we looked at the video and chat interactions, as well as drew on data from a group interview with the youth. In the video, we looked at how the youth constructed themselves transmodally to be perceived by the audience. Additional insights from the group interview helped to understand how they imagined their audience. Positioning at level two is important to examine because it provides further insights into how the youth present themselves to their imagined audience, and in a sense how they construct their identities in this project agentively in response to how they imagine they may be perceived, given that identities are socially negotiated (Norton, 2013).

Positioning at levels one and two help us to get a fuller sense of how the youth constructed identities and positioned themselves within the video narrative and in relation to their imagined audience. As Bamberg and Georgakopoulou (2008) explained, level three examines 'how the speaker/narrator positions a sense of self/identity with regards to dominant discourses or master narratives' (2008: 385) and how the narrator 'makes these relevant to the interaction in the here and now' (2008: 391) to portray themselves. Level three then helps us understand how the youth positioned themselves in relation to discourses such as consumerism in holidays, cultural ideals, and national identities. This level is especially important in transnational communication because it is the level where the youth negotiate who they are and position themselves in relation to discourses that are not only locally produced but are located in a broader social world (De Fina, 2013). Transmodally, we approached analysis at level three by investigating the source of different modes, such as still images and music used in the video. We also looked at the sequence of the video and how the modes worked together to reference or further certain discourses. At this level, the content and form of the narrative alone is insufficient to fully understand the discourses being cited. Understanding the context in which the narratives were produced, from a narrative and transmodal perspective, is key (De Fina & Georgakopoulou, 2015; Hawkins, 2018). Insights from the original facilitator (the third author) and from the group interview of the youth provided more information on the context and were used to triangulate our findings at this level.

Researcher Positionality and Roles

All three authors are part of an international research team for Global StoryBridges that works collaboratively to share data and build understandings through meetings and regular e-seminars held through email. As a team, our various positionalities allowed us different insights in the data (see more on this in the discussion section). Gordon's (first author) positionality in this project, as a white male from the United States who spent years working as an English language teacher in Korea, allowed him to look at the data and ask questions from a more outside perspective and to connect with youth in the site around their interest in K-pop music. Bingjie (second author) is a scholar from China who has lived in the United States for several years while attending graduate school. Her experiences of living, teaching, and studying in China and the United States provide her with an opportunity to compare social discourses and traditions in different societies. For both Bingjie and Gordon, their more etic perspectives allowed them to see and question aspects of the video that an insider might not notice, while also blinding them to observations that only an emic perspective could provide.

Trang (third author) was formerly the facilitator of the Riverbank group and helped to launch the site; she currently attends graduate school in the United States. She facilitated the group during the production of the video analyzed in this study. In that role, she led the group discussions, and observed roles and responsibilities of individual students during the film-making process. Trang was born and raised in the Mekong Delta region of Vietnam, and shares cultural commonalities with the youth participants. Her background as a middle-class woman is different than the socioeconomic status and background of the youth. While her positionality as facilitator and being from the same region as the youth afford her some insights into their references and video production process, her higher socioeconomic status and role as an authority figure also limit her understandings of the youth experiences, references, and ways in which they utilize transmodal resources.

All of us have transnational experiences of living, studying and teaching in various cultural settings that inform our interpretations of the data from our unique, personal histories. We also come from middle-class socioeconomic backgrounds relative to where we grew up. These histories are inflected by different racial, class, and gender positionalities. Working as a team allowed for emic perspectives from the researchers to mix with insights that others had from different positionalities to reach deeper understandings of the data. We understand also in our work that there are 'spectrums of emicity' (Ratanapraphart *et al.*, this volume) wherein even emic perspectives are necessarily limited and cannot represent the full range of emic understandings in the research process.

Findings and Discussion

In the following sections we lay out the findings of our narrative analysis of the video. Before going into the analysis, we first give a description of the video. We then look at the way meanings are made and positioning is accomplished using individual modes. We also investigate how the ensemble of modes is orchestrated by the youth holistically to position themselves and convey meaning at each of Bamberg's (1997, 2004) levels. A detailed analysis of the data helps us to answer our questions of how the youth use modes to transmodally construct narratives, and how they position themselves at the three levels in those narratives.

Description of *TET HOLIDAY IN VIETNAM*

The video, entitled *TET HOLIDAY IN VIETNAM*, was uploaded onto the GSB website in 2018 and is seven minutes long. Two other groups, one from Kenya and one from Uganda, posted questions and comments in response to the video, to which the Riverbank youth replied. Our data, then, include both the video and the ensuing discussions.

The video opens with a title screen with the title given in all caps. The music, '*Ngày Tết quê em*' (Tết in my village), begins immediately. The title screen is followed by a shot of fireworks for the holiday which was videoed by one of the youth using her smart phone. A brief tracking shot walking through the market follows. About 20 seconds into the film, a female youth (a project participant) appears, performing a pre-written script on the theme 'What is Tet?', which also appears as a subtitle over her section. This begins a sequence of segments in which youth appear individually, delivering a pre-written and rehearsed monologue in English on different aspects of Tết (i.e. 'what is Tet', 'when is Tet', 'the importance of Tet', 'why I like Tet', etc.). These are filmed at various locations in the city center and appear without background music, although there is background noise from traffic that at times overpowers the audio level of the youth's spoken language. Still images, at least one per monologue, are used. The subtitles and still images, in addition to the video segments and spoken language, serve as additional modes to extend, or give additional information (Martinec & Salway, 2005). The images, in addition to the spoken language, provide additional visual context of homes or of families, different from the city background shown where the youth are speaking into the camera. They also serve to show aspects of the fable that is shared about the holiday. The subtitles serve to frame each segment of spoken monologue from the youth.

About 4 minutes and 45 seconds into the video, the sequence of student monologues is interrupted by another tracking shot through the Tết market, where flowers and other goods for sale are shown, with the background music resuming and playing throughout the shot. The market shots serve as a sort of recurring chorus in the video. After the 30-second shot, the sequence of student monologues resumes, following the same format as the first set of monologues. This is followed by another tracking shot of the market, with background music, approximately 6 minutes and 30 seconds into the video.

After approximately 10 seconds of the final market shot, we see one group photo of the Riverbank youth and their facilitator. A title screen follows, saying, 'Behind the scene', and another group photo of the youth in front of the martial arts center appears. This transitions to a wide photo, taken from a distance, of the youth filming one of the segments for their video (see Figure 6.7). Finally, we see two of the boys riding a small merry-go-round at the edge of a park that was one of their filming locations. The background music continues from the last market shot throughout the final sequence of scenes.

Level one

In our analysis of the storyworld, we can see the youth playing roles as cultural ambassadors, in particular of ambassadors from an idealized sort of national culture as embodied in the Tết holiday. We can see this through their use of images of idealized settings and families (see Figures 6.1 and 6.2), their scripted performance as a sequential chorus of characters, and the choice of background music to help establish the atmosphere of the film.

The youth establish themselves as cultural ambassadors of an idealized national culture from the beginning of the video with the selection of Tết, the major national holiday, as the subject that they introduce and focus their narrative on. The locations in the city that they chose to film are quite far from the martial arts center where they meet. These spots were a square where public concerts and events are often held that is next to a statue of a famous leader who was from the city, and a park next to the river with two bridges that is considered representative of the city and the Mekong Delta region, with its many rivers and canals and the biggest outdoor market of the city.

Figure 6.1 A southern Vietnamese family celebrating Tết

This careful selection of the filming locations helps to set a storyworld that portrays an idealized holiday by showing the main, most desirable areas of the city, including the Tết market. None of the filming was done in the less prosperous neighborhood the youths lived in or where their martial arts center was located. Partly this was due to the constraints of film as a mode, since one of the youth was unable to obtain permission to film a '*bánh Tết*', or sticky rice maker, near the martial arts center, because the rice maker felt uncomfortable being filmed. Another constraint was the length limits for videos that was mandated by what the project website could accommodate.

Their selection of still images (Figures 6.1–6.4, as captured in screen shots from the video) served to elaborate and extend the meanings being made in their film (Martinec & Salway, 2005). This is especially true when the images are being used to show generalized aspects of the holiday, such as decorations or what happens during Tết. The image in Figure 6.1 is representative of this type of image, showing a family in southern Vietnam (as evidenced by the type of flowers used to decorate, and the types of offerings on display), depicting the elders giving a red envelope of money (one of the traditional Tết activities). These youth live in southern

Figure 6.2 A southern Vietnamese family celebrating Tết, wearing traditional clothing

Figure 6.3 Family in a rural area playing '*lô tô*'

Vietnam, and this would represent their Tet experience. Other images, such as in Figure 6.2, show families wearing more traditional clothing for the holiday, something that the youth themselves do not do during Tết. Most of the families shown in still images are middle to upper-middle class, and through their displays of wealth, in their decoration and dress, they help construct the storyworld around an idealized holiday, different than the way the project youth actually experience it. The fact that some northern Vietnamese families (as evidenced by different types of decorations and flowers, see Excerpt 2 for examples) are shown also helps set the holiday as a national event, which the characters in the storyworld, despite never having been to the northern part of the country, can then represent.

There are a few exceptions to the still images shown, such as in Figures 6.3 and 6.4. These exceptions appear in relation to more personal and specific aspects of Tết presented. Figure 6.3 represents a rural family from a socioeconomic background and location similar to those of the youth who produced the video playing '*lô tô*', a bingo-like game played with tamarind seeds to cover the numbers. This image appears during a monologue on what a particular student likes about Tết. Figure 6.4 shows a group of mostly young people, who work in an industrialized urban

Figure 6.4 A large group of people from an urban center waiting for a bus back home for Tết

center, waiting for a bus back to their hometowns for the holiday. This image more closely represents the type of travel that the youth and their families might experience, although none of them had personally experienced this. While the image does not depict more affluent means of travel for Tết, it does serve to establish a more dramatic atmosphere for the holiday, emphasizing its importance for people in Vietnam by helping us see the lengths to which people go to travel back home for the holiday.

The setting of the storyworld is that of a national holiday which is portrayed transmodally as an idealized cultural event. This setting is furthered by the choice of music that the students use in the background of the chorus-like market scenes that recur throughout the film, and also backgrounds the opening and closing scenes. The song played in this video is 'Ngày Tết quê em', written by Từ Huy in 1994. This is one of the most popular Tết songs in Vietnam. It has been recorded by various singers over the years. The song has a catchy tune with a strong upbeat pop tempo that gives a feeling of energy and youth and creates an atmosphere of celebration in the video. There are other, more traditional sounding versions of this song, but by using this pop version, the youth use the modality of music to add a layer of celebration to the setting of the storyworld in the film.

This setting then allows the youth to take on their role as characters in the film where they act as cultural ambassadors, representing this idealized national culture. In contrast to videos from other sites, where youth are often shown on screen at the same time, interacting and playing distinct individual roles, the Riverbank youth in this video appear individually throughout until the very end of the film. Despite appearing individually, however, their role in the storyworld is that of a sequential chorus, playing parts of a whole and working from a shared script. During the planning phase of the video, when the group decided to portray the Tết holiday, they then outlined what they wanted to talk about in the video and divided the content of the video into sections (i.e. definition, when and how long the holiday is, the main activities, how they feel about Tết, etc.). After collectively brainstorming and individually writing their sections, and then getting help editing the scripts, the students practiced their scripts until they had memorized them. Their main concern in editing was in maintaining the same amount of screen time for each student. Through this careful planning and scripting process, we see the youth as characters acting as a sequential ensemble. While they do not appear at the same time on screen, even when they appear individually they are working purposefully from the same planned script, which gives cohesiveness to their message and their character as cultural ambassadors. Videos have been shared by other groups on Global StoryBridges that share short, individual segments that do not necessarily connect with each other. Initially, the Riverbank group's video appeared to be in that style; however, through this sequential chorus format, they manage to highlight individual voices while also positioning themselves strongly as a cohesive group of cultural ambassadors.

Level two

At level two, we look at the ways in which the youth are positioning themselves in the telling of their narrative in relation to their imagined audience. The Riverbank youth position themselves as guides to an imagined audience that is foreign to and unfamiliar with Vietnam. This positioning largely reinforces their positioning in the storyworld as cultural ambassadors presenting an idealized national culture. We see at level two then how they work to guide us as an audience through the Tết holiday, using it to teach us about Vietnamese national culture.

We start by looking at the recurring market scenes to see how this positioning is being accomplished transmodally in their film. The market scenes are point-of-view tracking shots through the market with no youth participants visible. Rather, the viewer sees the market from the perspective of someone walking through it. Through this sort of point-of-view framing and the cinematography of the scenes, the viewers are directed to see what the filmmakers would like them to focus on (Halverson et al., 2012). While they are invisible, the youth are still functioning as guides, walking the audience through the market, using the modality of moving images to guide the audience (Burn, 2016).

Another way in which we see the guide/foreigner positioning is in the still images that the youth choose to display in the course of the video. The choice could have been made to use pictures of their own homes and families celebrating the holiday. Instead, the choice was made to show other families celebrating the holiday, often those of a particular socioeconomic status. At level one, this serves to help construct an idealized storyworld of Tết. At level two, we as an audience feel distance from the youth as guides who are anonymizing the holiday, and thereby also generalizing the culture. The effect is to give distance between the youth and the audience, where we do not know them as individuals or learn about the holiday as they experience it, but rather are presented with a version that is preferable for outsiders to consume.

An important mode through which the youth further their role as guides to an unfamiliar audience is using English language subtitles. The subtitles are visible in Figures 6.1 through 6.4 and serve to remind viewers of the theme of each monologue, and at times perhaps to help in understanding the meaning that is being made when background noise at times overpowers the youth's spoken language. The subtitles are instructional, directing our attention and priming us for what we are meant to learn from each student as they speak and share images to teach us about Tết and Vietnamese culture.

This positioning is taken up by participants at other sites as well in the chat spaces under the video on the GSB website. Figure 6.5 shows questions and a comment from the group in Kenya in response to the video. In questions #2 and #3, we can see that the youth from the Kenya group explicitly ask questions about Vietnamese national culture, aligning to the

Comments

Hi team Vietnam we have some
Submitted by   on Fri, 04/13/2018 - 11:43

Hi team Vietnam we have some questions.

1. Do you share cards during Tet holiday?

2. Is your country one religion state?

3. how many other major holidays d o you have apart from tet?

Thank you we will soon post our next video

reply

Figure 6.5 Questions from the Kenya site in response to the Riverbank Tết video

Thanks for your questions,   ! Here are our answers.
Submitted by   on Sat, 04/14/2018 - 12:03

Hello!

1. We rarely send cards during Tet holiday. People who live far away from their families send card to their beloved people

2. No it isn't. We have many religions such as Buddhism, Christianity, Islam

3. We have several big holidays, for example Hung King death anniversary, Independent Day.

Best wishes.

reply

Figure 6.6 Riverbank youth responses to the questions from the Kenya site

Riverbank youth's positioning as cultural ambassadors and guides. In Figure 6.6, the group from Riverbank reaffirms their earlier positioning by responding directly to the questions about national culture.

The first question from the group in Kenya, responding more directly to the content of the video, is representative of many of the questions that the group from Uganda asked. Since the content of the video, the storyworld, was carefully crafted to represent an idealized national culture, these questions further reaffirm the Riverbank youth's positioning in the video and align to that positioning. This can be read as a successful accomplishment of asserting the positioning and identity that the Riverbank youth wished to claim. They were able to orchestrate the various modes available, despite constraints, to accomplish this act of meaning-making and positioning transmodally through their film.

A final, interesting aspect of the video is the 'behind-the-scenes' sequence at the end of the film that breaks the so-called fourth wall, or the conceptual barrier between the performer and the audience. In this case, the footage here breaks that wall between performer and audience by taking the youth out of the roles they had been performing as cultural ambassadors. It functions similarly to blooper reels, or a genre of series-ending shots in some Asian dramas, where the cast and crew are shown in group pictures and in the process of filming. It is meant to show the 'true' personas of those on camera to build a sense of solidarity with the

Figure 6.7 Youth from Riverbank filming one of their monologues

audience in ways that allow the performers to do so in a controlled manner without losing face (Matwick & Matwick, 2020). This scene comes after the final market scene and is introduced by a formal title screen announcing it as behind-the-scenes footage. Two full group photos of the youth with their facilitator are shown, followed by a photo of the youth filming one of the monologues (Figure 6.7).

Immediately after the photo shown in Figure 6.7, the two boys are shown riding a merry-go-round. While there is no audio other than the background music, the group was being yelled at by an older woman at the park for riding the merry-go-round, which was meant for younger children. The image and the video segment of two boys on the merry-go-round serve to break from the previously shown storyworld. Through this behind-the-scenes sequence, the youth position themselves as filmmakers, showing us their process and a scene of what they were doing beyond the process of filming. While this different positioning is not referred to by the other groups in the comments section under the video, it marks a departure from their previous positioning in the video. Whereas in the rest of the video the viewers are positioned as outsiders and are kept at a relative distance by being shown idealized families and celebrations, this scene, in limited ways, allows the viewer to see the youth in different roles than as cultural representatives. At the same time, it provides what could be read as a more intimate view of the youth as themselves, while also positioning themselves as savvy, fun filmmakers through their choice of images and the merry-go-round shot. While small, it cannot be excluded from the complexity that it adds in understanding the youth's positioning toward the audience as multi-dimensional.

Level three

For the third level of positioning, we found ways in which the youth positioned themselves in relation to dominant discourses around national identity and consumerism in the Tết holiday. Following De Fina, we conducted a close examination of talk and text, expanding our analysis to a more complete accounting of the transmodal nature of the narrative, to show narrators' 'stance toward the ideologically laden categories and constructs' (2013: 45) of national identity and consumerism. Elements that we drew on from the videos, interviews, and chat spaces to understand this connection included: open referential categories, the presence of indexicality through still images, spoken dialogue, other visual references, and repetitions of music, themes, and cinematography. How discourses are collectively represented in narratives at the third level can in turn show the social process of discourses, including social and cultural struggles in society. In the video, dominant discourses are referenced, but rather than being challenged directly as they are in other studies of positioning (Bamberg, 1997; De Fina, 2013), those discourses are embodied by the youth in their video about Tết. This is in alignment with their positionalities as cultural ambassadors of an idealized national holiday (level 1), and as guides to a foreign audience outside of Vietnam (level 2). Those dominant discourses are not challenged in clear ways, but the narrative is transmodally composed of references to those discourses.

In positioning themselves within a larger, unified national identity through the video of the Tết holiday, we found that the youth's descriptions and representation of the holiday through repetition of cultural stories and historical references work to build their positionality transmodally within a dominant national Vietnamese identity. This cultural-historical situating of the holiday within a discourse of unified national identity is evident when the youth introduced the ancient story of the kitchen god (Figure 6.8). The story of the kitchen god in particular is contested, with several versions of the story used in various ethnic and national Vietnamese and Chinese discourses as a way to build identity closely associated with the Lunar New Year holiday (Xu, 2006). Using a reverse image search, it is possible to trace back the image in Figure 6.8 to where the youth found it online on a Vietnamese website discussing the story of the kitchen god in a way that makes clear its place in traditional Vietnamese customs and

Figure 6.8 The picture presented when narrating the 'Kitchen god' story

Figure 6.9 Family traditions and customs on the Tết holiday

traditions around the Tết holiday. The students' own recontextualization of the image and story within their video narrative (see Excerpt 1 below for the oral narrative accompanying Figure 6.8) shows how the youth not only take up this cultural-historical narrative, but also reshape it transmodally to construct their own narrative of the holiday within the larger context of their video narrative.

We also see this cultural-historical positioning within a national identity in the cultural symbols related to the holiday including signs, food, clothing, and holiday traditions (Figures 6.1, 6.2 and 6.9). The traditions shown with the alters of food offerings, the food shown for those offerings, the banners hanging in the background, and the clothing worn in the images all index and draw on cultural-historical narratives of a culturally defined national identity. As mentioned earlier (evidenced in Excerpt 2), the inclusion of traditions from multiple regions in Vietnam is a way in which the youth position themselves not simply as representatives of their region of Vietnam, but rather as representatives embodying a unified national identity.

We see this further as, when introducing these cultural practices and traditions, the youth make frequent use of linguistic markers including inclusive pronouns like 'we', and the pictures that show family events, such as cleaning, playing games, and praying also seem to demonstrate a sense of affiliation that is shared within certain social groups. The youth also included scenarios in their video to demonstrate that people from different parts of the nation celebrated the holiday. For example, the narrators elaborated on the different flower preferences for different regions, but with the common practice of purchasing flowers from flower markets for the Tết holiday in the north and the south of Vietnam, depicting this holiday as a nation-wide celebration and as a shared national tradition in both major regions. All of these elements are used as open referential elements that are representations of their national holiday, and the particular selection of these elements shows their process of reasoning: they bring the elements of the holiday that are shared by people all over the nation and thereby represent a national identity.

When presenting the Tết holiday and identifying themselves with the holiday as a national identity, the youth also drew on various linguistic and semiotic resources. Some of the resources were drawn from their everyday encounters and some were drawn from their own experiences. One way they presented Tết holiday was to select images from online resources (i.e. image searches), since none of these youth had traveled outside of their own region, as they described during our group interview. They make use of online resources in order to extend the visual representation of the holiday to include different areas of the country. In this sense, they are positioning themselves as part of the constructed national identity reflected through these online resources. While introducing the kitchen god story for the Tết holiday, for instance, the youth picked several pictures and constructed their own stories (see Figure 6.8). As one youth describes:

Excerpt 1: The fifth youth narrator in the video telling the kitchen god story.[2]

Youth #5: Sending the kitchen god to the heaven is the habit of the Vietnamese people so far and it take place on the 23rd of the last month of the lunar year uh this symbol is the carp because it help the kitchen god to the heavens and reporting news from earth. (TET HOLIDAY IN VIETNAM, 1:29–1:55)

Here, the narrator seems to repeat the story as being part of Vietnamese history in order to represent their cultural identity. In taking this narrative and recontextualizing it to their own video narrative of the holiday, they are both drawing on a specifically framed collective national memory, but also working to build a collective memory of the holiday for themselves that they then share with others (Halbwachs, 1992). In Halbwachs' (1992) understanding of collective memory, this story can be seen as a cultural element used to construct a national history.

When presenting the holiday, the youth co-construct their identities with the holiday through their own interactions with the holiday. For example, when describing cultural practices for the Tết holiday, the youth selected many pictures from online sources, but they also took turns to describe their everyday encounters with the holiday, including the food they cooked, some of the family activities they do, and fables like that of the kitchen god. In the video they presented their trip to the local market and showcased artefacts such as red envelopes for lucky money, fruits, and decorations for the viewers. In this case, their identification of the holiday also shows how the cultural entities and resources are social-historically contextualized and re-contextualized in the modern society, but at the same time these resources are taken up and narrated by the narrators' own creativity and unique interaction with the holiday. Agha (2003: 231) proposed 'enregisterment' as a process 'through which a linguistic repertoire becomes differentiable within a language as a socially recognized register of form'. De Fina highlights the importance of attending to this enregisterment (2013: 43, following Agha, 2003) process of identity in the third level of analysis, where narrators position their identity in relation to macro-level discourses. While there is freedom in the process of enregisterment, macro-level discourses and social identities can be reified as well (De Fina, 2013). We find that happening here in the way that the youth use the modalities available, in a process of enregisterment, to reify a national Vietnamese social identity and discourse of unified nationalism.

In addition to the youths' positioning within a dominant discourse of a unified national Vietnamese identity, other discourses are also represented, most clearly that of consumerism as a means of properly celebrating the holiday. Here, the discourses are not 'sets of organized propositions' (De Fina, 2013: 45) but are seen as 'materially mediated ideational phenomena' (Blommaert, 2005: 164). From a transmodal approach, we see how social discourses around consumerism are represented and indexed through the orchestration of various linguistic and visual modes of narratives. First, we notice that many semiotic resources in the video demonstrate how consumption happens during the holiday. For example, narrators emphasized the flower market when introducing the holiday. The images selected online demonstrate the extensive presence of fruits and food purchased for the holiday. The guided tour to the local markets also reveals the presence of luck money and the habits of consumption for the holiday. The images selected by the narrators seem to depict an idealized holiday where colorful decorations and a wide range of material goods are exhibited and exchanged. When presenting these resources, the group of students narrated their affiliation and association with the holiday, as in the following verbatim transcriptions from their spoken language:

Excerpt 2: The sixth youth narrator in the video talking about why he loves Tết.

> Youth #6: I love Tết because I and my parents get together there at our house, do shopping, and cook traditional food Vietnamese ah Vietnamese. On Tết ah we play we play a lot of game, fun game together. (TET HOLIDAY IN VIETNAM, 1:58–2:15)

Excerpt 3: The seventh youth narrator in the video talking about Tết decorations.

> Youth #7: Tết is so diverse, one that we could gain weight after the holiday, one of the special food is 'bánh tét' which is from sticky rice, mung bean, uhm and fatty pork or banana. After shopping for Tết, we usually decorate our house, such as apricot blossom in the southern and central part or peach blossom in the northern part [inaudible – wind] in addition and kumquat tree are also popular decoration in the south. First if you want to buy flower to decorate your house you will go to flower markets

because it's very exciting, funny, beautiful, and have many flowers for you too. (TET HOLIDAY IN VIETNAM, 2:16–3:05)

As the oral narratives above show, the students love the holiday for different reasons, one of which is the experience of shopping, purchasing materials and decorating the house with family members. As De Fina stresses, level three positioning often involves 'individual stances towards discourses [...] but such stances may turn out to be common among different members of a community and point to collective positioning processes' (2013: 46). These narratives and what's visible through visual modes seem to index a naturalized discourse of the commodification of culture and cultural events and values in the society. This discourse of consumption for the holiday was highly visible although the youth themselves would not be capable, given their socioeconomic position, of participating in the types of opulent consumption and decoration that they show in their video. Youth in other sites picked up on this discourse also, with youth from both Uganda and Kenya sites posting questions online about the habit of purchasing flowers and gifts during the Tết holiday (see Figure 6.5 for one example).

In looking at positioning at the third level, the youth position themselves as participants in, and contributors to, a unified national identity which is represented by the history, online images and cultural events, no matter whether they are physical or directly interacting with elements. When positioning their identities, the information that they presented reflects macro-level discourses.

Methodological Implications

In this section, we share methodological implications for this study, both in terms of the contribution transmodal narrative analysis can make and how working as part of an international research team informs this methodology.

Transmodal narrative analysis

As we show, our analysis investigates modes and resources holistically rather than privileging certain modes or resources, such as spoken or written languages, as has traditionally been the focus in narrative studies. Taking a transmodal approach to narrative analysis provides greater insights into the multimodal construction of narratives, and particularly for this study, positioning within those narratives. Without looking at the ways in which the various modes are utilized at the different levels (e.g. still images of upper-middle-class families to show an idealized holiday in addition to subtitles and spoken narration), we would not be able to understand the full range of how these positions are taken in narratives.

At a time in which digital narratives and interactions are ever more common, expanding our tools of analysis in this way is vital to understanding the complexity of meaning-making and narratives as they are being constructed online (De Fina & Perrino, 2017).

For our analysis, we approached the data with a micro-level transmodal narrative analysis, using an ethnographic angle. When analyzing the video, we focused initially on the first complexity of transmodalities that Hawkins (2018) underlined: the intertwined nature of modes. We adopted different approaches to viewing it so as to minimize the possibility of privileging certain semiotic and linguistic resources. For example, we sometimes muted the video to help focus on other modes beyond the spoken language. Sometimes we focused on specific sets of resources (e.g. language, artifacts, or color) to detect nuances and make sense of the cues. We did, though, always start with and return to viewing the video, to ensure that we were analyzing the ensemble of modes holistically. In attempting to isolate and view different modes in different ways (i.e. muting sound), our goal was not to analyze each individually but rather to find ways to see what we may not have otherwise noticed. Even in viewing modes holistically, we understand that different modes may be privileged or more salient than others, and so to fully understand the ensemble of modes, and how they work together, it was helpful to view them both in isolation and in varied configurations together. By adopting various approaches rather than a predetermined set of protocols, we attempted to capture the nuances and fluidity of the resources as a way to deal with the complexity of the intertwined nature of modes in constructing narratives.

We used tools from multimodal analysis (Bezemer & Kress, 2016; Martinec & Salway, 2005), while also pushing to expand on how those tools may be used within a transmodal narrative analysis. Most multimodal analysis takes a micro-level approach to data that offers more of a taxonomy and accounting for the modality of meaning-making rather than looking beyond the micro-level to understand how broader discourses may shape meaning-making (Bezemer & Kress, 2016). Positioning (Bamberg, 1997) allowed us a tool to examine a further complexity of transmodalities: how context and culture influence meaning-making (Hawkins, 2018, Complexity #4). We were able to do this by looking at how youth position themselves in relation to the audience and how broader discourses of national identity, culture, and consumerism shaped meaning-making in their narratives.

Transmodal narrative analysis proved useful in this study to examine positioning and as a way to expand notions of both interactional narrative analysis and multimodal analysis. It also was useful in exploring some of the complexities of transmodal meaning-making, providing insights on the perceptions of the youth about the topic and on the understandings that were conveyed, interpreted, and negotiated in transnational communications.

Researching as an international team

While the video and online chats were analyzed by team members who were from a variety of backgrounds, including researchers from non-Vietnamese backgrounds who were located in the United States, emic views from the former site facilitator and youth (from the interview) added additional layers to clarify the three levels of positioning, and constantly challenged interpretations of all team members. As a group, since we came from different cultural backgrounds and perspectives, we constantly challenged each other in our meaning-making and used our own experiences with the modes to understand the interactions and positioning work being done in the narrative. For example, Bingjie tended to compare the Vietnamese cultural symbols presented in the video (e.g. the decorations, the characters) with the ones she was familiar with in Chinese contexts. Sometimes she also used her own experience growing up in China to make sense of the issue of urbanization and commodification. While doing so during the analysis, the team constantly commented on, supported, or challenged each other's views, which ultimately led to closer and more critical reflections on our own perceptions and positionality in the research. This process is crucial: it helps researchers to develop a critical eye in viewing, listening to, and analyzing the narratives and positioning, as also discussed in Hawkins (2018; this volume) and Ratanapraphart et al. (this volume).

All researcher positionalities bring with them tensions and complications, whether one is studying 'others' or 'her own kind', as Lee and Simon-Maeda (2006) have reminded us. Each positionality brings with it different constraints and allowances. Self-reflexivity on the part of the researchers is critical to understanding how understandings are filtered through their own experiences and perspectives. Working in a diverse group of researchers on this project allowed for a range of views and understandings to come from our interaction with the data.

When engaging in this approach, we developed a greater critical awareness in exploring the relationships between different cultures and developed a critical eye for cultural symbols, languages, and meanings as embedded within historical flows and global interaction. Rather than positioning cultural traditions and identities as fixed, the combination of group research and transmodal narrative analysis offered us a space to explore connections between some cultural elements and social discourses, as they are interactive and hybrid.

Conclusion

This chapter drew on a transmodal narrative analysis of one online video narrative about the Tết holiday to examine youth positioning and identity. Through our transmodal narrative analysis, we have shown how the Riverbank youth positioned themselves in relation to other groups and broader discourses in their video about the Tết holiday. At level one, they create a storyworld setting of an idealized national holiday and culture, with themselves playing ambassadors for this idealized national culture as part of a sequential ensemble. At the second level, they take the role of guides in relation to an imagined audience of foreigners. Other groups align to this positioning in the questions they post in response to the video. At the same time, the youth at level two also present themselves with complex and multiple positionalities, not only as cultural ambassadors to outsiders, but also as savvy, fun filmmakers through their 'behind-the-scenes' segment. Finally, the positionality of the youth as embodying larger discourses of a unified Vietnamese national identity, and consumerism as a way to celebrate the holiday, align with their identities at both level one and two to give better understanding of the depth of positionality expressed transmodally in the narrative.

By connecting three major theoretical frameworks around narrative, identity, and transmodality, we were able to investigate the complexity of analyzing transmodal online data and making sense of narrative positioning. Applying Bamberg's (1997, 2004) three-level analytical framework and drawing on a team-based, reflectively-focused transmodal narrative analytical processes, our analysis emphasizes how semiotic modes (e.g. images, music, spoken narratives, and text) are orchestrated such that they convey certain messages, present certain images, and index certain discourses and ideologies within a narrative framework of meaning-making.

Notes

(1) All names of people and places are pseudonyms to protect the privacy of research participants.
(2) All transcribed excerpts are verbatim from the spoken language of the youth in the video.

References

Adami, E. (2009) 'We/YouTube': Exploring sign-making in video-interaction. *Visual Communication* 8 (4), 379–399.
Adami, E. (2015) What I can (re) make out of it. *Participation in Public and Social Media Interactions* 256, 233–257.
Agha, A. (2003) The social life of cultural value. *Language and Communication* 23, 231–273.
Armour, W.S. (2004) Becoming a Japanese language learner, user, and teacher: Revelations from life history research. *Journal of Language, Identity, and Education* 3 (2), 101–125.
Bamberg, M. (1997) Positioning between structure and performance. *Journal of Narrative and Life History* 7, 335–342.
Bamberg, M. (2004) Narrative discourse and identities. In J.C. Meister, T. Kindt, W. Schernus and M. Stein (eds) *Narratology beyond Literary Criticism* (pp. 213–237). Berlin: Walter de Gruyter.

Bamberg, M. and Georgakopoulou, A. (2008) Small stories as a new perspective in narrative and identity analysis. *Text & Talk* 28 (3), 377–396.
Barkhuizen, G. (2009) An extended positioning analysis of a pre-service teacher's better life small story. *Applied Linguistics* 31 (2), 282–300.
Barkhuizen, G., Benson, P. and Chik, A. (2013) *Narrative Inquiry in Language Teaching and Learning Research*. New York: Routledge.
Bateman, J. and Schmidt, K.H. (2013) *Multimodal Film Analysis: How Films Mean*. New York: Routledge.
Bernal, D., Burciaga, R. and Flores Carmona, J. (2012) Chicana/Latina testimonios: Mapping the methodological, pedagogical, and political. *Equity & Excellence in Education* 45 (3), 363–372.
Bezemer, J. and Kress, G. (2016) *Multimodality, Learning and Communication: A Social Semiotic Frame*. New York: Routledge.
Blommaert, J. (2005) *Discourse: A Critical Introduction*. Cambridge: Cambridge University Press
Bruner, J. (1991) The narrative construction of reality. *Critical Inquiry* 18 (1), 1–21.
Bruner, J. (1997) A narrative model of self-construction. *Annals of the New York Academy of Sciences* 1, 145–161.
Bucholtz, M. (1999) 'Why be normal?': Language and identity practices in a community of nerd girls. *Language in Society* 28 (2), 203–223.
Burn, A. (2016) The kineikonic mode: Towards a multimodal approach to moving image media. In C. Jewitt (ed.) *The Routledge Handbook of Multimodal Analysis* (pp. 375–385). New York: Routledge.
Butler, J. (1990) *Gender Trouble: Feminism and the Subversion of Identity*. New York: Routledge.
Cervantes-Soon, C.G. (2017) *Juárez Girls Rising: Transformative Education in Times of Dystopia*. Minneapolis: University of Minnesota Press.
Cervantes-Soon, C.G. (2012) Testimonios of life and learning in the borderlands: Subaltern Juárez girls speak. *Equity & Excellence in Education* 45 (3), 373–391.
De Fina, A. (2009) Narratives in interview – The case of accounts: For an interactional approach to narrative genres. *Narrative Inquiry* 19 (2), 233–258.
De Fina, A. (2013) Positioning level 3: Connecting local identity displays to macro social processes. *Narrative Inquiry* 23 (1), 40–61.
De Fina, A. and Georgakopoulou, A. (2015) *The Handbook of Narrative Analysis*. Chichester: Wiley-Blackwell.
De Fina, A. and Perrino, S. (2017) Storytelling in the digital age: New challenges. *Narrative Inquiry* 27 (2), 209–216. DOI: 10.1075/ni.27.2.01def.
De Fina, A. and Perrino, S. (eds) (2019) *Storytelling in the Digital World*. Philadelphia: John Benjamins Publishing Company.
Delgado, R. (2000) Storytelling for oppositionists and others: A plea for narrative. In R. Delgado and J. Stefancic (eds) *Critical Race Theory: The Cutting Edge* (2nd edn, pp. 60–70). Philadelphia: Temple University Press.
Duff, P.A. and Uchida, Y. (1997) The negotiation of teachers' sociocultural identities and practices in postsecondary EFL classrooms. *TESOL Quarterly* 31 (3), 451–486.
Georgakopoulou, A. (2007) *Small Stories, Interaction and Identities*. Amsterdam: John Benjamins Publishing.
Halbwachs, M. (1992) *On Collective Memory*. Chicago, IL: University of Chicago Press.
Halliday, M.A.K. and Matthiessen, C. (2014 [1985]) *An Introduction to Functional Grammar*. New York: Routledge.
Halverson, E.R., Bass, M. and Woods, D. (2012) The process of creation: A novel methodology for analyzing multimodal data. *The Qualitative Report* 17 (Article 21), 1–27.
Hawkins, M.R. (2018) Transmodalities and transnational encounters: Fostering critical cosmopolitan relations. *Applied Linguistics* 39 (1), 55–77.

Higgins, C., Furukawa, G. and Lee, H. (2016) Resemiotizing the metapragmatics of Konglish and Pidgin on YouTube. In S. Leppänen, E. Westinen and S. Kytölä (eds) *Social Media Discourse: (Dis)identifications and Diversities* (pp. 310–334). New York: Taylor and Francis.

Holland, D.C., Lachicotte Jr, W., Skinner, D. and Cain, C. (2001) *Identity and Agency in Cultural Worlds*. Cambridge, MA: Harvard University Press.

Jewitt, C., Bezemer, J. and O'Halloran, K. (2016) *Introducing Multimodality*. New York: Routledge.

Kress, G. (2016) What is mode? In C. Jewitt (ed.) *The Routledge Handbook of Multimodal Analysis* (pp. 60–75). New York: Routledge.

Lee, E. and Simon-Maeda, A. (2006) Racialized research identities in ESL/EFL research. *TESOL Quarterly* 40 (3), 573–594.

Martinec, R. and Salway, A. (2005) A system for image–text relations in new (and old) media. *Visual Communication* 4 (3), 337–371.

Matwick, K. and Matwick, K. (2020) Bloopers and backstage talk on TV cooking shows. *Text & Talk* 40 (1), 49–74.

Norton, B. (2013) *Identity and Language Learning: Extending the Conversation* (2nd edn). Bristol: Multilingual Matters.

Norton, B. and Toohey, K. (2011) Identity, language learning, and social change. *Language Teaching* 44 (4), 412–446.

O'Halloran, K.L., Tan, S. and E, Marissa K.L. (2015) Multimodal analysis for critical thinking. *Learning, Media and Technology* 42 (2), 147–170.

O'Halloran, K.L., Tan, S., Wignell, P., Bateman, J.A., Pham, D.S., Grossman, M. and Moere, A.V. (2016) Interpreting text and image relations in violent extremist discourse: A mixed methods approach for big data analytics. *Terrorism and Political Violence* 31 (3), 454–474.

Page, R., Harper, R. and Frobenius, M. (2013) From small stories to networked narrative: The evolution of personal narratives in Facebook status updates. *Narrative Inquiry* 23 (1), 192–213.

Perrino, S. (2017) Recontextualizing racialized stories on YouTube. *Narrative Inquiry* 27 (2), 261–285.

Ritchie, J.S. and Wilson, D.E. (2000) *Teacher Narrative as Critical Inquiry: Rewriting the Script*. New York: Teachers' College Press.

Somers, M.R. (1994) The narrative constitution of identity: A relational and network approach. *Theory and Society* 23 (5), 605–649.

van Lier, L. (2008) The ecology of language learning and sociocultural theory. In N. Hornberger (ed.) *Encyclopedia of Language and Education* (pp. 53–65). New York: Springer.

Vásquez, C. (2011) TESOL, teacher identity, and the need for 'small story' research. *TESOL Quarterly* 45 (3), 535–545.

Weedon, C. (1987) *Feminist Practice and Poststructuralist Theory*. London: Blackwell.

Xu, F. (2006) Comparing kitchen god worship between ethnical Chinese and ethnical Vietnamese. *Southeast Asian Studies* 3, 87–91.

Zembylas, M. (2003) Emotions and teacher identity: A poststructural perspective. *Teachers and Teaching* 9 (3), 213–238.

7 Critical Cosmopolitanism and Sustainable Education: Primary Educator Perspectives from Uganda and the United States

Sara J. Goldberg and Sarah Nazziwa

Introduction

As we move through the 21st century, education is at a crossroad. There often exists a juxtaposition, rather than a synergy, between standards-based, college and career-ready curricula and 21st-century learning skills. Furthermore, definitions and interpretations of 21st-century learning characteristics are dependent upon those leading the charge. As academic innovation advocate Ken Robinson put it, 'Current systems of education […] were developed to meet the needs of a former age. Reform is not enough: they need to be transformed' (Robinson, n.d., as cited in Assadourian, 2017: 130).

This chapter provides perspectives and experiences from two primary school educators who each facilitate a Global StoryBridges (GSB) site, one from Uganda and one from the United States, on the education of diverse learners in the 21st century. We address the question: How might education be transformed to move beyond the four walls of the classroom? Through transnational learning opportunities like those found in the program GSB, this chapter explores how even young learners' educational contexts can respond to globalization through developing global understandings and relationships, supporting the linguistic and cultural backgrounds of all students, and building on local strengths and needs that provide a nuanced approach to international humanitarian and education efforts. Additionally, it provides a space for a complete educator paradigm shift that changes how we approach and structure education, which has the potential to impact the entire educational landscape in its current forms.

Literature Review

The challenges in 21st-century education

Stakeholders and educators in K-12 and higher education increasingly recognize the need for educational change, but contestation exists around how to define and support development of skills for 21st-century learners. 'Whilst it has become in some ways a catch-all phrase that tends to stand in for a collection of ideas that may vary from site to site, the "21st-century learner" is also associated quite literally with a particular "brand" in many of its recent articulations' (Williams *et al.*, 2013: 794). This is tied up with the corporatization of education in a neoliberal era. While numerous publications and organizations exist to 'support' educators in implementing skill development necessary for a globalized world, the reality is that we live in a society often defined by economically-driven motives marked by post-industrial production and marketing (Raworth, 2017). There is a 'relentless corporatisation of education policy, schooling and the "21st century learner" globally' (Williams *et al.*, 2013: 799).

Hawkins claims that there is a trend in education worldwide to provide packaged curricula and materials, yet the most effective educational approaches involve responding to the 'specifics of students and places, rather than as imported or imposed curriculum and pedagogy' (Hawkins, 2014: 109). Luke writes that while there have been attempts to create pre-packaged, single-step materials to deliver critical learning opportunities in the classroom, there is 'no formula for "doing" this type of learning' (Luke, 2000: 453–4). Equity, engagement and responsiveness must drive decisions on pedagogies, learning and outcomes in order to make impactful change in educational environments.

Learning sites too often look for guidance from large-scale organizations and curriculum companies focused on a one-size-fits-all approach, versus building a system that supports local needs and assets. Sund and Öhman (2011) note that one of the challenges with organizational giants like UNESCO or the World Bank is that, while they promote a specific set of goals aligned with values that speak to bettering humanity and our planet, concerns have been raised regarding homogenization and the necessity for localized interpretations of a community's complexities. In order to develop a sense of intrinsic, universal values, they suggest a cosmopolitan perspective that considers the tension between the universal and the particular.

Finally, there are conflicting fields of thought surrounding globalization and 21st-century learning. From one perspective, including in the US, there is the push toward 'college and career ready' (Common Core State Standards Initiatives, 2019), with an emphasis on standards and accountability. One indicator is the strong and growing emphasis on accountability. High-stakes testing is now worldwide, including in both the US and Uganda (focal locations for our research), driven in part by global development organizations. Placing an emphasis on data does provide a snapshot of trends in student growth, and sheds light on ways to better support students through analysis of quantifiable information. Caution must be taken, though, to avoid a mechanistic approach that may result from a narrowed vision in which teachers are framed as 'providers', principals as 'managers', parents as 'employers', and students as 'consumers' (Sterling, 2001).

Williams *et al.* (2013) point out that the main differences in the specifications of the '21st-century learner' seem to turn on the weight given to economic versus democratic or equity imperatives. In a recent examination of the shifting education system in Australia, there were some perhaps unsurprising observations made between corporate sites and government education systems. While corporate sites focused on the desired self-managing, self-educating, entrepreneurial, neoliberal characteristics of the '21st-century learner', documents generated by government education systems such as those in Australia, the UK and Scotland gave equal weight to civic and social capabilities, with both commitments and competencies relating to equity and social justice. The presence of both individualist and collectivist perspectives provides evidence of the competing discourses regarding the '21st-century learner'. How the tension between the two is to be negotiated and managed practically in curriculum and pedagogy is rarely discussed (Williams *et al.*, 2013).

One clear way that '21st-century learning' has been taken up is an acknowledgement of the importance of technology in learning. In an effort to address the changing needs of the classroom and beyond, some schools, especially in 'developed' countries, are often equipped with the latest gadgets, but not necessarily with the methods to transform learning environments. In many US schools, initiatives toward 1:1 technology have become commonplace, providing even the youngest learners with access. Yet the fact remains that there is the issue of access, especially in communities of poverty both within and outside of the US. In Uganda, for example, where Sarah, the second author of this chapter, teaches, computers have been placed in a small number of city schools by the government ministry of education (the Uganda Ministry of Sports and Education), NGOs, religious organizations and international donors, but many teachers and students, especially those who live in rural areas – where the majority of Ugandans live without electricity – have never encountered a computer.

As educators, we consistently see the challenges and pressures teachers face to address curriculum, standards, and data-driven assessments, all within the very compartmentalized structure of the traditional school day. As Sterling notes, there are around 60 million teachers in the world, with very few experienced in or given the autonomy to create a re-imagined classroom context, one that is multifaceted and speaks to a 21st-century society – one of complexities and interconnectivity. The challenge is that, even if teachers are provided the tools to create environments that are more transformative in nature, it is less likely that educators are provided with the professional development to gain an understanding of the deeper conceptual or pedagogical foundations (Sterling, 2001: 70).

The 21st-century learner and global learning

How can we move from 'ticky-tacky' curriculum and instruction 'that all look just the same', to preparing youth for an 'increasingly globalized, intercultural, and multimodal world' (Shannon, 2013: 60)? The composite of a 21st-century learner involves a complex set of interwoven skills. What does that look like?

There have been many efforts in Western education to increase the importance of STEM (Science, Technology, Engineering and Mathematics) or STEAM (with the inclusion of the Arts) initiatives for diverse learners. Collaborative work environments, project-based or problem-based learning and critical thinking have also become buzzwords. While the 'Framework for 21st-Century Learning', developed by the (US-based) National Education Association, outlined 18 different skills that are important to student learning and development in a globalized society, four overarching skills emerged as 'The 4Cs of Education': *critical thinking, communication, collaboration* and *creativity* (National Education Association, 2012).

The implementation of these four skills in authentic and innovative ways is the key to moving beyond 21st-century learning skills as pawns in the 'business of education'. While true 21st-century learning contexts may encompass standards-based, college and career-ready curricula, they must also encourage global relationships, civic engagement, and critical literacy skills. Too often, standardization correlates with rote methods and uniformity. Schooling in the 21st century can and should address localized expectations for learning that often come in the form of specific educational standards but must also reach beyond these in a transformative and multifaceted nature. Additionally, they must not only prepare students for post-secondary education but also equip them for navigating our current and future interconnected world – replete with environmental, social, and economic complexities.

In a shift toward enhancing global education initiatives, *Global Awareness* is listed as an important theme to be interwoven across the curricular areas within the 'Partnership for 21st Century Learning' framework (Partnership for 21st Century Learning, 2015). This definition of global awareness includes these objectives:

- Use 21st-century skills to understand and address global issues.
- Learn from and work collaboratively with individuals representing diverse cultures, religions, and lifestyles in a spirit of mutual respect and open dialogue in personal, work, and community contexts.

- Understand other nations and cultures, including the use of non-English languages.

From an international perspective, the United Nations Sustainable Development Goal #4 aims to 'ensure inclusive and quality education for all and promote lifelong learning' (UN Sustainable Development Goals, 2019). The goal is:

> By 2030, ensure that all learners will acquire the knowledge and skills needed to promote sustainable development, including, among others, through education for sustainable development and sustainable lifestyles, human rights, gender equality, promotion of a culture of peace and non-violence, global citizenship, and appreciation of cultural diversity and of culture's contribution to sustainable development. (UN Sustainable Development Goals, 2019)

In recent decades, research, efforts and goals have begun to recognize the need to address society's interconnectivity that has emerged from the convergence of globalization and technological advances in more nuanced ways, providing a heterogenized approach to developing the aforementioned broadened skills and perspectives. Many educational institutions, especially in the United States, have the power and reach to either further the status quo or renew the vision and practices of education in previously unimagined ways. Work done in GSB, which integrates transmodal approaches supported by a critical cosmopolitan framework, provides one model, albeit an out-of-school one, of a transformative context that develops academic rigor and a skillset that develops a sense of civic responsibility and global citizenship.

Transforming Education: Critical Cosmopolitan and Transmodal Approaches

How can a systems approach to learning, one that entails both a big picture perspective and attention to patterns, parts and processes across disciplines (Assadourian, 2017), draw on research in the areas of transmodalities and critical cosmopolitanism? And how might this modernize curriculum and educational opportunities to fit our changing times, abilities and resources?

Steven Sterling (2001) writes that education that is participatory, learner-constructed and meaningful provides a space that values 'diversity, relative autonomy, community and integrity' and draws out elements of 'differentiation, empowerment, self-worth, critical thinking, cooperation, creativity and participation' (2001: 55). A critical cosmopolitan framework offers a foundational approach to creating a learning context that encompasses these attributes. Various theorists have looked to cosmopolitanism, an ancient and philosophical perspective, to deal with our world's multidimensional challenges and to address the relationship between universal claims and varying contexts of diversity (Öhman & Sund, 2011). Globalization is an inevitable force, infiltrating homes, schools and communities in both developing and developed countries alike. And, while the impact of this process certainly can bring out negative consequences for humanity and our earth, how it is addressed makes all the difference. Hawkins writes:

> Although cosmopolitanism is taken up in various ways and ascribed various meanings within diverse disciplines, I differentiate it from globalization (following Appiah, 2006, and in literacy studies, Hull, Stornaiuolo, & Sahni, 2010) through understanding it to refer to how humans encounter each other within forces of globalization. (2014: 91–2)

Therefore, it is imperative that education not only includes those aspects that Sterling (2001) laid out, but moves beyond the physical classroom to develop transnational, global interactions. As Hawkins (2014: 97) explains:

> It is the cosmopolitan aspect of education – the engagement with global others in service of an expansion of students' 'skills, competences, and knowledges' (following Luke), but also for an expansion of creativity, imaginings, openness, and affiliations – that is key to the educational endeavor if the goal is to create citizens of the world.

Öhman and Sund (2011) suggest that a critical cosmopolitan perspective turns toward an inquiry into the ethical grounds of our shared responsibility by recognizing that values are connected to those who *are* connected – through both community and a local context. Learning occurs through alternative ways of thinking that develop when local/global interactions are allowed to flourish.

Furthering this aspect of an expanded community of learners, Hawkins (2018) describes the necessity for these interactions to occur, and to be understood, through transmodalities. As Hawkins outlines, 'transmodalities' acknowledge 'the fluid integration, and mutual informativity, of repertoires of resources in meaning-making processes across local and global encounters and interactions in our globalized world' (2018: 56).

It is these cross-boundary collaborations (transdisciplinary, transmodal and transnational) that are pivotal in developing a sense of global citizenship for both educators and learners alike. What might a 21st-century learning environment look like that includes a critical cosmopolitan framework and transmodal learning and communication approaches? Is it possible, particularly in a primary education context?

Settings

Global StoryBridges

We need, briefly, to highlight some key features of GSB, in order to provide some context for our discussion of learning in our project sites.

GSB is a project that currently has 16 sites around the world. All are located in poor communities. Some, as in the US site discussed here, are comprised of mostly immigrant youth, and others, as in the Ugandan site discussed here, are in communities where youth participants and their families have lived for many generations. All participants, though, are English learners, whether because they live in communities where the local language is not English, or because they live in English-speaking communities but they (and/or their families) come from other places.

Each site is comprised of local youth and an adult facilitator. Some sites are located in community-based venues, others in schools, but meetings are held outside of formal instructional time. The process, in brief, is that youth are tasked with creating digital stories of their lives and communities. All steps in the production process are done collaboratively within the site, and then the finished video is posted to the GSB website. Youth in other global sites then watch it, discuss it together (within their sites) and post comments and questions to the youth who made the video. In this way, the youth learn together about each other and the world.

One important component is that decisions are made by the youth, including the video topics, their content, the process of making them, the roles each youth has in that process, and the decision about what to post, with all tasks carried out by the youth. There is a facilitator, but this is a task-based, collaborative, dialogic learning process, and the facilitator is there to support the youth, not to formally 'teach' them.

This chapter highlights two sites that are both at the upper primary school level (with youth at approximately 4th to 5th grade), one in Uganda and one in the US, that participate in GSB. It illuminates the many positive educational aspects of a transnational digital project such as Global StoryBridges, versus a critical analysis of the project itself. Despite their differences, both sites' work illuminates the powerful outcomes that emerge from learning environments premised on critical cosmopolitan concepts that enable transmodal transnational interactions. It is important to remember that GSB is an out-of-school program, and not part of formal school curriculum. Still, although there is no recipe for what this might look like in every context, we can glean much from the evidence that has been acquired through participation in this project by two primary school teachers (the chapter authors, in the US and Uganda respectively, who serve as facilitators in GSB sites), and our students.

Our findings have implications for classroom as well as out-of-school teaching and learning.

Ugandan context

In Uganda, GSB meetings are held in after-school times, and sometimes on weekends, in a community-based government-aided day school that serves students from Kindergarten through Grade 7. The school is located in a small village on the outskirts of a large town. The people in the community have different (Ugandan) ethnic backgrounds, although the majority are Baganda. Luganda is the language spoken widely. Most of the students in the school come from within the community; all are students from disadvantaged socioeconomic backgrounds. Primary teaching methods are mostly 'traditional', with a teacher-fronted classroom in which students receive information from the teacher and take notes. There are currently eight students working with GSB (although the numbers have varied over the years, and usually there are 12), and they are between 11 and 13 years of age. These children only get access to technology at school, using the equipment provided by GSB, as there is no other technology in the community or in their school. They all speak only Luganda at home and within the community. They are not introduced to English until they are in school, where they all learn it because the language of schooling in Uganda is English. Because there are mandates for local language instruction through Grade 3, these students have been immersed in English education since Grade 4, and they are currently in Grade 6. They have lived their entire lives within the community and have never traveled to any other part of the country or of the world.

US context

The US GSB site is located in a primary school in a mid-sized community located in the upper Midwest. The school district of which they are a part is culturally and linguistically diverse. Project work occurs in an after-school context of an elementary school where the majority of students come from families of poverty. Over half of the student body identifies as one or more race other than white, and linguistic backgrounds include Hmong, Spanish, Chinese, Laotian, Teluga, Thai and Vietnamese. Students in GSB are English language learners with diverse interests and identities. There are currently 12 participating students. Students have family ties to Mexico and China, along with countries in South America and Southeast Asia. While these students have global connections, many have not experienced much mobility beyond their local community. Nonetheless, their identities have been shaped by these global affiliations, as many still communicate with family outside of the United States through the use of technology. While their home access to technology varies and may be limited, there is a one-to-one technology initiative within their school district, so students utilize technology in a school setting on a daily basis.

Discussion

One of the primary goals of GSB is for students to engage in a project that is pertinent to their lives. Students learn best in a space that is meaningful and encompasses where they live, learn, and play (Wheeler et al., 2008). The following discussion shines light on this, and examines how learning contexts like GSB can provide a critical cosmopolitan, transmodal educational experience, thus having a profound impact on students' emotional, social and academic development.

Students' Perspectives on GSB

US

Over the course of the years as a facilitator for GSB, students have voiced enjoyment about the opportunity to make new friends, to meet students in other parts of the world, to gain cultural knowledge, to have choice in what they represent to their global peers and to have the opportunity to explore their communities. Some themes have also emerged in terms of what students feel is important to share with global peers through their videos, such as the following: family-owned or culturally connected businesses; events or places connected to cultural or linguistic backgrounds; traditions; school life; the environment; and seasonal activities. Students' pride in their racial, linguistic and cultural backgrounds has emerged through their participation in GSB.

Students' responses to videos posted by their global peers have provided further insight into their perspectives about schooling and learning. One particular conversation reiterated the need for change in academic settings. Following a video posted by a peer group from Mexico, in which most students articulated a sense of happiness in regard to their feelings about school, US students shared a different perspective. When asked about their feelings about school, some students stated that 'It is boring', and that 'the teachers do a lot of the talking while all we do is sit'. They also voiced that if teachers perceive that they are not paying attention, often a misconception with English learning students, then the teachers will call on them, furthering their embarrassment or feelings of inability.

In response to what students do like, they noted gym, lunch and recess as favorite parts of their day. Notably, those aspects of the day involve movement, interaction and choice. When asked to expand upon academic areas that they most enjoyed, students responded that they liked math because they could figure out and solve problems, which speaks to critical thinking. Students also noted enjoying writing time because it involved different projects, and the ability to write about what was important to them. This addresses the need for creativity and the importance of tapping into students' knowledge and identities. Students expressed pride and confidence about being in GSB, and shared particular enjoyment about expanding their knowledge of cultures and having an opportunity to explore their community. One student noted, 'Being in Global StoryBridges has changed me from when I first began. I got smarter!' As UNESCO delineated in their goals set forth for learning programs that encourage the development of lifelong skills, imperative is the combination of creativity and critical thinking, oral and written communication, collaboration and cooperation, conflict management, decision-making, problem-solving and planning, and practical citizenship (UNESCO, 2007). GSB offers these to students.

Following the viewing of a video from Uganda (a different Ugandan site/community than that of Sarah, the second author) titled *Girl Child Education*, US students had a conversation that further spoke to the importance of learning environments like GSB. One US student began the conversation by noting that the girl in the video voiced wanting to go to school so that she could follow her dreams. She stated that she is not like other kids in that she wants to go to school.

Many students in my site agreed that their families felt happy about the opportunities afforded to them in attending school. They also noted that there were commonalities with Gloria – the girl in the Ugandan video – in their aspirations following their K-12 experience. They mentioned wanting to lighten the load for their own families. One student voiced that families in the US struggle with money and that taking care of one's family is a concern for many. US students saw value in school and voiced their appreciation regarding the opportunities in attending so that they can learn, have friends, and be able to support or help their families in the future by obtaining a job following their schooling.

Several US participants noted that school is important to achieving their goal of learning English for the following reasons:

- 'Getting to meet people'
- 'You can return to your country of origin and have understanding of English for travel'
- 'It is easier to communicate within your community'
- 'The majority of people speak English and almost everyone knows English, so that is why we choose this language'
- 'I felt like I was forgetting my home language and wanted to keep learning Hmong so that I could help translate for people'
- 'I feel happy knowing more than one language because I can talk with my friends who speak the same language as me'

They added that there is comfort in knowing one can explain everything fully in the language your family speaks.

When asked how Global StoryBridges is different from school during the day, one student noted being able to learn about different cultures more than school allowed. Another also added that she liked getting to learn more about her own culture. Finally, one student mentioned that GSB and school are similar in that you get to learn things, but that school is sometimes boring, while GSB is 'super fun to be in'.

Uganda

Students in the Uganda site view GSB as a unique opportunity for them because they are the only ones in the entire school who get access to technology and the internet. Participating in the video-making process has enabled them to build confidence to explore and become competent users of the different forms of technology, such as computers and videocameras, provided by GSB. They are aware of the importance of technology in the 21st century, and eager to learn technology skills. In comparing GSB to school, here is what they said: 'In GSB we make our decisions and do what we feel like, which is not the case in school. We express our views and ideas freely without fear of being laughed at or even shut down by anyone.' This speaks directly to the 4Cs: *critical thinking, communication, collaboration* and *creativity* (National Education Association, 2012), and the ability of a project like GSB to provide opportunities for students to learn and leverage the 4C skills in ways that schools may not.

One of the tasks the children have for the project is to identify themes for their videos. They know that the videos are supposed to represent their lives and communities to their global peers. In our site, children have chosen to focus on places that are important to them, such as their school and the village market, but mostly on activities that they enjoy or that are done as part of life in their community. They have, for example, made videos about netball (a game girls play), cooking, and dancing – all representing activities they enjoy – and also about sanitation, farming, making brooms and drip irrigation – all of which are traditional within the community way of life. At one point, because a US site (different than the one focused on in this chapter) asked about language, they made a video called *Luganda Our Language*, introducing their global peers to their language. They displayed pride in their language, multilingual skills, and heritage.

Students in our site have said that GSB has helped them in the following ways:

- *Improved spelling.* As they ask questions about videos posted by their global peers and respond to questions asked of them in response to videos they post, they want to make sure that they type the correct words.
- *Improved listening skills.* As they watch the videos to understand what their peers are expressing, they must listen carefully to different varieties of English and different accents than those that they hear in school.
- *Improved speaking skills.* English is the medium of communication in the project; however, Luganda is widely spoken in school. While schooling is in English starting in 4th grade, the predominance of teacher-fronted, lecture-driven teaching, where students' role is to listen and take notes, denies them opportunities to practise speaking in English. GSB students practise speaking English while holding

discussions about the videos they are creating and about the videos posted by others. Further, the videos they create and post must be primarily in English so that other youth around the world can understand them – English is the lingua franca of the project. So they are held accountable for incorporating English into the multimodal online communications.

This view of learning, with its focus on discrete language skills, reflects how teaching and learning are perceived and taken up in the Ugandan educational environment, and equally, the importance of mastering English. These language skills, as well as those of the 4Cs reflected in the earlier quote, juxtapose formal schooling in Uganda with the environment and engagement processes of GSB, demonstrating how this project enables 21st-century learning in ways not accomplished in Ugandan government schools. In both the Ugandan and US sites, albeit for different reasons, students are clear that they are more comfortable, and less shut down, in communicating their thoughts and ideas than they are in their school classrooms.

Students in Uganda further noted that school and English are important because you learn to communicate with other people from different parts of the world and to continue with education and obtain a job. Thus, similarly with their US peers, they believe that schooling and learning are important to their futures, although in the Ugandan context the technology skills alone that they gain from the project are enough to ensure employment.

One concept that matters here is place. Hawkins (2014) claims that place mediates what can be seen, understood and learned. This is evident in the differences in how the students in each site view learning. Additionally, students in the US site mentioned learning about cultures – both the cultures of others and also their own. The US students were a diverse group, with many being immigrants. Thus culture, as an important part of their perceptions of themselves and others, was foregrounded in their thinking and perceptions. The Ugandan students live in a relatively monocultural community. Everyone shares a sense of place, language and ethnicity. For them, cultural differences were not as readily noticed until their attention was drawn to differences by participants from other sites and places, which enabled them, as in the example of the language lesson video, to demonstrate pride in their linguistic and cultural identities, whereas the US students from the start explicitly chose to make videos focused directly on theirs.

As a final note, the Ugandan students directly noted that if learning environments like GSB were taken into school, where they would then be free to express their ideas and views in their formal learning experiences, learning would be fun. This aligns with the US youths' views of GSB as fun.

Cultivating a Transmodal, Critical Cosmopolitan Education

Uganda

Modernizing school contexts through the utilization of technology within the learning environment has engaged learners in a positive way. There has also been a sense of renewed motivation on the part of both teachers and learners, and the development of more advanced pedagogical methodologies, which is engaging learners and shifting the role of educators from teacher to facilitator, thus promoting overall improvements in learning. GSB is providing an opportunity for students to acquire computer skills. The project computers are the only computers in the school, so it has improved access for the student population. The opportunity of accessing the computers, technology and the internet has helped the students who are part of the project look at education in a different way, despite a perspective of some parents – that is prevalent in the community – that education is a waste of time and money. The project has served to open students' eyes to new possibilities, because of new understandings of education and because they come to feel that they have shown success in education, and a direct outcome is that some have continued their educational careers beyond primary school in different institutions. To illustrate the importance of this, less than 25% of all children in Uganda attend secondary school (Forwerck, 2017), and only 40% are literate by the end of their primary schooling (UNICEF, 2019). The children who have participated in GSB attribute their success of pursuing further education to their participation in the Global StoryBridges project.

Through connecting with other students in the different global sites, the students develop a sense of belonging to a large world community, and they develop global awareness as they come to understand and appreciate the cultures and different ways of life of different people in the world. A sense of teamwork, cooperation, confidence and respect of others' views is strengthened among students as they discuss what to share with their peers in the different sites. The students acquire new skills and knowledge together as they explore the technology, which they integrate into their learning.

This demonstrates the power of a critical cosmopolitan education, where students engage with others from stances of openness, curiosity and equity, learning about and building connections with global others as they come to understand others and themselves as global citizens. It also demonstrates the power of transmodalities, as students use all of the semiotic modes made available through the technology and literacy tools they have to represent, convey and interpret meanings of themselves and others. If more projects existed like GSB in different places around the world, particularly in poor communities and communities that place little value on education, this would benefit curriculum development and overall educational spaces, leading to a true instantiation of 21st century education.

US

The Global StoryBridges project takes on the themes of globalization and expands global learning. The bedrock of this project involves participant-centered, transmodal learning opportunities within a critical cosmopolitan framework. Participants in this project utilize traditional communication strategies through speaking and writing, while also expanding their creativity through video creation and representations from start to finish. By experiencing this process, students have the opportunity to select what they feel is important to share, decide upon video content, utilize technological tools to record and edit their work, and further this learning by including elements such as music creation by navigating music production tools. It is evident that these transmodal opportunities not only support academic learning and encourage creativity, but students display confidence and an acknowledgement and appreciation of their unique identities. Even for students like mine, who have varied access to technology in their homes and classrooms, it supports the development of technological literacy and representational skills through relevant and collaborative methods, something they otherwise may not experience.

Throughout the GSB process, participants develop communicative competence and social skills as they collaborate and make ongoing decisions with their peers. While students noted not knowing everyone in the group when we began the year, they have articulated that our group feels 'like a family' where they feel safe and supported. This, in turn, has developed a community where students' voices and ideas are received without judgement, and builds a sense of belonging and kinship. All of this learning speaks to what is occurring at a local level (which also embodies critical cosmopolitanism, especially among these diverse youth), but there is much happening at a global level, as well.

Amplified learning ensues through the shared work done with their global peers. Students navigate interactions and negotiate meanings through continued communication via the affordances of technology. More specifically, it speaks to the point Hawkins (2018: 65) makes about transmodal learning spaces in that:

> Transmodalities attends to meaning-making across the arc of transmodal communications, such that, while production and assemblage may be the starting point, the spaces and timescales traversed, as well as the contexts and processes of reception and negotiation, are given equal weight. And lastly, transmodalities references transcendence and transgression, where inequitable relations of power can be dismantled and reconfigured, affording equal access, value, and representation to all participants in transmodal interactions.

It is in these relationships with global peers that the true power lies. This program purveys what it is to be 21st century learning, as delineated above. It encapsulates the 4Cs of education within a space for cross-curricular, interdisciplinary connections to be made. Furthermore, it develops the sense of global awareness, as outlined by the *Partnership for 21st Century Learning*, and above all, provides a tangible example of how transformative learning can look and how an environment such as this can provide a model for achieving The United Nations Sustainable Development Goal 4 on education. This type of learning environment is a biome of sorts-replete with dimension and interrelation, illuminating imagination and possibility. Although it is clear that the learning and perceptions differ between Uganda and the US, educational goals, engagement in the project, and most of all the power of forging relations with global peers, is clear in each.

Educator Transformation through GSB

Uganda

From a Ugandan educator's perspective, facilitating GSB provided newfound computer and technology skills. Teaching methods shifted from viewing myself as a source of knowledge to that of facilitation, which has led to an increase in full participation of learners during daily lessons in my 6th grade classroom. For example, I used to do all of the talking and explanations while conducting lessons, not giving students a chance to take part. Students, as mentioned above, were expected only to take notes on the information I delivered. That is how I, and all Ugandan teachers, are trained to teach. Facilitating GSB transformed my lessons. They are now learner – centered; I teach through asking a few guiding questions that help students to generate and explore their ideas on any given topic. I give them time and space to discuss ideas together in open dialog in my classroom. GSB has provided tools in research, as well; I am able to learn from the project researchers and other facilitators, thereby continuing to improve my facilitation and teaching skills. Therefore, the ways in which I teach – my curriculum development and pedagogies – reflect the development of 21st century learning skills and updated content that is multidimensional. The components of the curriculum need to be closely coupled with the 4Cs to support student learning, and to help them think critically, communicate effectively, collaborate with diverse peers, solve complex problems, adopt a global mindset and engage with technology.

US

As a facilitator for Global StoryBridges, I have grown as an educator in a number of ways. It has provided me an opportunity to see the impact technology can have when implemented in creative, authentic ways. It has offered me an improved skillset with technology, as well as a new vision.

A concern that emerges with increased utilization of technology is that meaningful, interactive, collaborative work may be taken away. Global StoryBridges has countered that by proving technology to be the tool that enables endless possibilities for meaningful, interactive, collaborative work with an expansive local/global peer group. I continue to develop my skills in facilitation, and my abilities to ask critical questions that further student dialogue.

While transnational projects are intended to create learning experiences that develop academic skills and cosmopolitan dispositions in students, an additional facet are the affordances in cross-cultural educator collaboration. Being a part of GSB has expanded my worldview greatly, but has also brought me a sense of closeness to communities, students and educators globally through the navigation of local systems and an emphasis on communicative and collaborative practices. This program has enabled some facilitators and researchers to participate in a transnational professional group in which we share experiences and research and develop facilitative strategies appropriate for local and globally connected contexts.

This has provoked me to look at curriculum from a different lens by encouraging me to not only critically examine content, but also to reframe and restructure existing curricula and learning opportunities to be cross-disciplinary, cross-cultural and globally-framed, and to push beyond traditional constructs in US classrooms that tend to further the status quo and inhibit the full potential of learning opportunities. It has enabled me to consider transnational opportunities as real possibilities during the regular school day. Finally, it has encouraged me to challenge myself by continuously thinking of learning environments as permeable and dynamic, thus creating a space in which the 4Cs of education may flourish and, most importantly, that supports students as learners and global citizens. Fazal Rizvi (2008: 29) writes:

> I believe that our focus ought to be on understanding the nature, scope and consequences of global transformations, rather than on some generalised principles of cosmopolitanism, global citizenship, or indeed the skills required in the global economy. In this way, I want to argue that learning about interconnectivity itself needs to become cosmopolitan.

And for me it has.

Conclusion: Implications for Schools and Classrooms

Cortese (2003) notes that, 'Students retain an estimated 80% of knowledge, skills, and values from active participation, in contrast to only 10% to 20% of what they hear or read' (as cited in Redman & Larson, 2011: 11). Contrary to the belief that only standardization leads to improved academic scores, research has proven that collaborative projects and problem-based activities have actually been associated with improved test scores as well, and they contribute to the development of competencies focused on sustainable education (Garrett & Roberson, 2008; Barron et al., 1998, as cited in Redman & Larson, 2011: 14).

We believe that there are implications from GSB that provide tenets for what a transmodal, critical cosmopolitan education might look like in school classrooms, and that these tenets would support the development of 21st-century skills and learning, while globalizing curriculum. They are:

- engagement with globally-framed projects that are culturally and linguistically responsive;
- development of critical literacy skills and global citizenship through locally-grounded initiatives that transcend global spaces;
- utilization of technological tools that explore everyday interactions and offer opportunities for negotiation of meanings (Hansen, 2010);
- a focus on peer relationships in a globally-oriented classroom;
- participation in project-based, cross-curricular learning through digital media.

Given the fact that outdated school structures persist everywhere, spaces for project-focused, inquiry-based learning are often isolated to after-school programming or weekend community service learning projects (Redman & Larson, 2011). Nonetheless, infusing approaches into the regular school day such as those found in GSB is achievable. One worthwhile goal of educators should be to develop curriculum that increases students' global perspectives and celebrates students' linguistic and cultural competencies even while connecting to curriculum, district and national goals, and standards.

References

Appiah, K.A. (2006) *Cosmopolitanism: Ethics in a World of Strangers*. London: Norton.
Assadourian, E. (2017) *EarthEd: Rethinking Education on a Changing Planet*. Washington, DC: Island Press.
Barron, B., Schwartz, D., Vye, N., Moore, A., Petrosino, A., Zech, L. and Bransford, J. (1998) Doing with understanding: Lessons from research on problem- and project-based learning. *The Journal of the Learning Sciences* 7 (3&4), 271–311.
Common Core State Standards Initiative (2019) See http://www.corestandards.org/ (accessed April 2021).
Cortese, A. (2003) The critical role of higher education in creating a sustainable future. *Planning for Higher Education* 31 (3), 15–22.
Forwerck, M. (2017) 10 important facts to know about education in Uganda. The Borgen Project. See https://borgenproject.org/10-facts-about-education-in-uganda/ (accessed Apil 2021).
Garrett, S. and Roberson, S. (2008) Systems thinking and students: Relationships, student achievement, and the curriculum. *AASA Journal of Scholarship and Practice* 5 (1), 21–26.

Hansen, D.T. (2010) Cosmopolitanism and education: A view from the ground. *Teachers College Record* 112 (1), 1–30.
Hawkins, M.R. (2014) Ontologies of place, creative meaning making and critical cosmopolitan education. *Curriculum Inquiry* 44 (1), 90–112.
Hawkins, M.R. (2018) Transmodalities and transnational encounters: Fostering critical cosmopolitan relations. *Applied Linguistics* 39 (1), 55–77.
Hull, G.A., Stornaiuolo, A. and Sahni, U. (2010) Cultural citizenship and cosmopolitan practice: Global youth communicate online. *English Education* 42 (4), 331–367.
Luke, A. (2000) Critical literacy in Australia: A matter of context and standpoint. *Journal of Adolescent & Adult Literacy* 43 (5), 448–461.
National Education Association (2012) Preparing 21st century students for a global society: An educator's guide to the 'Four Cs'. See http://www.nea.org/assets/docs/A-Guide-to-Four-Cs.pdf (accessed April 2021).
Partnership for 21st Century Learning (2015) P21 Framework Definitions. Batelle for Kids Frameworks & Resources. See http://static.battelleforkids.org/documents/p21/P21_Framework_Definitions_New_Logo_2015_9pgs.pdfRaworth, K. (2017) *Doughnut Economics: Seven Ways to think Like a 21st-Century Economist*. London: Chelsea Green Publishing.
Redman, E. and Larson, K. (2011) Educating for sustainability: Competencies & practices for transformative action. *Journal of Sustainability Education* 2 (March).
Rizvi, F. (2008) Epistemic virtues and cosmopolitan learning. *The Australian Educational Researcher* 35 (1), 17–35.
Shannon, P. (2013) *Closer Readings of the Common Core: Asking Big Questions about the English/Language Arts Standards*. Portsmouth NH: Heinemann.
Sterling, S. (2001) Sustainable education: Re-Visioning learning and change. *Schumacher Briefings*. Schumacher UK, CREATE Environment Centre, Seaton Road, Bristol, BS1 6XN, England.
Sund, L. and Öhman, J. (2011) Cosmopolitan perspectives on education and sustainable development: Between universal ideals and particular values. *Utbildning och Demokrati* 20 (1), 13–34.
UNESCO (2007) *Annual Report 2006: UNESCO Institute for Lifelong Learning*. Hamburg: UNESCO.
UNICEF (2019) Education: For Every Child, an Education. See https://www.unicef.org/uganda/what-we-do/education (accessed April 2021).
UN Sustainable Development Goals (2019) Sustainable Development Goal 4. See https://sustainabledevelopment.un.org/sdg4 (accessed April 2021).
Wheeler, G., Bergsman, K. and Thumlert, C. (2008) *Sustainable Design Project Teacher Manual*. Olympia, WA: Office of the Superintendent of Public Instruction.
Williams, C., Gannon, S. and Sawyer, W. (2013) A genealogy of the 'future': Antipodean trajectories and travels of the '21st century learner'. *Journal of Education Policy* 28 (6), 792–806.

8 Developing Decolonizing Pedagogies with Mexican Pre-Service 'English' Teachers

Mario E. López-Gopar, Vilma Huerta Cordova, William M. Sughrua and Edwin Nazaret León Jiménez

Introduction

During the last three decades in Mexico, 'literacy', 'English', and 'technology' have been sold as the panacea for personal and social *progress* as well as the *development* of a *more* competitive nation (Hernández-Zamora, 2010; López-Gopar, 2016). The two sources cited with regard to these three concepts (literacy, English and technology) speak to the narrow, technical, apolitical and colonial meanings attributed to these concepts by both political and educational actors. The italics applied to the terms 'progress', 'development' and 'more' speak to the modernity/coloniality discourses present in Mexico. Coloniality is the other side of modernity, the tale that emerged from the expansion of European capitalism in the Americas and other parts of the world, positioning European males' ways of being and knowing at the top of human hierarchy (Dussel, 2002; Mignolo, 2000; Quijano, 2007). Within the logic of modernity/coloniality, other people's ways of being and knowing are considered inferior. This leads to 'colonial difference', which holds that these 'other people' should aspire to be European and to strive to be *better* by climbing the modernity hierarchy (Mignolo, 2000).

As such, the colonial difference has a lasting impact, as seen for instance in literacy, English and technology. Literacy, first of all, has been regarded from an autonomous (Street, 2003) and Eurocentric perspective (Menezes de Sousa, 2003) privileging 'alphabetic' literacy over other modalities (López-Gopar, 2007) and thus rendering most Mexican people as 'illiterate' in worst-case scenarios or as 'non-readers' or 'educationally behind' in the best cases (Hernández-Zamora, 2009). Secondly, English has been discursively constructed as *the* language to learn and *the* language that will 'open doors' (Sayer, 2015) and change Mexican people's future (López-Gopar, 2019). Thirdly, technology, which in Mexico has come to simply mean computers in classrooms loaded with software created by foreign companies or government institutions in Mexico City (López-Gopar *et al*., 2009), has been part of presidential campaign promises. In this political rhetoric, technology is portrayed as a way to reach the poorest children and provide them with a 'better' education, without acknowledging that many schools in Indigenous communities and impoverished areas lack electricity or the infrastructure to safely store a computer (Matías, 2007). Most importantly, technology has never been viewed as a means to share the knowledge that has been present in communities for centuries. Since the 1990s, presidential candidates have promised '*más lectura*' ('more reading') and '*Inglés y Computación*' ('English and computers') for all Mexican schools, which in effect reproduces coloniality and colonial difference (Mignolo, 2000).

Many Mexican teachers, along with low socioeconomic status (SES) children throughout Mexico, have been caught in the crossfire produced by the discourses constructed around literacy, English, and technology. It is commonly believed that if Mexican teachers and children were to read more books, and if Mexican teachers were to speak English and be adapted to technology, then the education in Mexico would be *better* (López-Gopar, 2016). These colonial discourses seem to subtly place the blame on Mexican teachers and children, disregarding the historical social inequalities and the discourses that have regarded Mexican teachers and children as lacking literacy, English, and technology. That said, it seems undeniable that literacy, English, and technology will prevail within educational initiatives, policies, and programs, to the approval of most Mexican parents. Hence, it is important to decolonize and reshape the deficit discourses surrounding these three concepts, so that both Mexican teachers and children can appropriate literacy, English, and technology on their own terms and in order to negotiate affirming identities and to challenge colonial difference. Consequently, it is imperative to work with pre-service English teachers in projects where literacy, English, and technology work *in favor* of Mexican children and to share with the world the local epistemologies and ontologies co-constructed by pre-service teachers and children.

Within this panorama, this chapter presents the experience of three Mexican pre-service 'English' teachers. Here, as well as in the title to this chapter, we have put the word 'English' in quotation marks to represent that the work of the pre-service teachers was not only to teach English *per se* but also to engage in critical issues such as identity and decolonization, as discussed below. The three pre-service teachers (Luz, Estela and Jorge), in the final year of their studies in the BA program in the teaching of English at Facultad de Idiomas at Universidad Autónoma Benito Juárez de

Oaxaca, completed their student-teaching assignment at BIBLOCA, a multilingual community library located in an urban neighborhood of the city of Oaxaca.[1] At this library, Luz, Estela and Jorge taught English to children from the local community. Part of Luz, Estela and Jorge's classroom activities involved co-creating videos with Global StoryBridges (GSB) youth participants about the daily lives of elementary school children in Oaxaca, Mexico, and exchanging these videos with children from other countries such as the US, Uganda and China. In these pre-service teachers' experience, literacy, English, and technology came together through GSB, developed by Maggie Hawkins. This project was initiated with three goals in mind:

(1) to increase English language and literacy skills for underserved, at-risk English learning students globally;
(2) to support the development of technology skills;
(3) to engage youth in transglobal, transcultural communications in order to increase awareness and understanding of global others and of themselves as global citizens. (Hawkins, 2014: 98–99)

For us (the authors of this chapter), as language teacher educators at a Oaxacan public university, the objective was to use English, literacy, and technology as an excuse and conduit to achieve the third goal set by Hawkins (cf. above). We also wanted our pre-service teachers to have the experience of working with children in order to co-create texts (in this case, videos) for real purposes and real audiences, to use English, literacy and technology for the children's own purposes, and to re-negotiate affirming identities for themselves as well as the children.

To achieve this purpose which centers on the fulfillment of Hawkins's third goal regarding the children's and pre-service teachers' critical cosmopolitanism (Hawkins, 2014, 2018), the present chapter consists of six phases. The chapter, first of all, addresses the geopolitical context of the project; secondly, it develops a relevant theoretical framework; third, it provides a succinct methodological section; fourth, it describes the video co-created between the children and the pre-service teachers; fifth, it presents and analyzes the feedback to the video provided by children from various international settings; and sixth, it reveals our views, as language teacher educators, regarding the pedagogical development gained by the pre-service teachers as a result of this project.

The Geopolitical Context of the Project

Latin American theorists Dussel (2002), Mignolo (2000), and Quijano (2007) have not only analyzed the modernity/coloniality narrative present in Mexico and Latin America but have also worked with the concept of geopolitics of knowledge. Mignolo, in an interview conducted and reported by Walsh (2003), states that, 'knowledge is not abstract and de-localized, but totally the opposite' (2003: 3, our translation). Mignolo goes on to argue: '[H]uman knowledge that is not produced in a certain region of the world (from Greece to France, to the North part of the Mediterranean), especially the knowledge produced in Africa, Asia and Latin America, is not considered knowledge' (2003: 3, our translation). Geopolitics of knowledge, then, refers to the value that certain geographical and political areas are given over others. As Mignolo concludes:

> Knowledge, as the economy, is organized through centers of power and subaltern regions. [...] The trap is that the discourse of modernity created the illusion that knowledge is dis-incorporated and de-localized and that it is necessary, from all regions of the planet, to 'climb up' to the epistemology of modernity. (in Walsh, 2003: 3, our translation)

In order to challenge this de-localization of knowledge, which hides the Eurocentric origin of modernity/coloniality discourse and its ways of knowing imposed on other regions, Hawkins (2014: 91) argues for ontologies of place. She states: 'The distinctive nature and features of each place where meaning making occurs shape what is and can be learned within it'. Hawkins also reminds us that we need to 'take into account ideologies, positionings, and power relations among people that are integral to and inherent in place, and represented, distributed, and reified through the movements and flows of specific resources among specific people in specific places' (2014: 91). This present section of the chapter, therefore, is much more than 'contextual background' information: it is about the geopolitics of knowledge of the *place* where valid knowledge (epistemologies) and identities (ontologies) were co-constructed through the creation and sharing of a video by the pre-service English teachers and the Oaxacan children.

The video, as mentioned previously, was co-created at the library BIBLOCA located in a low SES neighborhood in the city of Oaxaca, Mexico. Oaxaca is the most culturally and linguistically diverse state of Mexico. More than 100 Indigenous languages prevail in the state. Nevertheless, these languages have little power compared to the hegemonic presence of Spanish and, more recently, English. Spanish has been the *de facto* official language since the Spanish invasion in the 16th century. Spanish is not constitutionally the official language of Mexico, but rather a national language sharing the same constitutional status with Indigenous languages, due to the historical resistance of Indigenous groups (López-Gopar *et al.*, 2013). English has been taught in public middle schools since the 1970s (Terborg *et al.*, 2007) and in some public elementary schools since the 1990s (López-Gopar, 2016). The proliferation of private English institutes and elite bilingual schools in Mexico was connected to Mexico's signing the North America Free Trade Agreement (NAFTA) in 1991, and to Mexican people's imaginaries that learning or acquiring English will be necessary in order to succeed in the new North

American market economy. Since then, access to English has been a matter of social class and economic status, especially in poor states like Oaxaca, as we discuss below.

Oaxaca is the second poorest state in Mexico. Almost half of the wealth in Mexico is possessed by a very small percentage of the population (0.02%). Indeed, González Amador (2013) reports that Mexico is the country with the widest gap between rich and poor people among the countries belonging to the Organization for Economic Co-operation and Development (OECD). Eighty percent of the population is considered poor or vulnerable (Olivares Alonso, 2013). The Oaxacan Indigenous peoples struggle financially, more so than the rest of the Mexican population. Many Indigenous families survive on the minimum wage of US $4.00 for eight hours of work (Enciso & Camacho, 2013), and 76% of Indigenous children and young adults in Oaxaca live in poverty and suffer poor nutrition (Enciso, 2013). The poverty present in Mexico, and especially in Oaxaca, severely restricts access to books and technology, which tend to be very expensive and inaccessible to people living in poverty. The same occurs with English education.

Learning English is connected to economics in the country of Mexico, especially in its impoverished states. In Oaxaca, for example, English instruction begins in middle school. This means that 40% of the state population (1.2 million people) is excluded from public-funded English learning since this 40% does not finish elementary school education (INEGI, 2010). For the other 60% of Oaxacan youth, who have completed at least middle school and hence have participated in English classes, English language competency nevertheless seems unattainable, mainly because English language instruction seems largely ineffective in public Mexican schools where 'English teaching practices often reflect obsolete educational policies' as well as 'structural rather than social-related linguistic issues' (León Jiménez *et al.*, 2019: 101). Another reason for the Oaxacan youth being excluded from English language education is that the high tuition at English teaching institutes and private schools in Oaxaca makes English inaccessible to most Oaxacans. As López-Gopar and Sughrua (2014: 107) report:

> [A] low-SES Oaxacan family would have to invest their entire monthly income to pay one month's tuition for only one of their children in a private school where she/he could learn English. Equally expensive are the private English language institutes. Only 5% of the Oaxacan population can afford private schooling.

The inaccessibility of English instruction makes Mexican people desire English even more. Most Oaxacan parents wish to enroll their children in English classes. The library BIBLOCA has used the lure of English to attract children and engage them in different projects, such as GSB, as described in this chapter.

BIBLOCA is located in Candiani, an urban neighborhood located 3 km from downtown Oaxaca. Back in the 1970s, Candiani was founded by Indigenous and mestizo migrants relocating to the city from the countryside. This neighborhood soon became one of the very first low-SES neighborhoods outside the city center, and in its early days it was home to the municipal garbage dump. Currently, Candiani remains inhabited mostly by the low-SES families who moved to this undesirable neighborhood in the 1970s and 1980s. However, due to its geographic proximity to downtown Oaxaca, Candiani has become the internationalized area of the city, as within its parameters one can find transnational retail outlets such as McDonald's, Burger King, KFC, Sam's Club, Home Depot, Office Depot, automobile dealerships and department stores. These stores represent the materialization of the English language in Oaxaca with its connection to transnational companies and neoliberal practices.

BIBLOCA was founded by the first author of this chapter, Mario, and his family in 2002. Mario, whose family moved to Candiani in 1979, grew up in the neighborhood. BIBLOCA has received the support of Canadian and American benefactors who have donated English books as well as funds to purchase books and materials in Spanish and Indigenous languages. The library is run by pre-service English teachers, like Luz, Jorge and Estela, who offer free after-school language classes in English, Spanish and Indigenous languages to low-SES children, mostly from Candiani. BIBLOCA has four main objectives: (a) to develop critical literacy; (b) to foster Indigenous languages; (c) to teach English critically; and (d) to offer future English teachers the opportunity to work with children. BIBLOCA has used English as an excuse or as a medium to work on the first two objectives. In the next section, we describe the theories that drive the preservice teachers' BA program and that support the work that pre-service teachers like Luz, Jorge and Estela do in BIBLOCA and on different projects such Global StoryBridges (GSB).

Decolonizing Literacy, English and Technology

Mexico, as is true of most countries in Latin America, was invaded by the Spaniards in the 15th century. During the 300 years of Spanish colonialism, Mexican peoples' ways of knowing and being as well as their language and literacy practices were constructed as the 'other' (i.e. inferior), whereas the ways and practices of the Spaniards were positioned as modern or superior. In spite of Mexico's independence in 1821, colonialism has continued, somehow ingrained in Mexican peoples' thinking. This mindset is referred to as 'coloniality' by Latin American scholars such as Quijano (2007). In particular, Quijano (2007) argues that coloniality currently remains the most prevalent and widespread form of subjugation in the world, even though the actual political system of 'colonialism' has long since been replaced, for the most part, with independent nation-states. Mignolo (2009: 43, our translation) similarly argues that, 'the rhetoric of modernity (salvation, novelty, progress, development) appeared with the logic of coloniality'.

Currently, in Mexico, literacy still operates within the discourse of coloniality. With the inception of the alphabetic literacy by Spanish missionaries, books have remained as the only valid way by which knowledge can be reported and acquired (López-Gopar, 2007). Mexico is considered a nation of non-readers, especially because national surveys tend to pose such questions as 'how many books have you read (lately, this week, this year)'? Hernández-Zamora (2004: 4, our translation) states that '[a]ccording to the most common and superficial definition [in Mexico], a reader is a person who reads books [...] many, good ones, and for pleasure'. This definition of a 'reader' seems to drive national policies and initiatives to promote reading in Mexico while justifying the absence of inquiries as to the economic and the social inequalities preventing certain groups from having access to books. The definition, as a result, is rooted in coloniality and is thereby indicative of the historical exclusion of othered literacy practices with different (trans)modalities such as images, color, sounds, and so forth (Hawkins, 2018; New London Group, 1996). It therefore is important to historically understand, albeit succinctly, the colonial aspects of literacy in Mexico, in order to decolonize literacy.

At the onset of the Spanish invasion, American Indigenous groups had complex multimodal literacy practices through what is known as *codices*, which were colorful, multimodal texts recorded on *amate*, a paper made out of cotton or animal skin (Cifuentes, 1998). According to Restall *et al.* (2005: 11), codices 'combined pictorial representation (direct depiction by images) with a numerical and calendrical system, logograms or images (which conveyed a word or idea), and phonetic representation of individual syllables or roots of words' based in part on 'the use of homonyms or "tone puns"'. These codices, as Cifuentes (1998) states, could be read by people who did not share the same language, as in the case of Aztecs and Mixtecs, who spoke Nahuatl and Mixtec, respectively. This was possible because these texts were independent from the oral versions of the languages and because the people shared a broad cultural base. These multimodal texts, however, were seen as inferior when compared to the alphabetic texts used by the Spaniards.

This 'colonial difference'-related discourse regarding literacy practices was resisted by Mexican Indigenous peoples who began using Spanish and alphabetic literacy on their own terms. López-Gopar (2007) states:

> With the introduction of the Spanish language and its alphabetic writing system, Indigenous multimodal texts became dual language texts as well, especially in the sixteenth century. The authors would use pictorial writing combined with print in both Spanish *and* Indigenous languages. Robertson (1994), who has studied the *codices* extensively, sees this as a 'fusion whereby Spanish [designs] and native traditions [designs] meet

and create a new synthesis [the redesign]' (p. 34). The *Codice Florentino* and the *Codice Mendozino* are perfect examples of these redesigns (see León-Portilla, 2003 for examples). Unfortunately, the Spanish destroyed most of the *codices*, and print soon replaced the Indigenous available designs. (2007: 9, brackets and emphasis in original)

In current-day Mexico, though, one can find 'walking codices', and the multimodality present in the old codices has continued as part of Mexican peoples' literacy practices (López-Gopar, 2007), as for instance seen in some contemporary texts ingrained with Mesoamerican practices in which other modes are given more weight than alphabetic texts (Jiménez & Smith, 2008) as well as with Indigenous modes representing Indigenous cosmologies, epistemologies, and ontologies (Menezes de Souza, 2003; Jiménez & Smith, 2008, based on León Portilla's work on Nahuatl philosophy).

This view has oriented us towards the decolonization of literacy, which we attempt in our BA program and in the project we conduct at BIBLOCA with pre-service teachers. For this, we align with a multiliteracies (New London Group, 1996) and transmodalities (Hawkins, 2018) framework, not so much because 'new' digital communications have given more weight to other semiotic modes, but because (trans)modalities have been part of Indigenous peoples' literacy practices for centuries. We believe that both pre-service English teachers and children *are* in fact authors of their own histories and multimodal texts. For this reason, the BIBLOCA project considers decolonizing literacy

> as a fundamental practice of voice and a tool for self-authoring one's place in the world. [...] For the descendants of the colonial subservient castes, in particular, literacy and education are a means to stop depending on others (often the oppressors themselves) in order to speak and to be heard, seen and respected as citizens and human beings. (Hernández-Zamora, 2010: 9)

Hence, the co-creation of the BIBLOCA videos goes beyond assembling a multimodal text. It is about producing ways of knowing and being that can be shared and hopefully accepted by other groups in similar situations. (Multi)literacy, then, is not something we (Mexican language teacher educators, pre-service English teachers, and children – the actors in this chapter) 'need' in order to become 'better' but rather the semiotic means to show how creative and intelligent we already are. (Multi)literacy is also the conduit to learn from other decolonized or de-imperialized groups, as in the case of American, Chinese and African groups participating in the GSB project (Hawkins, 2014, 2018).

In a similar decolonizing approach, English serves the same purpose as literacy in our BA program and projects. Decolonizing English entails challenging the apparent world phenomenon that associates English with 'progress' and neoliberal practices. Currently, in Mexico, English is sold as *the modern* language to learn so as to obtain alleged benefits (Sayer, 2015). In contrast to the discourse of coloniality, Indigenous and 'minoritized' languages are connected with backwardness and primitivism (Maldonado Alvarado, 2002). Since 2007, the authors of this chapter, fulfilling our role as language teacher educators, have been conducting different university-based initiatives that bring together language teacher educators in collaboration with pre-service teachers of the English language. Under our supervision, the pre-service teachers conduct their teaching praxicum in different urban and semi-urban schools, community centers, and BIBLOCA, the context of this chapter. Our overall goal is to decolonize English language teaching.

The English language in Mexico is part of the modernity/coloniality discourse. English institutes and elite bilingual (English/Spanish) schools advertise English as the language that will *change* Mexican peoples' backward, primitive life. English is also portrayed as the language that Mexican people will use to communicate with 'the world'. These discourses do not specify who or what this world is. The spotlight that English receives obscures all the many other Indigenous languages existing in Mexico. Consequently, López-Gopar (2016: 10) has stressed that, 'it is important to decolonize [English] in order to move away from discourses that position their learners as needy and expecting to be saved by the English language'.

Decolonizing English is an ideological and transgressive stance. It uses English against the discourses surrounding it and in favor of othered languages and speakers. This, according to López-Gopar (2016: 10), means 'using the English language classroom as a space in which all the actors' identities [...] are renegotiated in order to value the different ways of being, speaking and knowing [...] and to transgress the inferiority imposed by coloniality'. In this attempt to decolonize English, our focus has been on how pre-service teachers and students *transgress* the discourses behind imposed languages and cultures as they bring their ways of knowing, culturing and speaking to the forefront. Transgressing means speaking and acting back to negative identities imposed on Mexicans by coloniality. Transgressive literacy, language, and technology projects must be situated in the material lives of pre-service teachers and students, who should be regarded as legitimate authors of multimodal texts, such as the video described in this chapter. In a decolonizing English approach, English is not the main goal, but the medium to create multimodal texts to be widely shared through technology in order to renegotiate affirming identities.

In the same way that literacy and English are connected to economics in Mexico, access to technology is constrained by poverty. Although technology and information technologies may be sold as democratic and egalitarian, caution is in order. For instance, Aubert *et al.* (2013: 14) warn:

> Let's not be naïve, societies with information technologies, even though they contain elements that can promote more democracy and equality, have not overcome economic and social inequities. [...] [These societies work] within a capitalist framework, and the consequence is new and more inequities.

In Mexico, since 2000, information technologies have been brought into the classroom through different projects such as *Enciclomedia*, which 'use[d] as its basis digitalized free textbooks to enrich these [traditional textbooks] with multimedia materials [such as still images and audio and video files produced by government and educational organizations]' (Prieto Hernández, 2005: 162, our translation).

Treviño Ronzón and Morales Landa (2006) rightly define *Enciclomedia* as 'an informational, educational, and *political* program' (n.p., our translation, our emphasis). Government officials advertised *Enciclomedia* as the policy that would 'change' national basic education (Comunicación Social SEB, 2008) and would 'close the gap for everyone' (Cavanagh, 2004: 13). During the planning stages, Mexico was supposed to invest 1 billion US dollars in this project (Cavanagh, 2004), but ended up spending 1.6 billion US dollars (Del Valle, 2008). This program was launched without realizing that many schools around the country would not even have the proper classrooms to safeguard the equipment (Sánchez, 2007) or electricity to be able to run the program (Matías, 2007). This is especially the case in many Indigenous communities in Oaxaca (Matías, 2007). Aviles and Vargas (2006), two reporters, mocked the validation report of *Enciclomedia* conducted by researchers from Harvard with their newspaper article entitled, '*Descubre* Harvard que Enciclomedia funciona mejor en escuelas con luz' (Harvard *discovers* that *Enciclomedia* works better in schools with electricity) (emphasis in original). Consequently, many academics and news reporters viewed this program as 'elitist, costly, exclusive, and presidential' (Elizondo Huerta *et al.*, 2006: 218, our translation).

Mexico is not alone in the debates concerning the use of Information and Communication Technologies (ICT). This is also a highly debated issue in the United States and Canada. For example, Cummins (2000: 537–8) states:

> Some see I[C]T as a new educational deity, a potential messiah set to rescue society from a moribund educational system, staffed by lethargic teachers. [...] On the pews facing the altar of computer literacy we find a predictable group of believers: corporate leaders and politicians genuinely anxious to ensure that the educational system delivers the intellectual resources to fuel the engines of the 'knowledge society'; other corporate and educational leaders, with lean and hungry looks, interested in using I[C]T as the lever to turn a profit on a privatized educational system; and

many in the public, primarily from the middle classes and including many educators, who have been convinced that computer literacy is the key to their children's social and economic advancement. [...] Outside the temple of the faithful, however, a noisy crowd of activists and academics has gathered [to argue that] there is not a shred of empirical evidence that the massive investment in computer hardware and software has improved achievement levels.

In Mexico, many government officials, educators, non-governmental organizations, and some in the general public have falsely believed that computers alone will do the job. For this reason, Cummins and Sayers (1995) argue that pedagogical discussions should precede discussions about computers and ICT.

Our approach to technology and computers in the classroom has been from a decolonizing approach. Following the successful experience of the Zapatista movement, which used ICT to let the world know about social inequalities and the discrimination suffered by Indigenous peoples in Mexico, in our BA program and projects like the BIBLOCA video as described in this chapter, we attempt to use technology as an amplifying device to share our stories with the world. Our BIBLOCA video project, like the GSB project, follows this principle and uses technologies to foster communication among different groups of children, who ideally see each other as worthy of being listened to. In the next section, we focus briefly on the methodology of the BIBLOCA GSB project.

Methodology

As already mentioned, Luz, Jorge and Estela completed the BA program in Language Teaching at the Facultad de Idiomas at Universidad Autónoma Benito Juárez de Oaxaca. The purpose of this BA is to prepare language teachers and researchers with a critical and transforming vision. Part of this vision is to be aware of the multilingual and intercultural context of the State of Oaxaca, where the hegemonic presence of Spanish and English prevails. As part of their program, as in any other BA program in Mexico, the pre-service teachers at the Facultad de Idiomas must complete a period of social service, which consists of 480 hours of professional/academic work connected to their area of study at a government institution or an NGO like BIBLOCA. The purpose of social service is for the BA students to give back to the community, who by way of tax contributions has funded the students' public university education. Taking this notion of 'giving back to the community' to heart, we, as language teacher educators, coordinate projects where young pre-service teachers like Luz, Estela and Jorge can collaborate with children in low-SES communities such as Candiani, where BIBLOCA is located. Consequently, our decolonizing agenda is based on *politicized qualitative research methodology* through a fusion of critical ethnography and critical action research.

The methodological underpinnings of politicized qualitative research, first of all, rely on the analysis and discussion of subjectivities related to the 'social problems of vulnerable groups' in order to make a 'contribution' (Flick, 2015: 122). In politicized qualitative research methodology, a socially committed desire or need almost always preludes the research project. In our case, we are aware that modernity/coloniality discourses drive literacy, English, and technology in Mexico. As a result, our socially committed desire is to provide all of the participants (language teacher educators, pre-service teachers and children) with the opportunity to challenge colonial difference, which, in the case of the project reported in this chapter, was by way of co-creating, sharing and discussing videos as part of the GSB project (Hawkins, 2014). In this video project, and similar projects of the pre-service teachers completing their social service at BIBLOCA, we fused critical ethnography with critical action research (cf. López-Gopar *et al.*, 2014).

We, as language teacher educators, work with the pre-service students during the final two years of their BA program, consisting of eight semesters in total. In the penultimate year or otherwise semesters five and six, the pre-service teachers are introduced to critical ethnography (Anderson, 1989), through which they, along with the language teacher educators, get to know the community and the children's lives before starting the teaching praxicum or engaging in projects like GSB. In most cases, the pre-service teachers spend part of semesters five and six in activities within the community in order to learn about its geopolitics. In semester seven, the critical action research component of the project is the pre-service teachers' praxicum, which included engagement in GSB. In the praxicum, the role of 'teacher' and 'learner' is not fixed since pre-service teachers are there not only to teach but also to learn from the children. In semester eight, the pre-service teachers finish their praxicum and write their graduating paper.

For the project described in this chapter, the data was collected and analyzed by both the language teacher educators and the pre-service teachers before and during the creation of the focal video with the children. In the pre-video phase, the collected data included participant observations of the community, ethnographic fieldnotes, and informal conversations with parents, pre-service teachers and children. While the video was being created, additional data was collected in several ways. The pre-service teachers kept a diary of all of the classes. On some occasions, they audio and video-recorded parts of their classes and took photographs. We conducted participant observations of the classes and engaged in personal and group dialogue with the pre-service teachers.

This dialoguing between the teacher educators and the pre-service teachers, along with the above-mentioned participant observation, fieldnotes, informal conversations, diaries, audio-recordings, video-recordings and photographs, generated a wealth of data. This diverse data, however, is not directly analyzed in this chapter, which instead relies on the produced video as well as the digital chats between the BIBLOCA children and other children within the GSB international panorama for its direct data base (cf. the following two sections of this chapter). Nonetheless, although the dialogue-based and other types of previously-mentioned data do not play an overt role in the analysis dimension of this chapter, we describe that data here, because it not only represents the pre-service teacher's learning but also indirectly informed our own reflection on and interpretation of the direct data base consisting of the video and the GSB chats. We hence consider the video and GSB chats as the direct data of this chapter, and the previously-mentioned data sets as indirect data.

The impact of this indirect data can be seen in the manner in which the data guided the socialization between the language teacher educators and the pre-service teachers. For instance, during the creation of the video, the language teacher educators and the pre-service teachers analyzed all of the data in order to identify emerging themes and adjust the collaboration with the children. The data was analyzed in a recursive and reiterative manner through weekly meetings the language teacher educators had with the pre-service teachers. In these meetings, we discussed the pre-service teachers' sessions with the children, planned ahead, and connected the co-creation of the video project with the general context of Oaxaca. This socialization led to the videos co-created by the pre-service teachers with the children as well as the feedback the children received from children of other countries by way of chats within the GSB panorama. In the next section, the analytical phase of the chapter, we focus on the direct data consisting of one video and ensuing GSB chats. Immediately thereafter, in the concluding section, we present our reflections as to how this project enabled pre-service teachers to develop a decolonizing approach in their current and future teaching. We now turn to the video.

BIBLOCA: Activities in Our Free Time

As previously mentioned, Luz, Estela and Jorge conducted their teaching praxicum at BIBLOCA, a multilingual library located in a low SES urban neighborhood of Oaxaca. They worked on a video project connected to Global StoryBridges (GSB). Luz, Estela and Jorge worked with 12 children, five boys and seven girls, ranging from 10 to 14 years of age. All of the children lived in Candiani. The pre-service teachers worked with the children for a period of four months, combining the co-creation of the video project with general English classes and literacy activities, both in English and Spanish. Most children had very limited knowledge of English when they started the course and had also very little experience with technology, including the handling of a video recorder and a computer. With the supervision and collaboration explained in the previous section, the pre-service teachers and the students spent many sessions deciding on the topic for their video, forming the storyline, setting the English language script, learning how to use a video recorder, shooting the video within and outside of BIBLOCA, and producing the video. Next, we describe the video the pre-service teachers and children co-created. The 'co' in 'co-created' speaks to the collaborative nature of the project, which was children-led, but with guidance and input from the pre-service teachers.

This video, which has a duration of 5 minutes and 48 seconds, is set in Candiani. Titled *BIBLOCA: Activities in Our Free Time*, the video features a group of children from the Candiani neighborhood who participate in the multilingual classes and literacy activities offered in BIBLOCA. In the video, these children talk about and show what they like to do in their free time. The video opens with a black screen, on which a cloudburst of purple dots vanishes into the title (cf. above) printed in white letters, giving way to a sweeping view of the colorfully-painted façade of the BIBLOCA library building and then to the image of a hand knocking on the front door. The door opens from the inside of the library to reveal a young girl wearing her physical-education school uniform. The girl says, 'Hello. Welcome to BIBLOCA, a bilingual library', gesturing to the film crew, and by extension the viewer, to enter into a room whose walls are lined with bookshelves and where a group of children, some in their school uniform and others in 'street clothes', are seated in a large circle on multi-colored floor matting, while reading books.

The video then pans back to the outside façade of the library, first to a sign whose main text reads 'BIBLOCA Est. 2002', and then to a group of children (the same ones from above) now standing together against the large image of a tree painted on the exterior wall and exclaiming in unison: 'We are BIBLOCA students!' This image shrinks to postcard size and falls into the depth of the screen as the next image emerges: that of the same students again sitting in the reading room of the library. One student, sitting near the corner of the room, says, 'How are you? We hope you are okay'; another student, standing in the opposite corner of the room, says, 'We will show you some activities we do in our free time'; and a third student, standing outside against the entrance to the library and holding out her arms, says, 'Enjoy'. She turns; says, 'Let's begin'; waves her right hand in a type of 'follow me' gesture; and walks out of camera range, as the scene shifts to another student, a boy, standing in the middle of an outdoor, cement-paved, soccer court located in an athletic field that belongs to the public university (where the authors of this chapter teach) and that is within easy walking distance from BIBLOCA library.

This boy on the soccer court says, 'We are in a field named '*El Gallinero*' ['The Hen House']', and the video shows some of the students walking around on the cement court and kicking a soccer ball to the sound of idyllic piano music, which after a moment suddenly gives way to a

Brazilian samba-inspired and industrialized-sounding hip-hop beat. This music fades away while four students, one after the other, state one sentence, introducing the activity to follow: (1) 'We will play soccer'; (2) 'First, we make teams'; (3) 'Then, we decide the rules, and the game starts'; and (4) 'The winner is who scores more goals.' The Brazilian samba hip-hop music then resurfaces with singing both in Portuguese and English as the screen fissures into a type of checkerboard, with each small square flipping over in succession and forming part of the next scene. This scene shows the students, both girls and boys, standing on the cement court and arranging themselves into two separate teams for the soccer game. A representative from each of the two teams then participates in the 'coin toss' overseen by one of the boys, apparently in the role of a referee, and then the game begins, the camera speeding up and the children thus moving in a type of hyper and cartoonish fashion to the sound of electronic percussion created by what seem to be synthesized bongos and snare drums. A goal is scored, a couple of students congratulate each other, and the video switches to a girl standing in the middle of the soccer court.

This girl says, 'Next, we will show you another activity', apparently as a way of introducing two other students, boys, who stand in front of a tree at the side of the soccer court. Each boy, one by one, describes what seems to be part of the same activity, while his comment appears in print (subtitled) along the bottom of the screen: (1) 'Sometimes in our free time, we like to walk'; (2) [and] '[l]ook for beautiful plants and pick up its flowers.' Each of the next two students, a boy and a girl, standing in front of a bush with purple flowers, collaborate on a description: (1) 'This is a bougainvillea plant'; (2) 'You can prepare tea with its flower for stomachache.' The next student, a girl, standing beside another tree near the soccer court, says: 'This is a jacaranda tree, one of the main trees you can see around the city.' The next student, a girl, standing beside a large plant near the front of what seems to be a private residence, says, 'This plant is named *pitiona*'; and the next student to appear on the screen, a girl who stands beside the same plant and who moves her hand in a circular motion as if stirring a large pot, explains that '[p]eople use it to cook.' The next student, a girl, is seen standing on the sidewalk, positioned between a parked pick-up truck and a banana tree. She says: 'Close to BIBLOCA, we can find a *platanar* [banana tree]. We eat banana plants.' The final student of this phase of the video is a girl wearing her public-school uniform. She introduces the viewer to the next phase of the video.

This girl, standing among the plants near the front entrance of the school, waves hello and then gestures for the viewer to follow her into the school grounds, saying, 'Hey, come on, guys', with a title at the bottom of the screen that reads, 'Break at the school.' The first area is the corridor, where another girl addresses the camera, saying, 'We are going to see the activities we do on break at the school.' The next student, a girl, standing beside the red-painted wall of the central patio, explains that during break time the first priority is to eat. Her comment is spoken while appearing in print at the bottom of the screen: 'Usually before we do other activities ... / we have a breakfast!' Another student, a boy who holds a plastic bottle of water, exclaims, while the corresponding subtitle appears on the screen: 'You can buy it [i.e. breakfast] at the cafeteria ... / Or bring it!' The image of this student shrinks to postcard size and vanishes into the next image, which is of another student, a girl, who says, as her words are printed out on the screen, 'Also during the break, we play different games.' Another girl, the same one who beckoned the viewer into the school grounds (cf. above), says, 'For example', just as the word 'SOCCER' in green letters appears on the screen, and in the center of the image one boy and three girls kick a soccer ball back and forth on the cement soccer court, which is shaded by a pavilion-like roof. The video then switches from the soccer court to a different area of the school grounds: an open-air courtyard between two double-storey classroom buildings. The first part of this phase of the video consists of the phrase 'ANTELOPES AND LEOPARDS' in capital letters and green print superimposed over the image of two girls and one boy standing with their faces to the white wall of the classroom building, apparently counting out the time allowed for the other children to hide away somewhere in the courtyard. These two girls and one boy then begin the game, running throughout the courtyard, engaging in the playful hunt for their classmates. The video, as before during the scene of the soccer game in the outdoor court in the university athletic field, speeds up while the children are seen running in hyper and cartoonish fashion to the sound of a similarly accelerated musical tone.

The screen then splits into separate panels, which drop down to reveal the image of a boy who stands at the wall of the classroom building and says, 'That is all for today.' To continue this farewell extended by this student, the video, as it has done previously, fissures into a checkerboard, with the small squares flipping over to form the next scene, which is the reading room of the BIBLOCA library. There one of the students, standing alone in the corner of the bookshelf-lined room, says, 'We hope you have enjoyed our video', as her words appear in a written caption that ends with the ':)' symbol. The next image shows seven of the BIBLOCA students posed in front of the bookshelves. They say in unison, 'We wish you the best. See you soon.' The screen then turns black, and the credits roll. In this 'credits' phase, the students are cited by their first names. At the end of the credits, the video freezes on a group photograph of 12 BIBLOCA students in the reading room of the library.

Analysis

This video, as stated previously, follows from the GSB project, which has three main objectives: (1) to increase English and literacy skills; (2) to support the development of technology skills; and (3) to engage youth in transglobal, transcultural communications. Even though we did not see English, literacy, and technology skills as our end goals, but rather as conduits to achieve the third objective by challenging colonial difference and negotiating affirming identities, the video reflects development in English, (multi)literacy, and technology. The children started the project with very limited English. Some of them knew some words in English, but they were not capable of producing sentences, and certain English sounds were unfamiliar to them. In the video, children use different grammatical structures (e.g. present verb tense, future verb tense, imperative commands, active voice, passive voice, and so forth) along with transition words (e.g. first, then, next) and vocabulary regarding their activities and the plants around the neighborhood. In fact, the children themselves, with the help of the pre-service teachers, composed the script. Despite not having the best equipment to capture high quality sounds, the English sentences they produce are quite understandable and the children also use gestures to communicate their message. It could be argued that the children simply memorized the phrases for the video; however, this alleged memorization would show the children being introduced to meaningful English sentence structures with a purpose. Typical English classes in Mexico do not expose children to a wide range of grammatical sentence structures right from the beginning; instead they focus on simple vocabulary categories (e.g. colors, animals). Hence, the video shows that the children developed English meaningfully in a short period of time.

In terms of multiliteracy, transmodalities and technology, the video is also a testament to the children's development in these two areas that cut across each other. Regarding multiliteracies, the children engaged in different multimodal activities and authored different texts, including the video. During the planning stages of the video project, the pre-service teachers and children had oral discussions to first determine the topic and then what to include and how to present it. These discussions were mediated by multiliteracies as children brainstormed topics and listed ideas on the board, talked about gestures to accompany oral speech, decided and wrote the written texts to be included in the video, and engaged in conversations as to what and how to shoot the video to convey the message they intended. These multimodal multiliteracy activities introduced and developed technological skills, as children had to use the video camera, the computer, and the video projector. While interacting with these three devices, for instance, children had to get familiar with different symbols such as the 'play' icon, the 'recording' icon, and images or icons for different software on the computer. During the video production, children learned to shoot and edit video, clip and join videos, and include effects, music, and written texts in the video. All of these technological skills are quite complex and intertwined with different modes (i.e. icons, images) and with different languages as some words are in English and others in Spanish. As a result, the pre-service teachers introduced and developed

English, literacy, and technology while engaging the children in the co-creation of the video. While doing so, the children, along with the pre-service teachers, challenged colonial difference and negotiated affirming identities, thereby accomplishing the third objective of GSB (cf. above).

Both the pre-service teachers and the children came from low-SES backgrounds and 'non-reading' families, as the literacy practices they engaged in were not considered valid by the mainstream (Hernández-Zamora, 2009), and they were not exposed to English and technology in their early years as they could not afford to attend elite bilingual schools or private English institutes (López-Gopar, 2016). Consequently, by standards of the modernity/coloniality discourse (Mignolo, 2000), they needed help, especially the children. Nevertheless, the pre-service teachers broke this providing-help pattern and saw the children as intelligent and creative right from the get-go. By doing so, the pre-service teachers also saw themselves as intelligent and creative teachers who broke the typical language teaching patterns and engaged in decolonial projects. As previously stated, BIBLOCA is located in Candiani, which has recently transitioned from an outskirt city neighborhood to a more 'modern' neighborhood hosting the newest, most expensive, transnational restaurants, supermarkets, and department stores with their connection to English and neoliberalism. One thus could have easily expected that the children would have jumped onto the modernity and progress wagon and showed their pride in their neighborhood and lives as bound up in this modernity development. Conversely, and with great hope for decolonial studies, the video revolved around *their* lives, *their* activities, *their* important places (e.g. BIBLOCA, the nearby university sports facilities, and the neighborhood public school). Unexpectedly, and as a deviation from the intended focus on free-time activities, the children brought into the video their family knowledge regarding plants for medicinal and cooking purposes (e.g. the bougainvillea plant for a stomachache) and by extension their epistemologies and ontologies of place (Hawkins, 2014). They *are* BIBLOCA students and showed not only what they do in their free time, but *what they know*, and they *used* English, (multi)literacy, and technology as conduits to share with other children around the world what is *important to them*. They also challenged English-only ideologies, by bringing Spanish (e.g. *el gallinero, pitiona, platanar*) and Portuguese (Samba, hip hop music) and its connection to the importance of soccer both in Brazil and in Mexico into the video. While doing so, the children engaged with youth in transglobal, transcultural communications, as we now discuss.

Through the video, the BIBLOCA children participated in online conversations with children from the US, Uganda, and China. The children started the video with a direct message to its main audience, both by opening the door not only to BIBLOCA but also to their own lives and practices, and by saying 'Hello. Welcome to BIBLOCA.' They directly addressed their audience many kilometers away from them by raising a question and stating a wish, 'How are you? We hope you are okay.' These two sentences, by bringing the 'you(s)' and the 'we' into intercultural exchanges, are a frontal challenge to the modernity/coloniality discourse, where *othered* people do not matter as they are seen as human *resources*. Decolonial attempts are rooted in the *subjectification* of languages and literacies, where people are more important than languages and literacies (López-Gopar, 2016). This video is not just a text; it is about children, *real* people, engaging with other (not inferior) children, who care for one another: 'How are *you?*' This genuine caring was paid back, as children in the USA suggest in their feedback: 'You have nice video; I see you paint and I think it is very cool!' The US children also wanted to get close to the children in BIBLOCA by finding commonalities among them and acknowledging the Mexican histories in their own lives in the US: 'I think I have the same coin as you do in the video', one US child says, referring to the scene of the 'coin toss' at the start of the soccer game.

Transglobal and transcultural communications are brought to life in the children's exchange regarding games, gender, and educational difference. Activities in their free time, and games in particular, sparked conversations and questions from the three places. The children in China asked, 'What's the rule of the game? How you make up of a team?' The US children asked, 'Do you guys and girls have fun playing soccer at school? Do you always play soccer? Do you play a soccer every time you go to recess?' Moreover, the children in Africa wondered, 'Why is your play field without grass? Don't you put on sports wear?' Their questions were also rooted in their epistemologies of place, as seen not only in the African children's curiosity about why the soccer court in the Oaxacan public school does not have grass, but also in their inquiry as to whether the BIBLOCA children 'have a national park with antelopes and leopards near your school' (in response to the name of the game, 'Antelopes and Leopards'), which preludes the African children's comment that 'our school is near them but leopards and lions are dangerous'. This geopolitical context, however, was not constraining. The children also emerged from their own context, where gender roles and rules may differ. The children in Africa asked, 'Why do girls play football, do they know how to play netball too?' The children in China wondered, 'Why do girls wear earrings?' They also stated their difference on this point: 'We don't wear them [earrings] in school.'

Children also raised questions about school practices, based on their own geopolitical contexts. The children in the US raised the question: 'Why do you have to buy the breakfast?' They are most likely receiving free breakfast in their schools in the US. This is, of course, not the case in Mexico. The children in the US wondered about school hours: 'When do you go to school and come home from school?' The children in Africa wondered more about BIBLOCA: 'Can everyone come in the reading room? Don't you have some rules?' Questioning difference, without viewing it as inferior, is the core aspect of challenging colonial difference, as it is of critical cosmopolitanism. It is recognizing the other as worthy, and as someone one wants to know more about and learn from. The US children's comment is a testament to this and what keeps us hopeful that decolonizing English, literacy, technology, and transglobal and transcultural communication is possible: 'Could you send us one [video] where we can see your community and your school? and hear your language?' Engaging pre-service teachers in projects like GSB can also be a way to develop their decolonizing pedagogies, as we discuss next.

Conclusion: The Development of Decolonizing Pedagogies

This chapter has presented the experience of Luz, Estela and Jorge, three Mexican pre-service 'English' teachers, in co-creating videos with BIBLOCA students and in exchanging these videos with children from other countries through the project Global StoryBridges (GSB). Having the intention to decolonize literacy, English, and technology as well as to promote transglobal and transcultural communications among these children, we conclude that these activities help develop decolonizing pedagogies with pre-service language teachers, while enabling the pre-service teachers to meaningfully use these pedagogies in their future praxis and research. Concurring with our pre-service language teachers, we, as language teacher educators, see the benefits that this project has brought to Luz, Estela and Jorge as well as to other potential pre-service language teachers who engage in similar decolonizing projects.

In decolonizing pedagogies and projects like GSB, pre-service language teachers come to see the children as producers of knowledge, while negotiating affirming identities and creating inclusive spaces in the classroom. Currently in most schools within a modernity/coloniality framework, knowledge is merely a transmission from teachers to children, who must be helped (Onrubia & Mayordomo, 2015). In addition, schools typically create student hierarchies, from the most to the least intelligent student as dictated by grades. To the contrary, Luz, Estela and Jorge did not view the children in a vertical hierarchy. In this project, Luz, Estela and Jorge witnessed how children imagined, planned, carried out, completed, and shared a video that was well-received by the intended audience and had an affirming identity effect whereby both the children and the pre-service language teachers felt good about who they are and what they know. As such, Luz, Estela and Jorge created an inclusive pedagogical space in which all children participated throughout the different stages of the project. 'Inclusion means welcoming all students, and all citizens with open arms in our schools and communities' (Díaz-Aguado, 2013: 16, our translation). As the video shows, all children were included and formed part of a commonly-shared goal. This is totally the opposite in schools where success is individually measured. Hence, in decolonizing pedagogies, actions involving epistemologies and ontologies of place originate from the children in a collective and inclusive nature, and one can learn from the other who is no longer inferior.

In decolonizing pedagogies, children contribute to the generation of knowledge, and they speak up in more horizontal relationships where their social and cultural spaces are recognized and valued. As previously discussed, colonial difference created a hierarchical order, which is still replicated in schools through the asymmetrical relations between teachers and students, and among the students themselves. To the contrary, Luz, Estela and Jorge engaged in a 'broader horizontal process which challenge[d] the norms, knowledge and institutional norms [of modernity/ coloniality]' (Corona Berkin & Kaltmeier, 2012: 18, our translation). Throughout the project, the pre-service teachers led and followed discussions, opined and listened, gave and took suggestions, taught *and learned*. Decolonizing horizontal relationships opened the door for the recognition of children's cultural and social ways of being and knowing. In the video, for instance, Luz, Estela and Jorge respected the importance that activities in children's free time and the community spaces played in children's lives. Through games, children go beyond having fun: they establish friendship, negotiate rules and conflict, and develop language and multiliteracies, among other things. We also witnessed in the video that the children brought in their families' ways of knowing in regard to medicine and nutrition. As suggested by the video, children seem to share parts of their familial or personal life only when they notice that their ways of knowing and being are accepted and valued, which occurs when horizontal relationships are established and the teachers are willing to learn from the children.

In decolonizing pedagogies, the role of the teacher must be dynamic and include different strategies in their didactic teaching repertoire. As could be inferred in this section, the pre-service teachers did not play a fixed, transmissive role. Traditionally, education has been teacher-centered, where teachers plan, teach, and evaluate on their own (Durán, 2014). Throughout this project, Luz, Estela and Jorge gave up their position at the center of the activities being carried out; instead, they became facilitators, guides, and providers of support when required by the students. Most importantly, the pre-service teachers learned from the students and from the GSB project. Luz, Estela and Jorge had never before implemented the creation of a video project led by children as part of their teaching practice. They realized that literacy, English, and technological activities can come together in meaningful, creative, critical, and purposeful ways. They also noticed the importance of creating multimodal texts, a video in this case, for a real audience and with a real purpose. Finally, they experienced the powerful effect of the sharing and feedback sessions. They witnessed that it is through engaging children in global and transcultural communication among similar others that decolonizing literacy,

English, and technology not only becomes possible but also allows other epistemologies and ontologies to thrive. This, in turn, leads to the much-needed critical cosmopolitan citizenship.

Note

(1) In order to protect the privacy of the three pre-service teachers as research participants in this study, we refer to them by the pseudonyms Luz, Estela and Jorge. Further, in order to ensure the anonymity of the other research participants, the children who participated in the English classes taught by Luz, Estela and Jorge, we do not refer to the children by name, instead using only generic referents such as 'children', 'students', 'girls' and 'boys'.

References

Anderson, G.L. (1989) Critical ethnography in education: Origins, current status, and new directions. *Review of Educational Research* 59 (3), 249–270.

Aubert, A., Duque, E., Fisas, M. and Valls, R. (2013) *Dialogar y transformar. Pedagogía crítica del siglo XXI*. Barcelona: Editorial Graó de IRIF.

Aviles, K. and Vargas, R.E. (2006) Descubre Harvard que Enciclomedia funciona mejor en escuelas con luz. *La Jornada*. See http://www.jornada.unam.mx/2006/11/07/index.php?section=sociedad&article=046n1soc (accessed 15 February 2009)

Cavanagh, S. (2004) North America. *Education Week* XXIII (35), 12–16.

Cifuentes, B. (1998) *Letras sobre voces: Multilingüismo a través de la historia*. México City: CIESAS, INI.

Comunicación Social SEB (2008) *Habilidades digitales para todos cambiará la educación básica nacional*. See http://www.enciclomedia.edu.mx/Para_saber_mas/La_SEB_dice/28_Agosto_2008.htm (accessed 20 September 2008).

Corona Berkin, S. and Kaltmeier, O. (2012) Introducción: En diálogo: Metodologías horizontales en ciencias sociales. In S. Corona Berkin and O. Kaltmeier (eds) *En diálogo: Metodologías horizontales en ciencias sociales* (pp. 11–21). Barcelona: Gedisa.

Cummins, J. (2000) Academic language learning, transformative pedagogy, and information technology: Towards a critical balance. *TESOL Quarterly* 34 (3), 537–548.

Cummins, J. and Sayers, D. (1995) *Brave New Schools: Challenging Cultural Illiteracy through Global Learning Networks*. New York: St. Martin's Press.

Del Valle, S. (2008) Pagan caro fiasco en *Enciclomedia. Reforma*. See http://www.reforma.com/nacional/articulo/931274/ (accessed 5 November 2008).

Díaz Aguado, M. (2013) *Educación intercultural y aprendizaje cooperativo*. Madrid: Ediciones Pirámide.

Durán, D. (2014) *Aprenseñar. Evidencias e implicaciones educativas de aprender enseñando*. Madrid: Editorial Narcea.

Dussel, E. (2002) World-system and 'trans'-modernity. *Nepantla: Views from South* 3 (2), 221–244.

Elizondo Huerta, A., Paredes Ochoa, F. and Prieto Hernández, A.M. (2006) Enciclomedia: Un programa a debate. *Revista Mexicana de Investigación Educativa* 11 (28), 209–224.

Enciso, A. (2013) En seguridad alimentaria, 51.5 millones de mexicanos: Coneval. *La Jornada*. See http://www.jornada.unam.mx/2013/08/01/sociedad/035n1soc (accessed April 2021).

Enciso, A. and Camacho, F. (2013) Enfrentan indígenas más carencias que el resto de mexicanos pobres. *La Jornada*. See http://www.jornada.unam.mx/2013/08/09/sociedad/033n1soc (accessed April 2021).

Flick, U. (2015) Qualitative data analysis 2.0: Developments, trends, challenges. In N.K. Denzin and M.D. Giardina (eds) *Qualitative Inquiry and the Politics of Research* (pp. 119–139). Walnut Creek, CA: Left Coast Press, Inc.

González Amador, E. (2013) En México la brecha entre ricos y pobres es la más amplia de la OCDE. *La Jornada.* See http://www.jornada.unam.mx/2013/05/15/economia/029n2eco (accessed April 2021).

Hawkins, M.R. (2014) Ontologies of place, creative meaning-making and critical cosmopolitan education. *Curriculum Inquiry* 44 (1), 90–113.

Hawkins, M.R. (2018) Transmodalities and transnational encounters: Fostering critical cosmopolitan relations. *Applied Linguistics* 39 (1), 55–77.

Hernández-Zamora, G. (2004) Pobres pero leídos: La familia (marginada) y la lectura en México, presented at *Seminario Internacional La lectura: de lo íntimo a lo público: XXIV Feria Internacional del Libro Infantil y Juvenil*. México: CENART.

Hernández-Zamora, G. (2009) Neocolonialismo y políticas de representación: La creación histórica y presente del analfabetismo en México y Estados Unidos. *Lectura y Vida,* 30 (1), 30–43.

Hernández-Zamora, G. (2010) *Decolonizing Literacy: Mexican Lives in the Era of Global Capitalism.* Bristol: Multilingual Matters.

INEGI (2010) *México en Cifras: Oaxaca.* See http://www.inegi.org.mx/ sistemas/mexicocifras/default.aspx?e 20 (accessed April 2021).

Jiménez, R. and Smith, P. (2008) Mesoamerican literacies: Indigenous writing systems and contemporary possibilities. *Reading Research Quarterly* 43 (1), 28–46.

León Jiménez, E.N., Sughrua, W.M., Clemente, A., Huerta Cordova, V. and Vásquez Miranda, A.E. (2018) 'The coin of teaching English has two sides': Constructing identities as critical English teachers in Oaxaca, Mexico. In M.E. López Gopar (ed.) *International Perspectives on Critical Pedagogies in ELT* (pp. 101–123). London: Palgrave Macmillan.

López-Gopar, M.E. (2007) Beyond the alienating alphabetic literacy: Multiliteracies in Indigenous education in Mexico. *Diaspora, Indigenous and Minority Education: An International Journal* 1 (3), 159–174.

López-Gopar, M.E. (2016) *Decolonizing Primary English Language Teaching.* Bristol: Multilingual Matters.

López-Gopar, M.E. (ed.) (2019) *International Perspectives on Critical Pedagogies in ELT.* London: Palgrave.

López-Gopar, M.E. and Sughrua, W. (2014) Social class in English language education in Oaxaca, Mexico. *Journal of Language, Identity and Education* 13, 104–110.

López-Gopar, M.E., Javier Reyes, C.E. and Lambert Gómez, B. (2014) Critical ethnography and critical action research: Dialoguing with Mexican children. In S. Marshall, A. Clemente and M. Higgins (eds) *Shaping Ethnographies in Multilingual and Multicultural Contexts* (pp. 201–224). London, ONT: The Althouse Press.

López-Gopar, M.E., Núñez Méndez, O., Montes Medina, L. and Cantera Martínez, M. (2009) Inglés enciclomedia: A ground-breaking program for young Mexican children? *Teaching English to Younger Learners [Special Issue]. Mextesol Journal* 33 (1), 67–86.

López-Gopar, M.E., Sughrua, W. and Julián Caballero, J. (2013) Análisis crítico de las políticas de lenguaje en Oaxaca, México. In N. Elias and S.S. Fidalgo (eds) *Diálogos, Lingu(agem) e Ensino em Prácticas Sociais* (pp. 17–27). São Paulo: Porto de Ideias Editora.

Maldonado Alvarado, B. (2002) *Los indios en las aulas: Dinámicas de dominación y resistencia en Oaxaca.* México City: INAH.

Matías, P. (2007) Demandan maestros de Oaxaca aclarar el destino de 4,142 equipos de 'Enciclomedia'. *Proceso.* See http://www.proceso.com.mx/noticias_articulo.php?articulo=48686 (accessed 5 November 2008).

Menezes de Souza, L.M.T. (2003) Voices on paper: Multimodal texts and Indigenous literacy in Brazil. *Social Semiotics* 13 (1), 29–42.

Mignolo, W. (2000) *Local Histories/Global Designs: Coloniality, Subaltern Knowledges, and Border Thinking.* Princeton, NJ: Princeton University Press.

Mignolo, W. (2009) La colonialidad: La cara oculta de la modernidad [Coloniality: The hidden face of modernity]. In S. Breitwiser (ed.) *Catalog of Museum Exhibit: Modernologies, Museo de Arte Moderno de Barcelona* (pp. 39–49). Barcelona: MACBA.

New London Group (1996) A pedagogy of multiliteracies: Designing social futures. *Harvard Educational Review* 66 (1), 60–92.

Olivares Alonso, E. (2013) Sólo 19.3 % de la población en el grupo de personas no pobres ni vulnerables. *La Jornada.* See http://www.jornada.unam.mx/2013/03/15/sociedad/045n2soc (accessed April 2021).

Onrubia, J. and Mayordomo, R. (2015) El aprendizaje cooperativo elementos conceptuales. In R. Mayordomo and J. Onrubia (eds) *El aprendizaje cooperative* (pp. 179–651). Barcelona: Editorial UOC.

Prieto Hernández, A.M. (2005) Programa educativo nacional: Enciclomedia, retos y perspectivas. In T. Bertussi (ed.) *Anuario educativo mexicano, visión retrospectiva* (pp. 161–177). México City: Miguel Angel Porrúa/UPN.

Quijano, A. (2007) Coloniality and modernity/rationality. *Cultural Studies* 21 (2–3), 168–178.

Restall, M., Sousa, L. and Terraciano, K. (2005) *Mesoamerican Voices.* New York: Cambridge University Press.

Sánchez, V. (2007) El aparato no funciona. *Reforma.* See http://www.reforma.com/nacional/articulo/759231/ (accessed 14 December 2007).

Sayer, P. (2015) 'More & earlier': Neoliberalism and primary English education in Mexican public schools. *L2 Journal* 7 (3), 40–56.

Street, B. (2003) What's 'new' in New Literacy Studies? Critical approaches to literacy in theory and practice. *Current Issues in Comparative Education* 5 (2), 77–91.

Terborg, R., García Landa, L. and Moore, P. (2007) Language planning in Mexico. In R. Baldauf, Jr. and R.B. Kaplan (eds) *Language Planning and Policy in Latin America, Vol. 1: Ecuador, Mexico and Paraguay* (pp. 115–217). Clevedon: Multilingual Matters.

Treviño Ronzón, E. and Morales Landa, R. (2006) *Enciclomedia en escuelas del Estado de Veracruz: Formas de usos y retos.* Unpublished manuscript.

Walsh, C. (2003) Las geopolíticas del conocimiento y colonialidad del poder. Entrevista a Walter Mignolo. *Polis, Revista de la Universidad Bolivariana* 1 (4), 1–26.

9 Positionality Revisited: A Critical Examination of Meaning-Making and Collaboration in a Transnational Research Team

Patricia Ratanapraphart, Lisa Velarde, Nikhil M. Tiwari and Suman Barua

Introduction

> Meaning is not a property of individual words or groups of words but an ongoing performance of the world in its differential dance of intelligibility and unintelligibility.
> Karen Barad (2007: 149)

Meaning-making, although a continuous human activity, is an elusive object of study. While meaning is constantly being made, how exactly that meaning is made is a complex question. In the fields of SLA and literacy studies, meaning made through interaction – its form and construction within and across various modes, its historical roots and cultural significance, and its (mis)interpretations and effects – takes a central position as *the* subject of study. In an increasingly globalized and digitally connected world, the ways in which we communicate and make meaning with one another has become an area that draws our attention as researchers, particularly as messages move across spatial, temporal, ideological and material borders to construct knowledge. In making sense of global communications, Hawkins (2018) has called for a more layered, complex view of meaning-making that accounts for the culturally varied and situated semiotics embedded within languaging. Research that attends to multiple modes (material and otherwise) by exploring how they are arranged and carry meaning relationally is one such way that this complexity has been explored. Beyond looking at the structural components of language and communication, Hawkins, in her transmodalities framework, draws our attention to the sociocultural aspects of communication: the negotiation, positioning, identity work, and power relations that occur as a result of communication, playing an active role in infusing the interactions with meanings in and of themselves (Hawkins, 2018).

Much like communication, research is a transmodal endeavor and, like the youth's digital interactions on the Global StoryBridges (GSB) platform, is in and of itself a meaning-making practice. As research, its pursuits, and products move across time, space, and communities around the globe, researchers must explore questions of (mis)representation, Western biases, and positionality in order to engage more ethically across the multitude of intersecting lines of unequal power. Feminist scholars have explored and continue to challenge the tendency in academic research to write 'about' or 'for' marginalized others as opposed to 'with' them (Sultana, 2007). Researchers are situated in communities of practice, influenced by different social and material environments, and are a part of a distributed practice. Within these distributed practices, we are bound to our positionalities, and influenced ideologically in our readings, analyses, and interpretations. Researchers therefore experience tensions in attempting to mediate between the knowledge they bring while simultaneously honoring the voices of those with whom they seek to research.

In this chapter, we explore nuances of the distributed meaning-making of our transnational research team in the analysis we conducted of the compositional choices of a group of youth in India in the GSB project. To begin this chapter, we provide context for the research we conducted. We then present a conceptual framework for our reflections and analyses. Following that, we share three pivotal moments in the research during which our differing and layered identities and positionalities shaped our meaning-making as we worked together in various configurations over the course of the study.

Context

The Global StoryBridges site in India is located in a large and densely-populated 500-acre 'slum' in Mumbai called Dharavi. Sources estimate between 300,000 to 1,000,000 people live in Dharavi, earning it the title of Asia's largest slum (Davis, 2006; Sharma, 2000), although the accuracy of this has been debated by some scholars (Arabindoo, 2011; O'Hare *et al.*, 1998; Weinstein, 2014). Established in the mid-to-late 19th century as a distant site for industries such as tanneries to work without polluting the air and water of the largely European-inhabited downtown areas of Bombay (Dwivedi & Mehrotra, 2001), Dharavi is today – as the 2014 Guardian Cities project called it, 'an informal economic powerhouse' (Fernando, 2014: 1) – at the geographical heart of 21st-century urban

Mumbai, with leather and recycling industries dominating its economy. Notably, unlike other more middle-class parts of Mumbai, which are self-organized along religious, caste, linguistic, and even dietary lines (Khan, 2007; Menon, 2012), Dharavi's demographics are fairly heterogeneous. Hindus, Christians, Buddhists, and Muslims all live in the area; families belonging to the government-defined categories of Scheduled Castes, Scheduled Tribes, and 'Other Backward Classes' live alongside one another; and the main ethnolinguistic groups found in the area are Marathi-, Gujarati-, Tamil-, and Telugu-speaking (Rajyashree, 1986). This heterogeneity is present in the demographics of the youth participants in the Global StoryBridges site.

In Dharavi, GSB is facilitated via a community organization, Youth Empowered Dharavi (YED)[1]. Over the past 10 years, YED's mission has been to provide youth in Dharavi's neighborhoods with educational and extracurricular experiences with the aim of breaking the cycle of poverty. GSB is run as part of the duties of Surya, an employee of YED. Surya facilitated the project with a group of 12 youth (10 self-identified boys, two self-identified girls), who published a 4:43 minute long video in November 2018 titled *Ganesh Festival in India* – referring to the festival celebrating the Hindu god Ganesh's annual visit to Earth. Youth from other project sites in Vietnam, Spain and the US responded to the video with questions in the website's comment section. We initially selected the Dharavi site's video for analysis because we found the comment chain between the youth and their viewers interesting, but our interests and focus shifted as we began to look more closely at their compositional choices – particularly, the ways they incorporated culturally-situated modes – in the video they produced. To understand how modes were assembled and meanings were made and communicated in the videos, we asked: How did the youth engage in digitally-mediated, multimodal, transnational communication? To interrogate the influences of our own cultural frameworks of understanding upon our answers to that question, we asked in turn: How did we, as a transnational team, make sense of the youth's composition as we drew from our own situated lenses of interpretation? Moreover, what were the affordances of a transnational team on this endeavor?

Literature Dive

As the authors of this chapter entered into this collaborative research, it quickly became apparent that we were noticing, or finding meaning, in different aspects of the video, and, as a result, each of us felt a sense of limitation as we developed our insights and interpretations. Questions emerged, such as: 'Is what I am noticing valid when it escaped my colleague's notice? Is it anything at all?' These reflexive questions were not so much a result of conflicting interpretations of the data as they were each member of the research team noticing and finding importance in different things altogether. As we engaged in the process of weaving a coherent story of what we were seeing, it became clear to us where each individual researcher's voice was coming through. When presented at the 2019 American Association of Applied Linguistics (AAAL) conference in Atlanta, GA, the work showed a unified analysis and story to the audience. We, however, saw our work as more of a multivocal tapestry in which individual ideas, insights, and interpretations were taken up, incorporated, and woven together. Accordingly, our meta-reflection on the research process operated on the premise that meaning-making occurs in relation to one's positionality, within communities of practice, and in fusion with the material world. We explored how our differing identities and positionalities influenced our collaborative meaning-making. We identified aspects from our own backgrounds, experiences, and culturally-situated practices – ways of seeing and being in the world – that played a role in how we interpreted the data. We examined our physical and material environments (access to technology, proximity to research participants, etc.) to consider their role in our collaborative construction of meaning. As a way of grounding our reflections, we build from three bodies of literature where similar topics have been explored by feminist, social anthropological, and literacy scholars.

Researcher positionality and reflexivity, communities of practice and material environments

Inclusion of positionality statements and calls for more reflexive practices in qualitative research have become not only commonplace, but a necessary and expected component of academic praxis. Though there have been critiques of this practice, with some scholars having described it as little more than self-flagellation, or a recognizable token of legitimacy amongst academics (Mountz, 2002; Sultana, 2007), the inclusion and continued focus on the positionalities and identities of researchers in qualitative work reflects the ontological and epistemological stance that sees research not as an objective practice, but rather as always and inescapably subjective (Berger, 2015). Feminist geographer Gillian Rose (1997: 306) described reflexivity in research as a way of 'situating knowledges' and 'avoiding the false neutrality and universality of so much academic knowledge'. Much of the work in the field of feminist geography aims at disrupting and re-thinking the relationships and power dynamics between researcher and research participants, with the goal of creating non-hierarchical relations between the two (Nagar, 2002). In our work together as a research team, we found that, much like Sultana (2007: 367) described, research, when reflexive in nature, becomes a practice where 'process and content can get blurred'. Differing positionalities not only influence interpretations of data, but researcher position and identity also play a large role in what and how data are generated. By not actively reflecting on the role researchers play in the knowledge construction process, researchers run the risk of unethically (mis)representing the experiences of their participants – a grave offense indeed when positions of power are unequal. As we analyzed the data, rather than identifying clean and linear cause and effect chains, the process felt akin to tracing the interwoven threads of meaning. Therefore, we understood that we were a part of the meaning-making process, and to be unaware of that would have the potential to forefront the Western gaze and perpetuate inequities.

Like feminist geographers (McDowell, 1999; Rose, 1997), scholars in the field of social anthropology have theorized on the situated nature of knowledge in the work around communities of practice (Lave, 1991; Lave & Wenger, 1991). Germinal studies exploring communities of practice have placed emphasis on the interactional nature of learning. Jean Lave (1991: 67) challenged the notion that any event, or situation, could be studied in isolation. As she described it: 'theories of situated activity bracket off the social world as something one can study – this negates the possibility that subjects are constituted in their relationships with and activities in that world'. In taking a reflexive approach to research, then, researchers need not only be aware of how their identity and positionality interface with those of their participants, but researchers must also understand and take seriously the variety of cultural, institutional, and societal factors that imbue their understandings of the world and the ways they (inter)act within it. Lave (1991: 67) claimed that, 'the social scientist's practice must be analyzed in the same historical, situated terms as any other practice under investigation'. This chapter is an effort to do just that. Seeing the nature of communities of practice as multiple and layered – with the understanding that individuals are simultaneously members of different communities to varying degrees – pushes us to reflect on our own situated knowledges and begin the work of tracing our knowledge back to its roots within each of our own differing communities of practice.

Given the virtual interactions that occur within this project and the way that communities and their practices weave together in different ways online, the concept of communities of practice when applied to transmodal work offers a unique perspective: that is, communities are not bound to a geographical location and their practices expand and reconfigure with each new interaction. Literacy scholars have theorized that communication and meaning-making are always shaped and have been shaped by the technologies and artifacts used and created (Brandt & Clinton, 2002; Haas, 2013). This scholarship became another lens through which we analyzed our own process as a research team. Like writing, we found our research activities (e.g. conducting interviews, drafting together on a shared document, generating and sharing data and notes, working through logistical matters, etc.) constantly mediated and influenced by the realities of our physical and material environments. Differing access to technologies, research participants, and time greatly influenced both data collected and the sense that was being made of it.

Much like the knowledge we each carried as a result of our socialization into various communities of practice, our situated positions in the material world influenced our meaning-making endeavors. This harkens back to Hawkins' transmodal framework where she described that all meaning-making is a result of the affordances and constraints of the multiple modes and material resources involved in the interactions (Hawkins, 2018). Each researcher's self – within their multiple and layered identities, situated knowledge and communities, and place in relation to the social and material world – shape the research. In this chapter we use these three layers as tools to reflect on the role our differing positionalities played in the research and to challenge the nature of knowledge production in transnational collaborative research.

Methods

Data collection

A qualitative approach guided the data collection and analysis of this case study (Bartlett & Vavrus, 2016) as a subset of Global StoryBridges. Data collected in the form of the youth-produced video artifact, semi-structured interviews, comment logs, and recordings of interactions served two purposes: first, it followed the Dharavi youth as they created, responded to, and reflected on the process of composing one digital story; and second, it tracked emergent understandings on the part of individual research team members to underscore similarities and differences in interpretations of the youth's work.

To support data triangulation (Denzin, 1978), two of the Western research team members (and chapter authors), Lisa and Patricia, interviewed the site facilitator from India, Surya, over a Skype conference call and through email; later on, Suman, a third research team member living in Mumbai, conducted an in-person interview. Lisa and Patricia also interviewed youth participants as a group over Skype. Suman conducted further interviews with the youth on site focused on the collection of footage, their production of the video, and their reflections on the process. The youth were interviewed by Lisa and Patricia in English, and by Suman in Hindi (a *lingua franca* in Mumbai), and Nikhil, an Indian research team member based in the US, translated transcripts into English for coding. We also collected chat logs among the Dharavi youth and their global peers on the topic of their video as an additional literacy artifact and conducted thematic coding, which we describe in greater detail below.

Drawing from work conducted by other international research teams (Hull *et al.*, 2010; Stornaiuolo *et al.*, 2017), the team for the present study engaged a reflective process during each phase of the research. Previous scholars' reflections on transnational team-based research (Creese & Blackledge, 2012) have addressed the significance of the modes and means of communication among team members, and we acknowledge its value in our own work. In this chapter, however, we have chosen to attend specifically to positionality and stance (Jaffe, 2009, 2015; Lee & Simon-Maeda, 2006; Rose, 1997; Sultana, 2007) both during analysis and in reflections on the research process. In addition to individual memos and group debriefs, data collection for this process consisted of semi-structured interviews of Nikhil by Lisa and Patricia and later of Suman by Lisa. The video composed by the youth served as a cueing tool during this process (Tobin et al., 2009). The goal of such a process was to elicit interpretations from each team member while, in turn, using members' reflections as an additional source for data triangulation and member checking in the coding of the video.

Analysis

Given the variety of data sources generated by this project, the team employed an iterative and systematic method of analysis in which memos, transcripts, and reflections were subjected to two rounds of open-ended and thematic coding (Saldaña, 2015). Of the dominant codes that were identified, themes such as culturally-embedded knowledge and researchers' own positionalities emerged from the data, which further highlighted the need to revisit the Dharavi youth's video compositions from both insider and outsider perspectives (DeWalt & DeWalt, 2011). The team was composed of three US-based graduate students – one Anglo-American (Lisa), one Asian American (Patricia) and one Indian national (Nikhil) – and a team member more intimately connected with and based at the site (Suman). Researchers' own assumptions were interrogated during this process, and the analyses were then used to further inform conversations that had been held with the site facilitator and youth participants.

The video analysis involved an additional set of steps. Using a modified version of Hull and Nelson's (2005) analytic, the research team parsed out the video artifact into brief 5 to 10 second segments and detailed their reflections and emergent understandings in four columns. In the first column, screenshots of the video segments were displayed, while the second column included details of modes employed by youth in their production (including sounds, written text, spoken language, and colors). The third column included notes about the researchers' own noticings and connections, and the final column detailed questions that emerged from viewing the segment. Drawing from Hawkins' (2018) five complexities of transmodalities, analyses of the interactions around the Dharavi video attended explicitly to the ways individuals drew from a variety of modes and fluidly moved between them in meaning-making, and identified relations of power embedded within those interactions and communications.

This video analytic supported both goals of the study: first, it allowed researchers to attend to the various modes employed by youth in the composition of their videos; and second, it fostered reflections for researchers to examine how meanings drawn from the videos were situated within each individual's own lens of interpretation.

Altogether, the coded memos, interview and video transcripts, and chat logs provided means through which the team could attend not only to the meanings that were being made through the video and in communication across sites, but also to the specific relations of power negotiated between sites and within the research process itself. The portrait rendered through the video analytic is a complex one, made doubly so with the inclusion of both youth and researcher perspectives. In the following section, examples drawn from the data reveal the central role of materials and community literacy practices in shaping youth's compositional choices, and also detail, more broadly, the inward lens that allowed researchers to unearth the affordances of multivocality in transnational work.

Discussion

To further elucidate how multivocality emerged and served as pivotal points in this work, we share three interactions during data collection and analysis, which demonstrate shifts in understandings and group configurations. The first of these moments highlights the affordances and constraints of approaching transmodal communication through different theoretical lenses, while the second delves into the findings that emerge when placing this work in conversation with emic and etic perspectives. The final moment traces the trajectory of this research to demonstrate the varied nature of 'the' emic perspective and argues for consideration of what we hereafter name 'a spectrum of emicity'.

First pivotal moment: The outside, Western gaze

The initial aim of this study was to more closely examine how youth engaged in global communications made meaning of one another and of each others' literacy artifacts. As such, we began our work by tracing the arc of communication (Hawkins, 2018) – i.e. composition, movement, reception and negotiation – between the Dharavi youth and their global peers, focused on the Ganesh festival video. The video, which features sprawling shots of Ganesh statues set to an upbeat track ('Deva Shree Ganesha' from the 2012 Hindi film *Agneepath*), takes viewers through the days leading up to the festival celebrating the Hindu god. From the process of painting statues, both large and small, to the steps taken in adorning them in jewelry, the youth capture a bevy of different colored statues situated across their neighborhood in various states of preparation. Towards the end of the video, the audience is taken through the entrance of the festival into a tent, after which a shot pans out showing the placement of the Ganesh statues on *pandaals* (raised platforms). Because we embedded conversational checkpoints throughout the data collection and analysis process, the first pivotal moment occurred early on during the research team's initial viewing of this video. For two team members, Lisa and Patricia, the video analytic that each engaged led to a realization that: first, their own theoretical lenses featured starkly in determining what they were and were not noticing; and second, their outsider, Western-based gaze on the work necessitated revisions to the data analysis process.

Lisa, whose work is based in literacy studies, approached the video from a new materialist perspective (Micciche, 2014). She viewed the video as a literacy artifact, attending especially to its composition processes, stylistic choices, and meaning-making potential. While meaning-making around the video served as a larger umbrella under which each of these elements was categorized, she asked: What did the youth want to make? How did the material actors guide the process? What was the ultimate effect? In attending to these aspects of composition, she sought to identify points of alignment and divergence in the production and reception of messages, especially when the artifact was viewed as an object imbued with agency (Barad, 2007; Ingold, 2010). Alternatively, Patricia approached the video with a focused lens on the languaging and literacy practices of the youth, raising questions around how such practices were situated within and mediated through an ever-changing and continually (re)negotiated landscape of experiences (Gutiérrez, 2008; Lave & Wenger, 1991). What modes the youth employed in their videos, how they assembled the modes to communicate particular messages, and how these messages were interpreted were of particular interest to her. To that end, she paid explicit attention to meaning-making as a situated activity, considering aspects of the youth's linguistic repertoires that emerged in the video, as well as questioning how and what meanings were made on the part of the global youth for whom the video topic proved foreign.

Based on these differing standpoints, Lisa and Patricia's initial viewing of the Ganesh video yielded nuanced points of contrast, an element that featured significantly in their initial codes. During the first 25 seconds of the video, a blue Ganesh idol was shown in a slow pan from top to bottom. The panning concluded with a zoom on the idol's face, which occurred in spurts, as opposed to the panning technique used moments earlier (see Figure 9.1). Both Lisa and Patricia agreed to call this a 'double zoom'; however, what they each understood the double zoom to be differed slightly. For Lisa, it was a technique that emerged as different parts of the idol's face pulled in the focus of the camera-youth assemblage. On the other hand, Patricia's analysis centered on the youth's intentions behind the double zoom, under the assumption that it was a choice made with the intention to support a particular meaning, tone, or message. Whether considered an emergence or a choice, both certainly *made* meaning of the

Figure 9.1 Double zoom shown between 0:21 to 0:23 in the video

zooming technique, and just as their backgrounds shaped their lenses and led to different interpretations of the double zoom, by extension, this too would be the case for any and all viewers. Thus, we argue that readings of that particular clip and meanings ultimately made by viewers would very possibly differ from youth's initial intentions.

The process of completing a video analytic proved particularly challenging, as, in line with concerns raised by Hawkins (2018) regarding the intertwined nature of modes, the researchers experienced difficulty identifying and coding the modes separately without considering the meanings that they signaled in conjunction with one another. Simultaneously, the process also necessitated a deeper understanding of the youth's community literacy practices, which was equally difficult to identify as researchers situated in the US. As Lisa and Patricia continued to view and individually code the video, they emerged with a greater number of questions. Patricia, who had homed in on the music selection and pieced together that the song, sung in Hindi, repeated the word, 'Ganesha', found it striking that the term differed from the video captions, which spoke in alternating clips of 'Ganesh' and 'Ganesha'. From a combination of these spelling variations and the shots of the multi-colored Ganesh statues in the video, questions for her centered on whether the multiple idols were representative of different genders, and if the youth's intent had been to highlight this through such multimodal composition. Lisa, on the other hand, focused on the way in which the video had been constructed, the shots that had been selected, as well as how they had been assembled together. What had been the youth's intent in panning from the multi-colored Ganesh statues to the sole Ganesh statue in black? What did the colors signify? What meanings did they want to convey, and how were meanings made of their compositions? Such questions ultimately shaped the next stage of the research, which expanded to fold in interviews and perspectives of additional team members more closely tied to the place and site itself.

Second pivotal moment: Our joint gaze

In a critical reflection of her own experiences studying southern Black youth's transactions at a community-based radio station, Green (2014: 150) noted the importance of 'consider[ing] and interrogat[ing] assumptions about the appropriate loci of the researcher in the research site, and question[ing] the relationship between such role(s) and research design and analysis'. Who researchers are, the histories and experiences they bring to bear on their work, as well as the epistemological beliefs they ground their work in are vital areas of consideration in transnational studies; and this emerged starkly following Lisa and Patricia's initial coding of the data. Among a number of factors, their geographical location, their knowledge of Indian customs and beliefs, as well as their own theoretical standpoints emerged in their analysis and worked to shape how they understood meaning-making as it occurred across global youth and among the researchers and participants. Upon identifying the limitations of their gaze, they sought input from additional team members, which resulted in the expansion of the core group of researchers to include Nikhil and Suman. This process, reflective of and in line with arguments made in anthropological studies regarding the emic and etic distinction (Harris, 1976), serves as the second pivotal moment, which we describe in further detail below.

For Lisa and Patricia, the questions that had emerged following the initial coding of the video were plentiful and diverse; and ultimately, the questions they asked of the video served as a launching point for the interview with the youth participants and site facilitator. However, in an attempt to interrogate their own assumptions and further identify the ways in which their positionalities shaped their orientation towards the work, they spoke first with Nikhil, who was geographically proximal. Having worked in classrooms and community-based education spaces in India across middle and lower-income groups, he offered valued and contrasting insider-based knowledge. Using the youth's video as a cueing tool, Lisa and Patricia interviewed Nikhil with the intention of unearthing the ways in which he made meaning of the various modes and stylistic techniques deployed by the youth in their composition. What emerged in that team interview were nuanced points of divergence in the readings of the video, and yet more interestingly, Nikhil's own reflections on what he understood to be intelligible to a broader audience.

The previously discussed double zoom came up in the interview with Nikhil, who identified the technique as a common one used in Indian soap operas. As he understood it, employing this method would produce a dramatic effect and draw the viewer's attention to a scene; and while this effect had been achieved on both Lisa and Patricia, the rich history influencing the youth's compositional choices was lost on them. Similarly, the youth had also chosen to incorporate clips of the Ganesh idols alongside a variety of figurines – mice, forms of women, and the Hindu god Shiva. While both Lisa and Patricia noted these in their codes as 'additional statues', neither made the connection of these figurines to the festival itself. Instead, they interpreted the depictions of the molding and painting of the mice, women, and Shiva idols as simply an additional example of the varied skill set of the Dharavi adults. However, instead of viewing the depictions in this manner, Nikhil suggested that what was likely being communicated was the full range of the symbolic forms rooted in the mythology of Ganesh as a god (e.g. the mice, or *mooshika*, as Ganesh's *vaahana*, or vehicle) and the celebration of the festival (which involves smaller scale worship of Shiva, his father, and Gauri, his mother, who are believed to visit with him during that time). Nikhil then raised observations of various elements he felt would be additional points of confusion for viewers situated outside of the Dharavi context. For example, he drew Lisa and Patricia's attention to the banners of sponsors around the *pandaals*, which they had not known were of local politicians seeking to build relationships with the community. Furthermore, he noted the varied linguistic groups indexed by the Ganesh/Ganesha distinction, which ran contrary to Patricia's assumption about gender distinctions. While Patricia had initially questioned the language of the song played throughout the video, Nikhil further brought their attention to additional lenses of interpretation, asking if others might read into the song as one reflective of religious practices or of Bollywood. Such sentiments were mirrored in the questions the Dharavi youth received from another site, in which youth situated in the US asked, 'Is the song that was played in the background connected to the statue or was it just for fun?' While the Dharavi youth had incorporated sophisticated literary elements and practices that would be read and understood by those within their own communities of practice, Nikhil demonstrated in his interview that much of this would have been, and in fact was, lost on their global audience.

Yet, despite the inclusion of Nikhil's perspective and interpretations on this work, additional questions lingered. In attempting to analyze how youth's communication and meaning-making were shaped by the literacy practices of their community, the researchers found it crucial to more closely understand the community itself. Given the interwoven nature of literacy practices and the bearing that multiple communities have on an individual's practices, the process of jointly creating a video was a complex task. It required negotiations among the youth not only about what to film but also how to collect footage, what techniques to use, and which scenes to include and exclude in the production. The interview with the youth and their site facilitator shed light on this process, but it also raised questions for the researchers about what more could be learned from this insider perspective while in the field with the youth themselves. Thus, Suman worked with both the youth and Surya, offering additional insight by shadowing their video-making process, asking questions of their compositional choices, and later interviewing the participants at the site.

As Suman and Lisa discussed the video, they sought to gain more insight on the youth's selection of the video's topic. They wondered: 'Why had the youth chosen to depict the Ganesh festival? What had they hoped to convey to their audience through their video?' For Suman, it was a particular point of interest to ask about why they had chosen to record only the days leading up to the festival, as opposed to the festival itself. None of the other team members had raised this point, and in the case of Lisa and Patricia, neither had known that the entire festival was not shown. Suman noted that a potential bearing on topic selection was the Dharavi site's location. Because the youth were situated near the workshops where the idols were created, he predicted that the proximity possibly influenced why the youth chose to depict what they did, and that time constraints may have likely played into why they chose the time period that they had.

Lisa and Patricia had initially interviewed the youth and asked them similar questions; yet, what emerged from Suman's interviews were more finely nuanced explanations. In his interview with the youth, he discovered that location and timing had, indeed, played a role in their topic selection, but that the youth had also felt that the idols' aesthetics would be appealing and attractive to global viewers. This interview, while illuminating, also became a point of contrast for the team. In Lisa and Patricia's initial interview with the youth, they learned from the youth that the topic selection was due to youth's desire to show a collective sense of 'culture' to their global peers. Despite additional questions asked, they did not receive as much detailed explanation as what the youth later told Suman. To him, they said, 'We thought we would show all that happens during a time [featuring] our India's tradition and culture, so that [our audience can] come to know all about how us Indians' culture is and [...] all its importance' (interview, 20 August 2019). They also added that the size of the pillars, their selection of particular idols, and later stages of production and editing were all tied to what they felt would be 'attractive' to viewers. This highlighted a sense of audience which had not emerged in the initial interview, where youth had said they wanted to 'show [their] lives' (interview, 19 February 2019).

Through the interview with Suman, what emerged was a striking image, one that showcased youth's awareness of those within and outside of their community. Their topic selection was based not only on what they (as youth) found personally interesting, but also what they felt others would not know, others both within *and* outside of their community. A part of these differing findings could be attributed to differences, such as Lisa and Patricia's interview being conducted in English over Skype at 4am in their (Lisa and Patricia's) local time, while Suman's interview with the youth was conducted in Hindi and on site. More significantly, however, these findings highlight how there were differences in relationships between the various research team members with the youth and their context, factors that contributed not only to how the team made sense of what youth produced, but also of how they made meaning with and of one another.

Third pivotal moment: Together, a broader perspective

More often than not, 'emic' and 'etic' perspectives have been treated as binaries in which researchers view themselves as possessing and offering either 'insider' or 'outsider' lenses in their studies (Headland, 1990: 4). In our experience, however, we did not feel that to be the case, and as a result we seek to complicate this notion by underscoring the immense value of diverse positionalities *within* a research site. The ways multiple emic perspectives contributed to our own analysis led us away from binary thinking (see Figure 9.2) and instead to conceptualize a 'spectrum' of emicity to an imagined and distributed center of meaning surrounding a lived event. We posit that what might be termed 'more centrally' emic is that meaning which is distributed amongst those closer (spatially and culturally) and more directly involved with one another in the lived event studied, and what is 'less centrally' emic – blending gradually to the etic – is the meaning that emerges the farther away one's positionality, and the higher one's hierarchical positioning to the event, is (see Figure 9.3). In imagining this on vertical (hierarchical) and horizontal (proximal) axes, we were able to achieve richer analytics and analyses, as this allowed us to attend to the individual and the influences of their communities of practice as related to their interpretations of the video. Each researcher's positionality is not unidimensional (not simply Western, not simply gendered), but is multidimensional and situated in the space between positions on both hierarchical and proximal axes. We conceive the hierarchical axis as being an actor's position in any figured chain of command or structure (e.g. principal investigator, graduate student researcher, participant) and class and cultural hierarchies (e.g. socioeconomic status, race and caste, gender, language, Global North/Global South positioning). Simultaneously, our conception of proximity to a lived event is both spatial (i.e. physical proximity to the social phenomena under study) and cultural (i.e. the degree to which individuals share models and practices of knowing and being in the world).

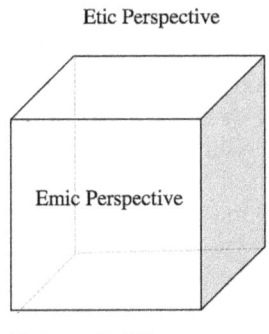

Figure 9.2 A traditional view of the emic and etic distinction

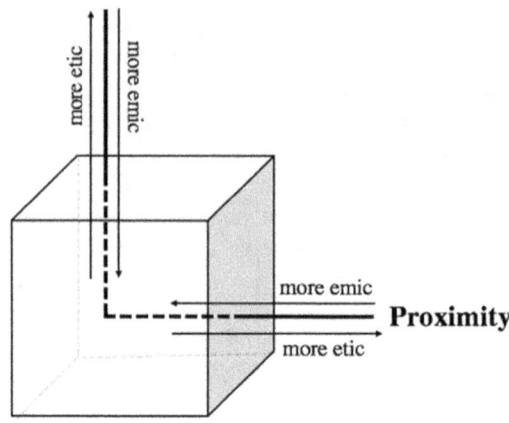

Figure 9.3 A re-envisioned spectrum of emicity

For example, when Lisa and Patricia asked the youth to talk about the different colors of the Ganesh idols they had observed in the video, a youth explained that the local Tamil community preferred darker idols while others preferred lighter-toned ones (and so both were available for purchase). But he offered an interesting personal understanding as well. To his community, the Tamil people, the darker idols were 'more auspicious' to worship. Prior to the youth's response, Nikhil did not attend to the differing colors of the idols, knowing beforehand that they were a common variant in his experience. However, what was striking to Nikhil was that no such understanding of the idols' colors is prevalent in the hegemonic priestly caste communities of practice he belongs to. Ordinarily, Nikhil's positionality as a cultural insider to a generally figured 'Indian' or 'Hindu' frame of reference would render his perspective an emic one. However, the fact that his interpretation did not align with the youth's is an example of why we want to trouble the binary category of emic and etic. Attending to these nuances in turn afforded him inroads to an analysis of the youth's ostensibly un-self-aware response to forces of Brahminical hegemony. It appeared to Nikhil that community remakings of meaning, ordinarily tightly controlled by upper castes, seemed to emerge in the youth's personal meaning-making of the mode of the idols' differing color. Issues of power via re-entextualization of modes could have been further explored. We did not choose to explore that idea, yet we hold that even the inroads to such a case would have been lost had the transmodalities framework not reoriented our stance to emicity – not as more valid/less valid, emic/etic binary positions, but themselves as methodological and epistemological sites where analytics and meanings emerge.

To demonstrate, the spectrum of emicity played a role in various researchers' meaning-making of the Ganesh/Ganesha distinction. As previously discussed in the first pivotal moment, Patricia was the first to notice and raise questions around the varied spellings. While Nikhil had interpreted this as indexing different linguistic backgrounds, different interpretations emerged in Lisa's interview of Suman. When asked, Suman first indicated that 'Ganesh' and 'Ganesha' were interchangeable, and that in fact he had not noticed the variation in the youth's video. As he thought aloud, however, he began to distinguish between the two spellings to describe 'Ganesh' as more formal and respectful and 'Ganesha' as more endearing and affectionate. He illustrated this understanding in some detail, describing how he, as director of an organization, would use the spelling 'Ganesh' in formal communications (e.g. declaring a work holiday on an internal memo), in contrast to more informal and devotional contexts where 'Ganesha' might be used. Interestingly, he concluded his thoughts by wondering out loud whether it had to do with the language the youth spoke at home, closer to the interpretations that Patricia and Nikhil had constructed.

These varied and nuanced interpretations further highlight the spectrum of emicity and illustrate how cultural and epistemological lines also intersect and factor into definitions of emicity. By traditional anthropological standards, Lisa and Patricia's perspectives would be considered etic and Suman and Nikhil's emic by virtue of culture, ethnicity, place and experience. However, we complicate this notion by tracing the hierarchical and proximal axes along which our interpretations were shaped. Patricia and Nikhil, for example, share a background in applied linguistics, which we believe may have played an influential role in the former's noticing and the latter's interpretation of the Ganesh/Ganesha distinction. Their shared, specialized disciplinary knowledge and status as graduate researchers positioned them as distant on both the proximal and hierarchical axes. Simultaneously, in comparison to Patricia, Nikhil's greater cultural proximity to and familiarity with the place afforded him an ability to provide an answer to the question/s she raised. Furthermore, Nikhil and Suman share cultural understandings, which we believe may have led to an overlap in their interpretation of the spelling distinction being tied to linguistic backgrounds. However, Suman's greater spatial and cultural proximity to the youth in his position as director of YED (which we associate with a more emic positioning) meant that his additional interpretations were based on his understandings of the youth's day-to-day interactions and language use. To further complicate this, Suman positioned himself as an individual who had 'lived [in Mumbai] forever' yet still found much of the content of the youth's video new and pleasantly surprising, indexing himself as more emically involved in the Bengali community (for whom Ganesh festival celebrations are less prevalent) – an identity not shared with any of the youth. The role his director position plays to hierarchically position him higher than participants, too, is something to be considered. Thus, we hold that at any given time, researchers and participants can be simultaneously positioned at different points in the axes of hierarchy and proximity – considering epistemology, culture and power – in complex, non-binary ways.

Conclusion

To recapitulate, we asked ourselves the questions: 'Why a transnational team?' and 'What does it afford us?' A transnational team offered a multiplicity of perspectives and vantage points from which to explore youth's experiences. Given our focus on studying youth's meaning-making in global communication, we recognized foremost that the complexities inherent in this endeavor are multi-layered. Questions of foregrounding and backgrounding perspectives arose; material and conventional affordances and constraints clearly shaped meanings made; and varied and incompatible agendas interacted. Thus, while studying how the youth's communities of practice influenced their compositions, we also looked inward and studied how our own communities of practice influenced our readings of their work. Simultaneously, we recognized how both researchers and participants are situated in socio-historical contexts imbued with stratified power relations and considered its impact on the research process: the gathering, analysis, and presentation of data.

There is nothing inherently special about any particular researcher's perspective; however, we recognize that meanings made – interpretations of data – are privileged differently across a multitude of contexts. Within academia, the interpretations of researchers are valued over those of participants, a point that has received much attention in feminist scholarship (e.g. McDowell, 1999; Rose, 1997). Western, Global-North interpretations and products of research are privileged over those in the Global-South periphery (Sultana, 2007; Wallerstein, 2001). With these inequities in mind, ethical engagement necessitates that we not only form transnational teams, but that within these teams, we: first, stay cognizant of the voices and perspectives foregrounded in the work; second, question the sociohistorical and sociomaterial processes involved in positioning individuals in the team; and third, contest our own tendencies to privilege certain interpretations over others as more valuable. Most importantly, we must be able to embrace the multiplicity of meanings made, whether or not they align with our own; for it is within the spaces of divergence that epistemological potential resides.

While such affordances of transnational research are, we believe, novel and exciting, we also recognize the constraints of this kind of work. Living across vast distances, far from our participants and their lived experiences, time and space played a central role in determining who could speak with whom, when, and through which medium. For the researchers located in the US, this meant that email and Skype were the two common mediums used for communication. Emails got buried; their asynchronous nature made it hard to ask and follow up on questions in a manner conducive to deep analysis. Skype froze often. Gaps and delays in the video and audio feed broke the conversations, which made them fragmented and frustrating to follow. Not all youth were always visible in the call, and street sounds often drowned out the voices of the participants farther away from the computer. Apart from the material constraints related to distance, time, and tools, we feel compelled to acknowledge the reams of data we consciously decided to exclude from this chapter as we considered the content, form, and stylistic expectations of this publication's (primarily Western, academic) audience. This may mean, therefore, in such a Western-based context, that some agendas are lost. It is fair to say that researchers have always had to bound their agendas per the expectations of academia, but more often than not, that is the end of the story. Work in such kinds of transnational teams, however, means that opportunities for reciprocity abound, in which Western-based researchers can, in other contexts, play a less central and more supportive role in the agendas and programs of their counterparts in the Global South.

Yet, how can more immediate work such as this chapter avoid perpetuating prevailing power structures? We posit that placing now-ubiquitous positionality statements in conversation with talk about choices made in data generation, analysis, and presentation is a means to critically locate oneself within a spectrum of emicity. Crucial to the process is an acknowledgement of the varying degrees to which each researcher on a team is hierarchically and proximally located in relation to the researched. This allows us not only to contest hierarchies of power, but to look at how power itself functions within meaning-making. We, therefore, call for participation in research processes which take into account the issues of power and inequity that have been present historically in academia and assert that transnational research teams, and consideration of spectrums of emicity within them, is one such way to achieve it.

Note

(1) All names of people and groups in this chapter are pseudonyms to protect the privacy of research participants.

References

Arabindoo, P. (2011) Rhetoric of the 'slum': Rethinking urban poverty. *City* 15 (6), 636–646.

Barad, K. (2007) *Meeting the Universe Halfway: Quantum Physics and the Entanglement of Matter and Meaning.* Durham, NC: Duke University Press.

Bartlett, L. and Vavrus, F. (2016) *Rethinking Case Study Research: A Comparative Approach.* New York: Taylor & Francis.

Berger, R. (2015) Now I see it, now I don't: Researcher's position and reflexivity in qualitative research. *Qualitative Research* 15 (2), 219–234.
Brandt, D. and Clinton, K. (2002) Limits of the local: Expanding perspectives on literacy as a social practice. *Journal of Literacy Research* 34 (3), 337–356.
Creese, A. and Blackledge, A. (2012) Voice and meaning-making in team ethnography. *Anthropology & Education Quarterly* 43 (3), 306–324.
Davis, M. (2006) Planet of slums. *New Perspectives Quarterly* 23 (2), 6–11.
Denzin, N.K. (1978) *Sociological Methods*. New York, NY: McGraw-Hill.
DeWalt, K. and DeWalt, B. (2011) *Participant Observation: A Guide for Fieldworkers*. Lanham, MD: AltaMira Press.
Dwivedi, S. and Mehrotra, R. (2001) *Bombay: The Cities Within*. Mumbai: Eminence Designs Pvt. Ltd.
Fernando, B. (2014) An urbanist's guide to the Mumbai slum of Dharavi. *The Guardian*, 2 April. See https://www.theguardian.com/cities/2014/apr/01/urbanist-guide-to-dharavi-mumbai.
Green, K. (2014) Doing double dutch methodology: Playing with the practice of participant observer. In D. Paris and M.T. Winn (eds) *Humanizing Research: Decolonizing Qualitative Inquiry with Youth and Communities* (pp. 147–150). Thousand Oaks, CA: SAGE.
Gutiérrez, K.D. (2008) Developing a sociocritical literacy in the third space. *Reading Research Quarterly* 43 (2), 148–164.
Haas, C. (2013) *Writing Technology: Studies on the Materiality of Literacy*. New York, NY: Routledge.
Harris, M. (1976) History and significance of the emic/etic distinction. *Annual Review of Anthropology* 5, 329–350.
Hawkins, M.R. (2018) Transmodalities and transnational encounters: Fostering critical cosmopolitan relations. *Applied Linguistics* 39 (1), 55–77.
Headland, T.N. (1990) Introduction: A dialogue between Kenneth Pike and Marvin Harris on emics and etics. In T.N. Headland, K.L. Pike and M. Harris (eds) *Emics and Etics: The Insider/Outsider Debate* (pp. 13–27). Newbury Park, CA: SAGE.
Hull, G. and Nelson, M. (2005) Locating the semiotic power of multimodality. *Written Communication* 22 (2), 224–262.
Hull, G.A., Stornaiuolo, A. and Sahni, U. (2010) Cultural citizenship and cosmopolitan practice: Global youth communicate online. *English Education* 42 (4), 331–367.
Ingold, T. (2010) Bringing things to life: Creative entanglements in a world of materials. *World* 44, 1–25.
Jaffe, A. (2009) *Stance: Sociolinguistic Perspectives*. Oxford: Oxford University Press.
Jaffe, A. (2015) Staging language on Corsica: Stance, improvisation, play, and heteroglossia. *Language in Society* 44 (2), 161–186.
Khan, S. (2007) Negotiating the mohalla: Exclusion, identity and Muslim women in Mumbai. *Economic and Political Weekly* 42 (17), 1527–1533.
Lave, J. (1991) Situating learning in communities of practice. *Perspectives on Socially Shared Cognition* 2, 63–82.
Lave, J. and Wenger, E. (1991) *Situated Learning: Legitimate Peripheral Participation*. Cambridge: Cambridge University Press.
Lee, E. and Simon-Maeda, A. (2006) Racialized research identities in ESL/EFL research. *TESOL Quarterly* 40, 573–594.
McDowell, L. (1999) *Gender, Identity and Place: Understanding Feminist Geographies*. Minneapolis, MN: University of Minnesota Press.
Menon, M. (2012) *Riots and after in Mumbai: Chronicles of Truth and Reconciliation*. Delhi: SAGE.
Micciche, L.R. (2014) Writing material. *College English* 76 (6), 488–505.

Mountz, A. (2002) Feminist politics, immigration, and academic identities. *Gender, Place and Culture: A Journal of Feminist Geography* 9 (2), 187–194.

Nagar, R. (2002) Footloose researchers, 'traveling' theories, and the politics of transnational feminist praxis. *Gender, Place and Culture: A Journal of Feminist Geography* 9 (2), 179–186.

O'Hare, G., Abbott, D. and Barke, M. (1998) A review of slum housing policies in Mumbai. *Cities* 15 (4), 269–283.

Rajyashree, K.S. (1986) *An Ethnolinguistic Survey of Dharavi: A Slum in Bombay.* Mysore: Central Institute of Indian Languages.

Rose, G. (1997) Situating knowledges: Positionality, reflexivities and other tactics. *Progress in Human Geography* 21 (3), 305–320.

Saldaña, J. (2015) *The Coding Manual for Qualitative Researchers,* 3rd edition. Los Angeles, CA: SAGE.

Sharma, K. (2000) *Rediscovering Dharavi: Stories from Asia's Largest Slum.* New Delhi: Penguin Books India.

Stornaiuolo, A., Smith, A. and Phillips, N.C. (2017) Developing a transliteracies framework for a connected world. *Journal of Literacy Research* 49 (1), 68–91.

Sultana, F. (2007) Reflexivity, positionality and participatory ethics: Negotiating fieldwork dilemmas in international research. *ACME: An International E-journal for Critical Geographies* 6 (3), 374–385.

Tobin, J., Hsueh, Y. and Karasawa, M. (2009) *Preschool in Three Cultures Revisited: China, Japan, and the United States.* Chicago, IL: University of Chicago Press.

Wallerstein, I. (2001) *Unthinking Social Science.* Philadelphia, PA: Temple University Press.

Weinstein, L. (2014) *The Durable Slum: Dharavi and the Right to Stay Put in Globalizing Mumbai.* Minneapolis, MN: University of Minnesota Press.

10 Coda

Li Wei

Almost 20 years ago, I had a phone call from a friend and fellow academic linguist in the north of England asking for recordings of nursery rhymes in Chinese. We had just had our first son and they had adopted a girl from Hunan, China. My friend knows some Chinese and was determined to provide their daughter with a bilingual environment where both Chinese and English were used. I gave them some videos and CDs that we got from China. Later on, my friend made videos of the daughter reciting some of the nursery rhymes and telling stories in Chinese, which he sent to the children's centre, an orphanage in Hunan where his daughter spent the first two and a half years of her life before coming to England. The children's centre sent back some videos of the children there singing and telling stories in Chinese. As the daughter grew up, my friend and his wife took her to visit China several times and established good friendships with the children's centre as well as with other families across the country. They started exchanging videos on a regular basis. Initially the videos were all made by the parents or the guardians and, in most cases, staged. Gradually, the children on both sides took the initiative to make the videos themselves, and involved other young friends of theirs in making the videos. It became an exchange of their everyday experiences in two very different cultures and in two languages. They discussed issues of gender equality, why girls tend to be abandoned in rural China, the schooling, or the lack of it, for children left-behind in the villages by parents who migrated to urban centres to make money for the family, amongst the more mundane topics of food, clothes, music, etc.

About 10 years ago, I met a researcher in China who had done fieldwork in Kazakhstan on the Dungans, the descendants of the Hui Muslims from the Northwestern provinces of China who fled to Central Asia in the 19th century after failed rebellions against the Han authorities. They are now a recognized minority community in Kazakhstan and other central Asian republics. While they have acquired Kazak, Russian and other languages, they have kept their Chinese to a very high level through the generations. I saw videos of young Dungan children reciting Chinese poems in perfect northwestern Mandarin accent. By chance I was invited to speak at a conference in Kazakhstan. I wanted to meet some Dungan people and learn about their life in Kazakhstan. It turned out that they had very close contacts with China and many of them frequently visited Xi'an, the former capital of China around where the Hui Muslims had their settlements. University students of Dungan origin told me stories of their experiences in China, including one in particular that I remember very vividly: a male Dungan student from Kazakhstan was in Xi'an and asked a girl at a street stall for directions to a place. He spoken Chinese in a perfect local accent. The girl thought he was trying to pick her up and told him to get lost. He had to explain to the girl that he was not local even though he spoke the local dialect, and he was genuinely asking for the way. The existence of the Dungan people in Central Asia has been largely unknown to the young people in China until fairly recently. There are now active links between the Dungans and their peers in Xi'an as well as other cities in the northwestern provinces of China, especially among the Hui Muslims. They exchange news and views through social media and often send each other videos. They are very much aware of religious conflicts, both historical and present-day, between the Chinese Muslims and others, and they talk about migration issues too.

When I first heard about the Global StoryBridge project from Maggie Hawkins, these two stories came to my mind immediately. They involve young people in different cultures exchanging their life stories via videos and learning about each other. I could see many similarities and connections between them, although of course Maggie's project is on a much bigger scale. The fact that she thought of creating such a project, in such an imaginative way, really impressed me. Her getting the Global Citizen of the Year Award from the United Nations Association in 2017 is testament of the impact of Maggie's work.

The theoretical underpinning of Global StoryBridges is the concept of critical cosmopolitanism which challenges globalization as the primary and universal mechanism for social change and instead focuses on the situated nature of the world order and on 'creating and sustaining just, equitable, and affirming relations with global (and local) others in global engagements and interactions through attending to the workings of status, privilege, and power between people and groups of people' (Hawkins, 2018: 66). Globalization is not a modern-day phenomenon, although its speed and scale have clearly been accelerated by modern technologies and transportation. Whilst it certainly has brought many positive benefits to human society, it has also contributed to inequality, injustice, and indifference. The last of these, in my view, is just as bad as the other two as it ignores and even tries to erase the causes of inequality and injustice. Critical cosmopolitanism recognises differences that exist between people and uses them as a point of departure in tackling the causes of inequality and injustice. It aims to develop a critical awareness of these causes by focusing on local developmental processes and cultural models whereby the social world is constituted. Global StoryBridges creates online spaces for young people in very different sociocultural contexts to develop critical cosmopolitanism through sharing their everyday experiences in self-made videos. The cases discussed in the present book cover vast and very different geographical areas: the US, Mexico, China, Vietnam, India, Spain, Kenya and Uganda. And I know that there are other sites the project has across the globe. While essentially the exchange is among young people, teachers and other adults do also get involved. Increasingly, educators and policymakers realise the deep engagement of the children in the project and the impact it has on these children's lives and their worldviews. It is an action project that develops the participants' critical cosmopolitanism through self-reflections as well as reflecting on the life of others.

Methodologically, the project advances the concept of transmodalities (Hawkins, 2018). Transmodalities is an integral part of the 'trans' turn in language, communication and education research and practice (Hawkins & Mori, 2018). Building on but also critiquing the existing work on multimodalities and multiliteracies among others, transmodalities offers a conceptual and analytical approach to the semiotic particularities of transnational, digital, and intercultural communication. The case study chapters by the transnational research team of the Global StoryBridges project illustrate how the transmodalities perspective enables us to gain a deeper understanding of the processes of language and literacy development of the participating youth, the role of technology and the development of technical abilities and expertise, and above all, how global citizenship can be fostered through engagement in everyday activities. As we can see in the chapters, the way data are analysed, presented and discussed gives us practical guidelines for our future work. The case studies in this book are not aimed at telling the reader facts of specific communities, although one can get plenty of information about some of the communities that have not featured in past research. They showcase how the Global StoryBridges project has brought people together and developed their critical cosmopolitanism through collaboration and participation, and how in doing so the lives of the young people (and adults) participating in the project have been transformed.

This last point is what I feel I have learned the most from reading the chapters of the present volume. I have indeed been reminded of the complexities of communication and learning in different sociocultural, geographic and political contexts. But the most important contribution of this book is the example it sets of how to do research with social impact. I see applied and educational research as part of social science. We social scientists need to constantly ask ourselves what our research is for and who can benefit from the research. The studies that are presented in this volume demonstrate that applied and educational linguistics research can transform people's lives. Through dialogic, collaborative, and task-based learning, the participants learned to negotiate meanings with emerging language, literacy and technology skills, to navigate identities and scales of differences that they come to realize through participating in the project, and to develop understandings of the sources of differences between them and the impact of the differences on themselves and their peers. These learning gains have come with struggles obviously. But on the whole, they have happened voluntarily, spontaneously and without formal content-focused teaching from adults in authority.

I am writing this short commentary amid the global coronavirus pandemic. Most major cities in the world have been locked down. Yet our everyday life goes on, albeit in a different style. A friend of ours recently sent us a short video clip of her teenage son trying to peel an apple with a knife. He is clearly struggling. So I asked the mother why he was doing that. She said that she simply wanted to remind him that when his parents were his age, they did not have fruit peelers. They either ate apples with the skin on or, if they wanted to peel the apple, they would do so with a knife. The mother also told us that in fact a group of Chinese schoolchildren made videos of themselves doing household chores without modern equipment or technology such as vacuum cleaner, dishwasher and microwave. They were fascinated by what they thought of as the creativity and inventiveness of their peers. But as this mother reminded them, human society developed these pieces of equipment and facilities over time; they were not always there. A sense of history needs to be part of the critical cosmopolitanism that we want to instil in the youth and in ourselves as well.

As Maggie promises in her Introduction, Global StoryBridges is an ongoing project. I am very much looking forward to hearing more of the insights from it.

References

Hawkins, M.R. (2018) Transmodalities and transnational encounters: Fostering critical cosmopolitan relations. *Applied Linguistics* 39 (1), 55–77.

Hawkins, M.R. and Mori, J. (2018) Considering 'trans-' perspectives in language theories and practice. *Applied Linguistics* 39 (1), 1–8.

Index

Agency 38, 46, 64, 72, 77, 184
Arc of communication 12, 13, 17, 113, 183

Bilingual/bilingualism 165, 196
　schools 155, 160, 169

Citizenship 78, 143, 150, 173
　global 78, 81, 138, 149, 150, 198
Civic
　capabilities 150
　engagement 23, 151
　identities/identifications 8, 18, 22, 23
　obligation 24
　responsibility 152
Coding 51, 181, 182, 185, 186
　thematic 181, 182
Colonialism/coloniality 6, 18, 152, 153, 154, 157, 158, 159, 160, 169, 170, 171, 172
　colonial discourse 18, 152, 153, 155, 160, 163, 169, 170
　colonial difference 18, 152, 153, 158, 163, 168, 169, 171, 172
　postcolonial 48
Community-based 1, 6, 16, 44, 48, 76, 140, 185, 186
Composition/compositional 18, 177, 178, 182, 183, 184, 185, 186, 192
Controversial Issues 8
Cosmopolitan/cosmopolitanism 9, 10, 11, 16, 17, 43, 47, 48, 51, 56, 57, 58, 59, 60, 61, 81, 89, 139, 149
Critical cosmopolitanism 2, 3, 8, 10, 13, 15, 17, 22, 28, 38, 39, 40, 44, 48, 59, 60, 80, 81, 82, 86, 89, 90, 98, 103, 104, 105, 106, 134, 138, 139, 140, 142, 146, 147, 150, 171, 173, 197, 198

Decolonize (ing)/decolonization 18, 152, 153, 157, 158, 159, 160, 162, 164, 169, 170, 171, 172
Dialogic
　cosmopolitanism 10
　engagement 102, 106
　learning 7, 140, 198

Ecology(ies) 4, 15
Emic
　perspectives 5, 14, 86, 115, 116, 183, 189, 190
　distinction 186, 189
　positioning 5, 190, 191
　spectrum of emicity 18, 116, 183, 189, 190, 191, 193
　views 130
Epistemology/ies 13, 40, 153, 155, 159, 169, 170, 172, 173, 186, 190, 191, 192
　epistemological potential 192
　epistemological stance 179
　narrative 110
Ethnicity 6, 48, 145, 191
Ethnography/ethnographic 14, 18, 38, 51, 61, 91, 92, 129, 162, 163
　ethnographic analysis 23
　ethnographic approach 40, 69
Etic
　perspective 115, 183, 189
　distinction 186, 189, 194

Gender 50, 116, 138, 170, 185, 187, 189, 196,

Intercultural
　communication 44, 198
　exchanges 170
Indigenous 4, 18, 90, 156-159, 161, 162
　communities 153
　languages 155, 157, 158, 160

Information and communication technologies (ICT) 80, 83, 85, 161, 162

Lingua franca 7, 145, 181
Linguistic repertoire/s 22, 38, 126, 184
Literacy 46, 84, 85, 100, 104, 152, 153, 154, 157, 158, 159, 160, 163, 168, 169, 171, 172, 198
    activities 164, 165
    artifacts 14, 181, 183, 184
    critical 137, 150, 157
    digital 7, 85, 161, 162
    education 81
    engagements 6
    multiliteracy/ies 11, 17, 18, 81, 83, 84, 85, 106, 159, 168, 169, 172, 198
    multimodal 100, 146, 158, 168
    performances 11
    practices 85, 86, 87, 88, 157, 158, 159, 169, 183, 184, 185, 187
    scholars 80, 103, 179, 180
    skills 7, 8, 82, 85, 90, 137, 147, 150, 154, 167, 168, 198
    studies 81, 83, 84, 85, 88, 139, 176, 184
    transliteracy/ies 83, 84, 85, 86, 87, 88, 103

Material/materiality/materialist 9, 12, 24, 80, 85, 87, 89, 97, 105, 106, 110, 127, 135, 157, 161, 176, 179, 181, 183, 192, 193
    actors 12, 184
    constraints 181, 192, 193, 181, 192, 193
    environments 177, 179, 180
    lives 160
    objects (goods) 98, 99, 101, 103, 113, 127, 128
    perspective 184
Migration(s) 24, 81, 197
Modernization/modernity 138, 146, 152, 154, 155, 158, 160, 169, 170, 171, 172
Multilingual/multilingualism 40, 87, 154, 162, 164, 165
    interactions 22, 24
    practices 24, 47
    resources 40
    skills 144
Multimodal/multimodality(ies) 11, 13, 23, 38, 40, 44, 45, 46, 72, 81, 82, 83, 86, 87, 91, 101, 102, 103, 111, 112, 128, 137, 159
    activities 168
    analysis 19, 20, 107, 111, 112, 129
    artifact 11, 47, 60, 88
    communication/s 6, 23, 60, 113, 145, 178
    complexes 65
    composition 185
    engagements 18, 91
    literacy 100, 158
    perspective 112
    texts 46, 100, 158, 159, 160, 172
    research/data 14, 51, 58
    stories 7
Multivocal 179, 183

Narrative/s 38, 44, 46, 109, 110, 112, 113, 114, 115, 116, 117, 121, 124, 125, 126, 128, 129, 130, 131
    analysis 17, 109, 111, 112, 113, 114, 116, 128, 129, 130, 131
    lens 112
    perspective 112, 115
Network(s)/networking 4, 8, 12, 22, 24, 39, 80, 85
New Materialist 12
    perspective 184

Pedagogy(ies)/pedagogical 135, 136, 148
    decolonizing 18, 152, 171, 172
    foundations 137
Positioning(s)/positionality(ies) 2, 3, 8, 10, 14, 30, 67, 77, 110, 111, 112, 114, 116, 120, 121, 122, 123, 124, 125, 126, 127, 128, 129, 130, 131, 152, 155, 177, 189, 190, 191, 192
    emic 5, 191
    positionality statements 179, 193
    researcher 179, 180, 181, 182, 186, 189
    transpositioning/transpositional 2, 3, 4, 5, 11, 12, 15
Power dynamics 3, 13, 179

Race 50, 141, 189
    Critical Race Theory 110
Reflection 3, 40, 69, 76, 91, 102, 164, 177, 179, 181, 183, 186, 198
    critical 19, 66, 75, 130, 185
Reflexive
    approach 180
    practices 179

research 179
questions 178
Rural 1, 17, 81, 82, 90, 99, 105, 119, 136, 196

Scale(s/Scalar 15, 16, 22, 24, 25, 34, 36, 38, 39, 110, 135, 187, 197, 198
   sociolinguistic 16, 22, 24, 38
   timescale 88, 110, 147
Semiotic(s) 2, 11, 12, 23, 176, 198
   assemblages 106
   identity 102
   modes 23, 80, 87, 89, 100, 109, 131, 146, 159
   representations 45
   resources, 7, 13, 23, 67, 88, 126, 127, 129
   understandings 11
   systems 46, 87, 100, 104
Sociocultural 19, 46, 80, 84, 85, 133, 177
   approach 8
   context/s 15, 16, 66, 67, 111, 197, 198
   identities 81, 105, 106
   process/es 3, 113
Socioeconomic 26, 68, 115, 116, 119, 121, 128, 141, 153, 189
Sociohistorical 111, 206
Sociolinguistic/s 24
   scale 16, 22, 38
Sociomaterial/socio-materially 110, 192
Sociopolitical context 15, 16, 67

Transcultural
   communication/s 2, 38, 89, 154, 168, 169, 170, 171
   lenses 102
   setting/s 89
Transglobal 3, 4, 9, 10, 13, 14, 19, 64
   collaborations 8
   communication/s 1, 2, 4, 6, 8, 13, 15, 16, 92, 154, 168, 169, 170, 171
   exchanges 9, 15
   flows 4
   interactions 2, 8
   perspectives 15
   research 1, 3, 13, 14, 15, 17, 18
Transgress/transgressive 18, 60, 88, 147, 160
Transidiomatic

communication 30
   practices 16, 22, 24, 27, 30, 39
Translanguaging 2, 23, 24, 46
Translingual/translinguistic/translingualism 7, 87, 100
   communication 7, 38, 99, 100
   practice/s 82, 87, 101
Transmodal 17, 58, 60, 61, 65, 66, 67, 70, 74, 76, 77, 78, 91, 109, 114, 115, 116, 120, 121, 122, 124, 127, 138, 147, 150, 177
   analysis 17, 64, 69, 64, 69, 71, 115
   communication/s 2, 7, 16, 22, 81, 83, 86, 88, 90, 92, 99, 183, 100, 103, 104, 139, 147, 183
   complexes 65
   design 72, 73
   encounters 38, 91
   engagements 82, 91, 102, 103
   framework 181
   interactions 16, 88, 104, 140
   language use 50
   meaning making 40, 67, 129
   moments 69
   narrative analysis 17, 109, 111, 113, 128, 129, 130, 131
   perspective 60, 115
   terrain 17, 80
Transmodalities 2, 3, 7, 1, 10, 12, 13, 14, 15, 17, 23, 24, 44, 45, 46, 47, 55, 64, 72, 81, 84, 86, 87, 88, 89, 90, 99, 100, 102, 104, 106, 111, 112, 129, 139, 146, 147, 159, 168, 177, 182, 190, 198
Transnational/transnationalism 17, 23, 38, 39, 40, 47, 65, 78, 80, 82, 87, 88, 89, 91, 100, 109, 111, 116, 134, 139, 140, 149, 157, 169, 183
   collaborative research 181
   communication 23, 81, 82, 83, 86, 90, 99, 100, 114, 129, 178, 198
   cultures 48
   engagements 64, 67, 82, 88, 91, 102
   research 18, 61, 64, 69, 192, 198, 199
   research team 176, 177, 178, 182, 192, 193, 198
   studies 186
   youth 58, 61, 109
Transpositioning/transpositional 2, 3, 4, 5, 11, 12, 15

For Product Safety Concerns and Information please contact our EU Authorised Representative:

Easy Access System Europe

Mustamäe tee 50

10621 Tallinn

Estonia

gpsr.requests@easproject.com